25,-

DŌGEN ZENJI'S

SHŌBŌGENZŌ
The Eye and Treasury of the True Law

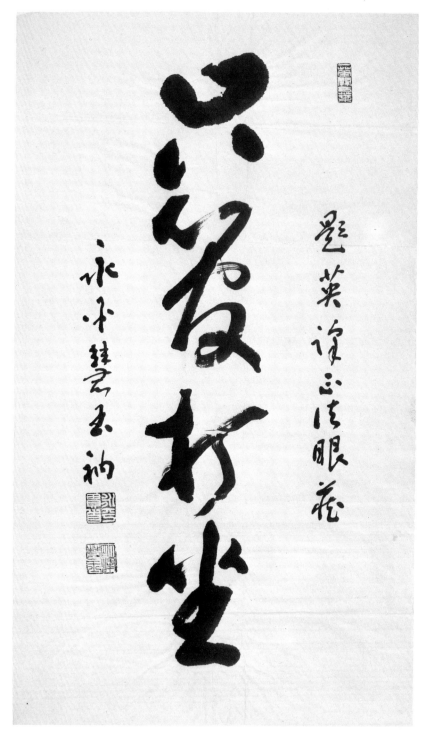

Shikantaza, single-minded sitting in zazen. Calligraphy by Hata Egyoku, Abbot of Eiheiji and Primate of the Sōtō Zen School.

A Complete English Translation of
DŌGEN ZENJI'S

SHŌBŌGENZŌ

(The Eye and Treasury of the True Law)

Volume II

TRANSLATED BY

KŌSEN NISHIYAMA

AND

JOHN STEVENS

PUBLISHED BY
NAKAYAMA SHOBŌ

Copyright © 1977 by Kōsen Nishiyama and John Stevens.

ISBN 0-87040-363-X

First Printing, 1977

Published by Nakayama Shobō
14-4, 2-chōme, Yushima, Bunkyo-ku, Tokyo, Japan

Overseas Distributor
Japan Publications Trading Co., Ltd. 1255 Howard St.
San Francisco Cal. 94103
200 Clearbrook Road, Elmsford, N.Y. 10523 U.S.A
P.O. Box 5030. Tokyo International, Tokyo 101-31, Japan

Printed in Japan by Kawata Press, Tokyo

Dedicated to all those seeking the True Way

CONTENTS

preface i
36. Butsukōjōji—Continuous development beyond Buddha 1
37. Kangin—Reading of the sūtras 8
38. Dōtoku—Speaking of the Way 17
39. Bukkyo—The Buddhist teaching 21
40. Arakan—The arhat 29
41. Shunjū—Spring and fall 33
42. Kattō—Spiritual entanglement 37
43. Hakujushi—The oak tree 43
44. Sangai Yuishin—The three worlds are only mind 47
45. Sesshin Sesshō—Explaining mind, explaining nature 52
46. Mitsugo—Secret teaching 58
47. Hosshō—Dharmatā, the real nature of phenomena 63
48. Dharani—The mystic formula 67
49. Sanjushichihon-bodai-bumpō—The thirty-seven conditions favorable to enlightenment 72
50. Senjō—Rules for the lavatory 87
51. Henzan—Direct study under a master 94
52. Ganzei—Enlightened vision 99
53. Jishōzammai—Self-enlightened samādhi 103
54. Kembutsu—Seeing Buddha 111
55. Hotsumujōshin—Developing the supreme mind 120

56. Tashintsu—Reading others' minds 126
57. Ōsakusendaba—The master's wish 134
58. Menju—Direct, face to face transmission 137
59. Baige—Plum blossoms 145
60. Muchūsetsumu—Explaining a dream within a dream 152
61. Raihaitokuzui—Making a prostration and attaining the marrow .. 158
62. Sansuikyo—The mountain and river sūtras 163
63. Shoakumakusa—Refrain from all evil 171
64. Shisho—The seal of transmission 178
65. Ango—The training period 187

PREFACE

BEGINNING with the publication of Oswald Spengler's *Decline of the West* and Nietzsche's pronouncement that "God is dead," the spiritual foundations of western society have been continually shaken. People like Ludwig A. Feuerbach wanted to do away with theology completely and establish a totally human-centered religion. In addition, the rapid expansion of technology and scientific knowledge has not given us all the answers; on the contrary, it has created more difficult and complex problems, e. g., the population explosion, shortages of food and natural resources, pollution, and destruction of the environment. Most of these problems have arisen because the natural balance of our world's life system has been disrupted by technological advancement and the development of civilization. Without exaggeration we may say that all those disruptions adversely affect the inner life of human beings and cause many serious spiritual crises. Consequently, we must both strive to create a new culture with a different set of ethics based on the harmony—spiritual and physical—of our life system and to re-establish correct observation of the nature of the world (i.e., the Buddhist chain of causation).

I strongly believe that Dōgen Zenji's interpretation of Buddhism is the most complete and that his concept of *shikantaza*, "single-minded sitting in zazen," is the best way for us to restore human life. As you know, the True Law began in India, was developed as the Dharma of the Buddhas and Patriarchs in China, and reached its culmination in Dōgen's *Shōbōgenzō*, the Eye and Treasury of the True Law. In that work, the Buddhist Way was crystalized; it has been the dominant spiritual influence in Japanese culture for more than seven hundred years. The world of the *Shōbōgenzō* is an extremely profound study, full of unsurpassed religious experience; it illumines Japanese thought like a brilliant pearl.

This supreme work of Japanese Buddhism has attracted the attention of foreign students, but due to its difficult and subtle nature it has not been as widely read as other Buddhist classics.

I am also continuing to lecture on the *Shōbōgenzō* in the English and French languages for my mission in Europe; I have already published in Paris a French translation of some parts of *Shōbōgenzō*, with my commentaries on it; however it is very hard to achieve this work without the help of some able collaborators.

But now, thanks to the efforts of Mr. Kōsen Nishiyama, assistant professor of Tohoku College of Social Welfare, and his able collaborator, Mr. John Stevens, an English translation is being made available. For me, this translation is especially valuable in helping establish real Zen practice among my many European students.

The *Shōbōgenzō* has the ability to nourish and refine the human heart and it is an excellent standard for a new world ethic. That is the reason for this publication and I encourage everyone to make use of it in their study.

TAISEN DESHIMARU
President of the Zen Association of Europe.

Paris, 23rd November, 1976.

[36]

BUTSUKŌJŌJI

"Continuous development beyond Buddha"

THE Patriarch Great Master Tōzan Gohon of Kinshū was the Dharma-heir of Great Master Ungan of Tanshū. He was the thirty-eighth Patriarch from the Tathāgata, and from himself to the Tathāgata he holds the thirty-eighth position.

One day, Tōzan gave a lecture to an assemby of monks. He said, "After experiencing continuous development beyond Buddha we are able to speak of the Buddhist Dharma somewhat." A monk asked, "What kind of speech can we make?" Tōzan said, "When I speak about it you won't be able to hear it." Then the monk said, "O Priest, can you hear it yourself?" Tōzan said, "When I'm not speaking about it I hear it."

"Continuous development beyond Buddha" was first used by this great master, a true Patriarch. Other Buddhas and Patriarchs have learned this saying from Tōzan, and then experienced continuous development beyond Buddha. You must clearly know that continuous development beyond Buddha is not contained within practice nor attained after enlightenment. Rather, it is experienced in "When I speak about it you cannot hear it." If we do not arrive at the state of continuous development beyond Buddha we can neither gain nor experience it. Also, if we do not speak about it, it cannot be gained. There is no opposition or concealment here and no reciprocal or symbiotic relationship. Therefore, when such speech is actualized it becomes continuous development beyond Buddha. When continuous development beyond Buddha is actualized it becomes "When I speak about it you won't be able to hear it." "You won't be able to hear it" means that continuous development beyond Buddha is involved with "not hearing." You must know that "When I speak about it you won't be able to hear it" is not polluted by hearing or not-hearing; therefore, there is no relationship between hearing and not-hearing.

Within hearing there is a "you" (the monk) and a "you" within speech. Meeting people is sometimes not to meet them, i.e., appearance differs from reality. In other words, speaking about it but not hearing it. The essence of not-hearing lies in not being able to hear because of the obstacles in our vocal cords [i.e., our individual, limited speech] and in our ears [i.e., our ability to hear the truth]. We cannot hear since our vision is narrow and our body and mind are in bondage. Due to these reasons we cannot hear. Nevertheless, do not take these things for speech; not-hearing is not true speech. There is only "When spoken, it is not heard." Tōzan said, "When I speak about it you won't be able to hear it." The beginning and end of speech is like a winding, tangled wisteria; speech is intertwined with speech, and speech obstructs itself.

The monk said, "O Priest, can you hear it yourself?" This question is not concerned with whether or not Tōzan can hear it, since speech cannot be expected to come from outside.

The point the monk was trying to make is whether we should study the principle of hearing when there is speech and when there is not. That is, the monk was asking if speech is speech and hearing is hearing. Speaking like that is not simply using the tongue.

The Patriarch Tōzan's "When I am not speaking I can hear it" must be clarified. That is, when it is spoken nothing can be heard. When hearing is actualized, there is no speech. Yet it is futile to disregard the everyday notion of "not speaking"; do not anticipate any special form of "not speaking." When we hear, there is no observation of speech, since real observation comes from outside. When we hear, it does not mean that speech is in some other place, nor does it mean that hearing is concealed in the essence of speech. Therefore, that is why even if the monk cannot hear it when he is speaking—or we can hear it when there is no speech—it is "speaking of the Buddhist Dharma somewhat" and "experiencing continuous development beyond Buddha." We can even experience this when no speech is heard. Therefore, we have "when I am not speaking I can hear it." Continuous development beyond Buddha did not exist prior to the seven past Buddhas; it is the seven Buddhas' continuous development beyond Buddha.

The Patriarch said to an assembly, "You must know that there is a man who possesses continuous development beyond Buddha." A monk asked, "What kind of man possesses continuous development beyond Buddha?" The master said, "Non-Buddha." Ummon said about this, "We cannot name or describe it; it is just 'non'." Hōgen said, "The word 'Buddha' is used as skillful means."

In general, the continuous development that occurs among Buddhas and

Patriarchs is similar to that of the Patriarch Tōzan. There are many so-called Buddhas and Patriarchs but none of them can even dream of continuous development beyond Buddha. If we were to explain it to Tokusan, Rinzai, etc. they would argue with us. Although Gantō, Seppō, and others have exerted themselves to the utmost, they can get only part of it. Tōzan's "After experiencing the continuous development beyond Buddha we can speak of the Dharma somewhat" and "You must know that there is a man who possesses continuous development beyond Buddha," etc. can be totally comprehended only after countless kalpas of practice and study. Only those who study and practice the profound and hidden Way can comprehend this.

We must know that one who possesses continuous development beyond Buddha possesses spiritual activity. We can find it in ancient Buddhas and manifest it in a fist. After observing and comprehending this, we can distinguish between those who have, and those who have not, continuous development beyond Buddha. What we find here is not that we should become men who possess continuous enlightenment beyond Buddha, or that we should meet these men with continuous development beyond Buddha; rather, we must be aware that such people exist. When we grasp this we can be liberated from ideas that there is, or is not, a man of continuous development. The man who possesses continual development beyond Buddha is "non-Buddha." What is "non-Buddha"? It is not a state prior to, or succeeding, Buddha. "Non-Buddha" is not simply that which has gone beyond Buddha. Why do we say "non-Buddha"? Because it is the original detached face of Buddha, and Buddha's liberated body and mind.

Zen Master Join Koboku of Tonkin (his secular name was Hōjō), the Dharma-heir of Fuyō Dōkai, once said to an assembly of monks, "When we realize that there is continuous development beyond Buddha and Patriarchs we will be able to explain it to others. O good Zen students! What is continuous development beyond Buddha? A single family has one child but he is lacking the six sense organs and missing the seven forms of consciousness. Such persons are called *icchantika*, beings who lack the seed of Buddha-nature. When they meet Buddha, they kill Buddha; when they meet a Patriarch they kill that Patriarch. Heaven refuses to accept them and even hell provides no gate for them to enter. Do any of you here have any idea of such people?" He went on, "That kind of person is dull-witted, always in a daze, and babbles foolishly in his sleep."

"Lacking six sense organs" means exchanging the pupils with the fruit of the Bodhi tree, the nostrils with hollow bamboo, and the skull with an excrement spatula. What is the principle of "exchanging"? It means a lack of the six sense organs. Since there is a lack of the six sense organs, we can pass through the blacksmith's furnace as a metal Buddha, emerge from the ocean as a clay Buddha, and rise from the flames as a wooden Buddha.

What is "missing the seven kinds of consciousness" like? It is like a broken ladle. They kill Buddha when they meet Buddha, because when they meet Buddha they kill Buddha. If they try to enter heaven, heaven will be broken; if they move toward hell, hell is shattered. Whenever they meet someone they smile foolishly; they do nothing but walk around in a daze and talk foolishly in their sleep. This is the principle of "mountains and rivers are unique in themselves, and jade and stone maintain their own independent existence." Reflect quietly on this saying of Zen Master Koboku and do not take it lightly.

Great Master Kōkaku of Mt. Ungo (Dōyō) studied under the Patriarch Tōzan. Once Tōzan asked him, "What is your name?" Ungo replied, "Dōyō." Tōzan then asked, "Tell me your previous name." Ungo said, "If I tell you, I will no longer be Dōyō." Tōzan said, "Your answer is no different from the one I gave Ungan when I was studying under him."

We must carefully study this dialogue. "If I tell you, I will no longer be Dōyō" refers to the Dōyō who exists beyond Dōyō. We should study the Dōyō who cannot be named, rather than the one who exists now. After this principle is actualized the real Dōyō emerges. However, we should not say that they are one and the same Dōyō. When Tōzan said, "Tell me your previous name," even if Ungo said "Dōyō," it still would have been continuous development beyond Buddha. Why? Because Dōyō's entire body transcends itself and he completely emerges.

Zen Master Sōzan Honjaku was also studying under the Patriarch Tōzan. Tōzan asked him, "What is your name?" Sōzan said, "Honjaku." Tōzan said, "Tell me your previous name." Sōzan said, "I can't say." Tōzan said, "Why not?" Sōzan answered, "I can't be called Honjaku." Tōzan said, "Good."

There is a word here that describes continuous development, i.e., "I cannot say." Hence, we have "Why not?" and the answer "I can't be called Honjaku." There is a "non"-Honjaku, a liberated "not-called," and a liberated Honjaku.

Zen Master Banzan Hōshaku said, "The path of continuous development has not been transmitted by thousands of Hinayana saints." "This path of continuous development" was only used by Banzan. He did not say "thing" or "person" of continuous development, only "path." The main point here is that even if thousands of competing saints appear, they cannot transmit the path of continuous development. "Cannot transmit" means that the thousands of saints preserve part of "not transmit." We must study this. There is another related saying: "There are thousands of saints and sages but the path of continuous development lies outside their world."

One day, a monk asked Zen Master Kōso of Mt. Chimon, "What is continuous development beyond Buddha?" The master replied, "Pointing at the sun and moon with the head of your staff." The staff does not obstruct the sun and moon; this is continuous development beyond Buddha. When we study the staff of the sun and moon it covers the entire world; this too, is the continuous development beyond Buddha. Do not say that the sun and moon are the staff. The head of the staff must become the entire staff.

Once, in the community of Great Master Sekitō Musai, Zen Master Dōgo of Tennō temple asked Sekitō, "What is the great meaning of the Buddhist Dharma?" Sekitō answered, "It cannot be attained nor comprehended." Dōgo said, "Is there any change in continuous development or not?" Sekitō replied, "The endless sky does not prevent the clouds from drifting."

Sekitō was the second Patriarch after Sōkei Enō. The Priest Dōgo of Tennō temple was a disciple of Yakusan. Dōgo asked, "What is the great meaning of the Buddhist Dharma?" Such a question cannot come from either novices or senior monks; it occurs only after we have comprehended the great meaning.

Sekitō answered, "It cannot be attained nor comprehended." We must know that a great meaning is contained in the very first thought as well as in the final stage of the Buddhist Dharma. It cannot be attained. Yet do not say that there is no resolve, practice or attainment of enlightenment—it is not attained. That great meaning cannot be comprehended. We cannot say that there is, or is not, practice and enlightenment—it cannot be comprehended, nor attained. Again, this great meaning is beyond attainment or comprehension. We cannot say there are no holy truths, practice, or enlightenment, nor can we say that there are holy truths, practice, and enlightenment. Nothing can be attained, nothing can be comprehended.

Dōgo said, "Is there any change in continuous development or not?" That is, if a change is actualized, is continual development actualized? "Change" here is a form of skillful means. Skillful means are used by all the Buddhas and Patriarchs. If we say this, change occurs. Yet even if there is change we must not overlook the aspect that does not change. We must speak like that.

"The endless sky does not prevent the clouds from drifting." This is Sekitō's saying. The vast sky cannot obstruct itself and clouds do not obstruct clouds. Drifting also does not obstruct itself or the endless sky. Here there is no obstruction of self or others. Yet it is not necessary, for each thing does not obstruct any other thing and each one possesses total freedom. Therefore, there is no obstruction. Then we will be able to locate the real nature of "The endless sky does not prevent the clouds from drifting." At such a time we must open the eye of study, look at the Buddhas, and meet the Patriarchs. We must also meet our own self and the self of others. This is the principle of "ten answers for one question." This means that the one who asked a question became the one who gave ten answers.

Ōbaku said, "Monks should know that they originally possess continuous development. Otherwise they will be like the Great Master Gozu Hōyū, a disciple of the fourth Patriarch, who freely proclaimed the Dharma but overlooked the essence of continuous development. If you possess real insight you monks will be able to clarify the difference between correct and incorrect principles."

Ōbaku's "originally possess continuous development" is the right transmission from Buddha to Buddha, Patriarch to Patriarch. It is called the Eye and Treasury of the True Law and Serene Mind of Nirvana. In order to possess it as our own, we must know it. However, there are cases when we possess it even though we do not yet know it. If there had been no right transmisson from Buddha to Buddha, we would not be able to even dream of it now. Ōbaku was the Dharma-heir of Hyakujō but ultimately surpassed his master and the other descendants of Baso. During that era, no one was equal to Ōbaku and he alone clarified the Dharma among those on Mt. Gozu. Even Buddhas have yet to clarify it.

Zen Master Hōyū of Mt. Gozu was a disciple of the fourth Patriarch. He freely proclaimed the Dharma, which is far better than lecturing on the sūtras and abhidharma like Chinese and Indian scholars; but unfortunately, he neither knew nor comprehended continuous development. And if we fail to understand that point how can we analyze the distinction between right and wrong in the Buddhist Dharma? Otherwise, we will just be linguists and philologists. Therefore, knowing, practicing, and enlightening the essence of continuous development is to go beyond the ordinary. When we have real practice, this will surely be actualized.

Continuous development beyond Buddha is to see more and more Buddhas after becoming a Buddha. This is not the same Buddha seen by sentient beings. If we see the same Buddha as sentient beings, then we are not "seeing" Buddha, much less seeing continuous development beyond Buddha. The continuous development of Ōbaku is to go beyond present day people. Someone may be equal to or surpass Hōyū, but he is still the Dharma-brother of Hōyū. How can we know the essence of continuous development, when even the ten saints and three sages, etc. cannot get it? How can we utilize it? This principle is the key point of our study. If we know the essence of continuous development we can experience, attain, and become the man of continuous development beyond Buddha.

This was delivered to the monks at Kannondōri- Kōshōhōrinji on March 23, 1242. Transcribed during the summer training period of 1259 at Eiheiji by Ejō.

[37]

KANGIN

"Reading of the sūtras"

In the practice and enlightenment of supreme and perfect awakening, sometimes we use the teaching of a master and sometimes we use the teaching in the sūtras. "Master" is the entire self of the Buddhas and Patriarchs; "sūtras" is the entire self of the sūtras. Therefore, we have the self of all the sūtras. "Self" is not some limited identity—it is active enlightened vision, and lively fists. Remembering, reading, chanting, copying, receiving, and possessing the sūtras together form the practice and enlightenment of the Buddhas and Patriarchs.

Nonetheless, it is difficult to come in contact with the Buddhist sūtras. In all the countries of this world even the name of the sūtras is rarely heard. Even among the Buddhas and Patriarchs and their descendants it is difficult to hear just the name. If you are not a Buddha or Patriarch you cannot see, hear, read, chant, or comprehend the sūtras.

Studying the Buddhas and Patriarchs gradually enables us to study the sūtras. Then the faculties of hearing, seeing, tasting, smelling, and the comprehension of the entire body and mind actualize hearing, receiving, possessing, explaining, etc. of the sūtras. Those who are only looking for fame or those who expound the doctrines of non-believers can never practice the Buddhist sūtras. Those sūtras have been transmitted by trees and stones and have become known in rice paddies and villages. They have been proclaimed everywhere throughout vast kingdoms and the entire universe.

The Great Master Yakusan Kudō had not given any Dharma talks for a long time. The general secretary of the monastery asked him, "All the monks are waiting to hear your compassionate teaching." Yakusan said, "Strike the gong and call an assembly." The general secretary did so, and soon all the monks gathered. Then Yakusan entered the Dharma Hall. He sat there silently for a time, then got up and returned to his quarters. The general secretary came after him and said, "O priest! You agreed to speak but left without saying even a single word. Why?" Yakusan said, "Sūtras have sūtra masters and abhidharma doctrines have abhidharma scholars. Why should you wonder at the action of this old monk?"

What Yakusan wanted to say is that fists have masters of fists and enlightened vision has masters of enlightened vision. However, the general secretary should have asked Yakusan, "I don't wonder about your actions. By the way, what kind of master are you?"

Once Hōtatsu, a monk whose main occupation was the continual chanting of the *Lotus Sūtra*, came to see the Patriarch Daikan [Enō] of Mt. Sōkei in Choshū. The Patriarch recited this verse:

> "If the mind is deluded, the *Lotus Sūtra* turns us.
> If the mind is enlightened, we turn the *Lotus Sūtra*.
> No matter how long we chant, if we do not clarify self
> Words and letters obstruct the essence.
> Thoughtless thought is true.
> Conscious thought is false.
> Abandon existence and non-existence
> And always ride the white ox cart [the Way of Buddha]."

Therefore, if the mind is deluded, the *Lotus Sūtra* turns us; if the mind is enlightened, we turn it; and if we transcend illusion and enlightenment, then the *Lotus Sūtra* turns the *Lotus Sūtra*.

After hearing this verse, Hōtatsu was overjoyed and recited his own verse:

> "Over and over, I chanted sūtras;
> Now, one verse of Sōkei's made me forget them all.
> If we haven't clarified Shakyamuni's emergence in this world
> We cannot be liberated from transmigration.
> There are sheep, deer, and ox carts;
> Beginning, middle, and end are full of goodness.
> Who knows that within this burning house [i.e., the body]
> Is the original Dharma kingdom?"

Then the Patriarch said, "From now on call yourself the monk who has memorized the sūtras."

We should know that there is such a monk in the Buddhist Way. This is the ancient Buddha Sōkei's direct pointing. "Memorized" is not consciousness nor unconsciousness, existence nor non-existence. Throughout unlimited kalpas we must keep and memorize the sūtras day and night; from sūtra to sūtra there is nothing but sūtras.

The Honorable Prajñātāra, the twenty-seventh Patriarch of East India was invited by the king for a meal. The king asked him, "Everyone is proclaiming all manner of sūtras but you. Why?" Prajñātāra said, "Forgive my poor words, but I will put it this way: When I exhale my breath is not affected by events or conditions; when I inhale I do not dwell in the world of conditioned form. Continually, I proclaim the sūtra of suchness; it has millions and millions of volumes, not just one or two."

The Honorable Prajñātāra sowed the seeds [of Zen practice] in East India. He was the twenty-seventh Patriarch descended from Mahākāśyapa. He transmitted the household effects of the Buddhas—their heads, enlightened eyes, fists, nostrils, staffs, mendicant bowls, robes, bones, marrow, etc. He is our Patriarch and we are his descendants. The essence of Prajñātāra's statement is that not only his breath is not affected by external conditions, but also that external conditions are not affected. Such external conditions as head and eyes, body and mind are not affected by external conditions.

"Not affected" here means "totally affected" [i.e., the identity of opposites]. Although exhaled breath is an external condition, it is not affected by external conditions. Although the meaning of exhale and inhale has previously been unknown for countless kalpas, it has now been made known for the first time through the expressions "not dwelling in the world of form" and "not affected by external conditions." In external conditions we have the opportunity to study "inhale." This occasion does not exist in the past or future but in the external present.

The world of conditioned form is the five skandhas, i.e., form, perception, mental conceptions, volition, and consciousness. Do not dwell in the five skandhas; you are staying in a world where the five skandhas do not appear. The main point here is that the sūtras proclaimed number not just one or two but millions and millions. "Millions and millions" is a huge amount but also has another meaning. One breath in which we do not dwell in the world of conditioned form contains millions of volumes. However, this is not a large amount of wisdom or a liberated state. It transcends the possession or nonpossession of knowledge and wisdom. It is simply the practice and enlightenment of the Buddhas and Patriarchs; it is their skin, flesh, bones, marrow, enlightened eyes, fists, head, nostrils, staffs, and fly whisks.

Once Great Master Shinsai of Kannon-in in Jōshū was asked by an elderly lady devotee who had made a large donation to read the entire Tripitaka. Jōshū came down from his seat and walked around it one time. Then he told the old woman's messenger, "I've finished reading the Tripitaka." The messenger returned to the old woman and told her what happened. The old woman said, "I asked him to read the entire Tripitaka. Why did he read only half?"

Now we can clearly see that both the entire Tripitaka and half the Tripitaka are the old woman's three sūtras [i.e., the three vehicles]. "I have finished reading the Tripitaka" is Jōshū's understanding of the sūtras. Generally, reading the Tripitaka is Jōshū's walking around his seat and the seat walking around Jōshū. Jōshū walks around Jōshū; the seat walks around the seat. Yet, the reading of the Tripitaka is not just walking around the seat, nor does the seat walk around.

There is another similar story. Great Master Jinshō of Mt. Daisai in Echū (his Dharma name was Hōsshin) was a disciple of Great Master Dai'e of Chokeiji. Once, an elderly woman disciple made a donation and asked him to read the entire Tripitaka. Daisai got up and walked once around his seat and said to the woman's messenger, "I have finished reading the Tripitaka." The messenger returned to the old woman and told her what happened. She said, "I asked him to read the entire Tripitaka. Why did he read only half?"

Here, we should not study Daisai's walking around his seat or the seat walking around Daisai. He was not trying to show the perfection [of Buddha's] fist and enlightened vision. His circle was the circle of the Dharma world. However, did the old woman possess the ability to understand it or not? "He read only half" is not sufficient, even if she transmitted it from her master; rather, she should have said, "I asked him to read the entire Tripitaka. Why did he come down so readily from his seat?" Even if she had said this unthinkingly, she still would be one who possessed enlightened vision.

Once, a minister invited the Patriarch Tōzan for a meal. The minister made a donation and asked Tōzan to read the Tripitaka. Tōzan came down from his seat and bowed to the minister. The minister returned the bow. Then Tōzan took him and they walked once around the seat. Tōzan bowed again, waited a short time, and then asked, "Do you understand?" The minister replied, "No, I don't." Tōzan said, "I have read you the Tripitaka. Why don't you understand?"

The meaning of "I have read you the Tripitaka" should be clear. We should not study that walking around the seat is to read the Tripitaka, nor should we study that reading the Tripitaka is the same as walking around the seat. We must listen carefully to the Patriarch's words.

Once, when my late master, an ancient Buddha, was living on Mt. Tendō a Korean pilgrim came to make a donation and to request that all the monks recite some sūtras for him. My master related the above story about Tōzan.

After finishing the story my master drew a circle in the air with his fly whisk and said, "Today I have read the Tripitaka for you." He threw down the fly whisk and left the hall.

We should carefully examine my late master's actions. They are beyond compare. When he read the Tripitaka did he use one bright eye or just half? We must clarify the manner in which Tōzan and my master used enlightened vision and Buddha's tongue.

The Patriarch Yakusan Kudō usually did not allow sūtra reading. One day, however, a monk found him looking at an open book. The monk said, "O Priest! Usually you do not allow us to read the sūtras so why are you reading the sūtras yourself?" "I just need something to rest my eyes on." The monk said, "May I use the same pretense?" The master replied, "If you look at the sūtras you'll burn a hole in the leather cover."

The meaning of "I need something to rest my eyes on" is that Yakusan became the object itself. This means abandoning enlightened vision, abandoning the sūtras. The eye is obstructed and becomes the obstructed eye. There is an active obstruction behind the eye; we add one more skin to the skin covering the eye. With "obstruction" we can enlighten the eye and vice versa. Therefore, if it is not the enlightened vision sūtra we cannot gain the merit inherent in the obstructed eye. "Burning a hole in the leather cover" means the entire cow is skin. Its skin, flesh, bones, marrow, head, horns, and nostrils form its lively function. When we learn about the master the cow becomes enlightened vision. This is the meaning of resting the eye on some object. Here, enlightened vision becomes the cow.

Zen Master Yabu Dōsen said, "Venerating all the countless Buddhas gives us unlimited happiness. But is it superior to reading the ancient teachings? The sūtras are black characters on white paper. Open your eyes and look at them!"

We should know that to venerate the ancient Buddhas and to read the ancient teachings possess the same virtue and happiness. There is no happiness and virtue beyond this. "Ancient teaching" is black characters on white paper, but who really knows the ancient teaching? We must study this principle carefully.

Once, one of the monks of Great Teacher Kōkaku of Mt. Ungo was reading a sūtra in his room. The master called out through the window, "What sūtra are you reading?" The monk answered, "The *Vimalakirti-nirdeśa Sūtra*." The master said, "I didn't ask you about the sūtra you have in your hands. What sūtra are you reading?" The monk was suddenly enlightened.

Kōkaku's "What sūtra are you reading?" transcends time and is extremely deep; it cannot be put into words. It is like meeting a poisonous snake in the road; hence, the central question of the sūtra emerges. Whenever we meet a master he will be able to explain the *Vimalakīrti Sūtra* without mistake.

In general, reading the sūtras should be based on the method used by all the Buddhas and Patriarchs. They use their enlightened vision. At that time all the Buddhas and Patriarchs become Buddhas; they proclaim the Dharma and Buddha. If you do not read the sūtras like this, you will never see the head or face of the Buddhas and Patriarchs.

In the present-day communities of the Buddhas and Patriarchs there are various occasions when the sūtras are read. For example, sūtras read for the benefit of all beings when requested by a lay devotee, the regular daily recitation, individual chanting by earnest monks, etc. Also, there is a special type of chanting for a monk's funeral.

After a lay devotee has come to the temple and requested the monks to chant the sūtras, this procedure should be followed: After the morning meal the head monk erects a sign board in front of the monastery and monks' quarters announcing the chanting. A cloth used for prostrations is placed in front of the image of Mañjuśrī. At the proper time the gong in front of the monastery is struck either one or three times [i.e., one sequence or three sequences], depending on the head priest's instructions. After the gong is struck the head monk leads all the others into the hall and they take their seats facing front. All should be wearing their kesas. Next the abbot enters the hall, makes a bow to the statue of Mañjuśrī, and takes his seat. Then an acolyte brings the sūtras. These sūtras should be prepared in advance and arranged properly in the repository.

The sūtras should be brought in either a special box or tray. All the monks reverently hold up the sūtras and begin chanting. Then the guestmaster brings the lay devotee to the hall. The devotee should pick up the censer, which has been previously placed at the temple entrance by an attendant monk. The sign for entering should be given by the guestmaster. Then they enter from the south with the guestmaster in front and the lay devotee behind. The devotee offers incense to the image of Mañjuśrī and makes three prostrations while holding the censer. During the devotee's prostrations the guestmaster stands at the upper corner of the prostration cloth, facing south with his hands folded across his chest. After finishing his prostrations the devotee turns to his right, faces the abbot and bows. The abbot remains seated, takes the sūtra in his hands, and makes a gassho. Then the devotee faces north and bows. After this, he walks around the hall beginning at the abbot's seat. The guestmaster leads him around. Once again the devotee stands before the image of Mañjuśrī, still holding the censer, and bows. While this is happening the guestmaster stands at the entrance, facing north with his hands folded across his chest.

After making his bow to Mañjuśri the lay devotee follows the guestmaster out of the monastery and walks around it one time. He enters again, makes three prostrations to Mañjuśri, goes to his assigned seat, and certifies the reading of the sūtras. His chair should either be next to the pillar to the left of Mañjuśri, or next to the southern pillar facing north. After the devotee sits down the guestmaster bows and then takes his own seat. On some occasions a monk will chant as the lay devotee walks around the monastery. That monk's seat should be either on the left or right of Mañjuśri depending on the circumstances. Only the highest class incense such as *jinko* or *senko*, etc. should be offered. The incense should be prepared by the devotee. When the devotee walks around the monastery all the monks should place their hands in gassho.

Next, the donation should be made. The amount or kind of donation depends upon the devotee. Sometimes things like cotton, fans, etc. are offered. The lay devotee can make the offering himself, or it can be done by the secretary general, or an attendant monk. The offering should be placed before the monks and not given directly to them. All the monks should make gassho when it is offered. (Sometimes the donation is brought in before the morning meal. In that case the announcement board is struck and the chief monk brings the donation in. The merit of the devotee's offering should be written down and placed on the pillar to the left of Mañjuśri.)

When the sūtras are chanted in the monastery it should be done in a low voice, not a high one. On occasion, the sūtras are not read aloud; they are simply opened and the monks only look at the characters. In that case, we generally use such sūtras as the *Diamond Sūtra*, several chapters of the *Lotus Sūtra*, or the *Golden Light Sūtra*, etc. A large quantity of those sūtras should be kept in the monastery.

Each monk should have his own copy. After the chanting is finished the sūtras should be put in the special tray or box carried by one of the monks. At that time, the monks should make gassho and chant the concluding prayer in a low voice.

If the sūtras are to be read outside of the monastery the general secretary can act as the devotee in the manner described above for handling the incense, making prostrations, walking, and arranging the donation. He must hold the censer in the prescribed manner. A monk may also request the sūtras to be read; in that case, he acts in the same manner as the lay devotee.

For the emperor's birthday, sūtra reading is done as follows: [The sūtra reading should begin one month prior to the birthdate.] For example, if the emperor's birthday is January fifteenth then the sūtra reading should begin on December fifteenth. On that day there is no Dharma talk. In front of the image of Shakyamuni in the Buddha Hall two platforms should be constructed. They should face the east and run from north to south. Between the two platforms a stand for the sūtras should be placed. On the stand place one sūtra such as the *Diamond Sūtra,* the *Ninnō Sūtra,* the *Lotus Sūtra,* the *Suvarnaprabhāvāsottama-raja-Sūtra* etc. Every day some small treat such as noodles, soup, or sweet cakes should be served to all the monks. The sweet cakes should be placed in a bowl with chopsticks, not a spoon. Eat the snack where the sūtras are being chanted and do not take it anywhere else. The food should be put with the sūtras and it is not necessary to prepare a special table. After finishing the snack all the monks should go to the lavatory and gargle. Then they return to their respective seats and begin to read the sūtras. They should read continuously from the morning meal to midday. When the drum is struck three times it signals the time for the midday meal, and marks the end of sūtra reading for that day.

From the first day a yellow sign board announcing the celebration of the emperor's birthday should be placed on the east side of the eaves in front of the Buddha Hall or the eastern pillar inside the Hall. The name of the abbot should be written on a small piece of red or white paper together with the year, month, and day of the celebration. The reading of the sūtras should continue in this way until the arrival of the emperor's birthday. The abbot gives a Dharma talk to mark the celebration. This is an ancient, established custom.

Sometimes an especially diligent monk will want to read the sūtras under his own initiative. Every temple should have a special room for sūtra reading. Those interested in sūtra reading should go there. Follow the rules for that kind of reading as laid down in the *Shingi.*

Once, Great Master Yakusan Kudō asked the novice Kō, "Which is more profitable—reading the sūtras or studying under a master?" Kō said, "Neither reading the sūtras nor studying under a master is of any value." Yakusan said, "You're pretty sharp. But if neither is of any value, how can enlightenment be attained?" Kō said, "I don't mean to say that no one can attain it, but neither the sūtras nor the teaching of a master can give the essence."

Some accept the essence of the teaching of the Buddhas and Patriarchs, some do not. Nevertheless, reading the sūtras and studying under a master are nothing but the everyday life of the Buddhas and Patriarchs.

This was delivered to the monks at Kōshōhōrinji, Uji, Yamashiro, on September 15, 1241. Transcribed on July 8, 1245 at the chief disciple's quarters of Daibutsuji, Yoshida, Echizen, by Ejō.

[38]

DŌTOKU[1]

"Speaking of the Way"

ALL the Buddhas and Patriarchs speak of the Way. Therefore, when Buddhas and Patriarchs choose Buddhas and Patriarchs as their Dharma-heirs surely they question them to see if they understand how to speak of the Way. This questioning is done with the body and mind, with a fly whisk and staff, with a pillar and stone lantern. If they are not Buddhas and Patriarchs they cannot be questioned nor speak about the Way since they lack its essence.

Speaking of the Way does not depend on others or on our own ability. By simply seeking the Buddhas and Patriarchs we will be able to speak of their Way. Within this speaking of the Way there is traditional practice and enlightenment which continues to be carried out and studied in the present. When Buddhas and Patriarchs practice and Buddhas and Patriarchs evaluate their speech, their speaking of the Way becomes the practice of three, eight, thirty, or forty years. It is continual speaking of the Way. One commentary says, "Twenty or thirty years of practice is accomplished through speaking of the Way." During all that time they practiced total speaking and attainment of the Way.

During such practice no time must be wasted. That is why observation based on enlightenment is always correct. Therefore, speaking of the Way in the present contains no doubt or error. The present speaking of the Way possesses the observation of the past. Observations of the past contain the present speaking of the Way. Consequently, observation and speaking exist in the past and present and there is no gap between them. Our present practice is based on speaking and correct observation of the Way.

---

[1] Dōtoku is used throughout the *Shōbōgenzō* to mean an expression used by a master. It has the dual meaning of "speaking" or "utterance" and "attainment of the Way." In this chapter it is used in both ways.

When such practice is continued for months and years all past evil karma drops off. After it is cast off our skin, flesh, bones, and marrow are renewed and countries, land, mountains, and rivers drop off. Then dropping off becomes the ultimate goal and we try to arrive there. That arrival is the emergence of our real self; ultimately the right time of dropping off occurs and speaking of the Way is actualized suddenly without expectation. Even if there is no effort in our body and mind we can naturally speak of the Way. There is nothing strange or unusual in this speaking of the Way.

However, when speaking of the Way is attained we must clarify which things are not spoken nor attained. If we recognize the attainment of our speaking of the Way but fail to clarify those things which are not spoken nor attained, we will miss the original face, bones, and marrow of the Buddhas and Patriarchs. Therefore, how can the speech of others and their attainment of the skin, flesh, or bones be equal to [Eka's] attainment of [Bodhidharma's] marrow by "speaking" with three prostrations and silently returning to his seat? The other disciples' attainment was nowhere near Eka's attainment. Here, Eka and the three other disciples each had a different experience of their master's teaching, and other beings will have still different ideas. Eka has a spoken word and a word that is not spoken; others also have a spoken and an unspoken word. There is a self and others in speaking and in not speaking of the Way.

Great Master Jōshū Shisai said to an assembly of monks, "You may stay in the monastery your entire life and concentrate on zazen for ten or fifteen years without speaking, but that does not mean you are mute. None of the Buddhas can surpass you."

Like this, living in the monastery for ten or fifteen years watching frosts and blossoms come and go, we practice the Way diligently throughout our life, thinking about how much speech there is in continuous zazen. Why do people think that the uninterrupted practice of kinhin, zazen, and sleep in a monastery is mute? Although we are not sure where our life comes from, once we entrust ourselves to the Zen life we will not want to leave the monastery. Life in the monastery is the only life to lead. Concentrate on zazen and do not worry about not speaking. "Not speaking" is the head and tail of speaking.

Continuous zazen must be carried out for our entire life, not just a few minutes. If you concentrate on zazen and do not speak for ten or fifteen years, all the Buddhas will recognize you. Truly, Buddha's vision cannot pierce its virtue, his power cannot move it, nor can he influence or destroy the merit inherent in continuous zazen and not speaking.

What Jōshū said about "continuous zazen without speaking" is not related to being mute or not mute. All the Buddhas say this. Not leaving the monastery for your entire life is to speak of the Way for your entire life. Concentrating on zazen and not speaking for ten or fifteen years is to speak of the Way for ten or fifteen years. Through zazen we can surpass a hundred thousand Buddhas, and they can surpass us through zazen.

Therefore, that is why the life of speaking of the Way of the Buddhas and Patriarchs is not to leave the monastery for your entire life. Even if you are always silent you are still able to speak of the Way. Do not study that a mute person cannot speak of the Way. Speaking of the Way is not always not mute; even a mute person can speak of the Way. Surely, we can hear a mute person's voice and listen to his words. If you are not mute how can you meet or talk to a mute person? Nevertheless, there are mutes that we must meet and talk with. Study like this to find the meaning of "mute."

In the community of Great Master Shinkaku of Mt. Seppō there was one monk who made a hut in the mountains and went to live there. Many years passed and he let his hair grow and no one knew what kind of life he was leading. His life there was solitary and quiet. He fashioned a ladle from a branch and lived simply. Like this, the days and months passed and gradually his way of life became known to outsiders. One day, a monk visited his hermitage and asked, "Why did the first Patriarch come from the west?" The hermit said, "The river is deep and the handle of the ladle is long." The monk could not understand and left without making a bow or any gesture. He returned to Seppō and reported the hermit's answer. After hearing the story Seppō said, "What a strange thing. His answer was quite correct. This time I'll go and question him myself."

Seppō's point is that the hermit's answer was too good and therefore a little strange. However, Seppō would go and see for himself.

After a while Seppō went to the hermitage with an attendant monk who brought along a razor. They arrived at the hermitage and Seppō said, "If you have attained the Way and are able to speak about it, why haven't you shaved your head?"

We must be careful about his question. It seems to mean that it is not necessary to shave your head if you have attained the Way. How about it? If that is attaining the Way, then it is not necessary to shave his head. Only those who listen to this question with a certain amount of understanding can grasp it.

After hearing Seppō's words the hermit washed his hair and appeared before him. Did he appear because he had attained the Way or because he had not? Anyway, Seppō shaved his head.

This story of cause and effect is truly the blooming of an udumbara flower. It not only shows us how to see, but also how to hear. It is not limited to the seven and ten stages of the Hinayanists nor the viewpoints of the three or seven sages. Scholars of the sūtras and abhidharma and those who denigrate supernatural power cannot even imagine it. Listening to this story is like meeting the Buddhas who have emerged in this world.

We should think over Seppō's "If you have attained the Way and are able to speak about it, why don't you shave your head?" Those who have not attained the Way, yet possess some level of understanding, must be surprised by this story and those who lack understanding will be indifferent. When Seppō spoke to the hermit he did not ask about Buddha, the Way, samādhi, or dharanis. He appears to be asking a question but actually he is revealing the Way through speech. We must clarify this in detail.

However, the hermit truly possessed ability, so when he was questioned about the Way he was not indifferent. He revealed his manner by washing his hair. This is an aspect of the Dharma that cannot be explained with even the wisdom of Buddha himself. His washing of his hair is a concrete manifestation of Buddha's body, the proclaiming of the Dharma, and the saving of sentient beings. If Seppō had not been the right man he would have thrown down the razor and roared with laughter. He was the right person, however, and possessed enough power to shave the hermit's head.

Truly, if the relationship between Seppō and the hermit had not been like that between Buddha and Buddha, this story could not have occurred. Also, if only one had been a Buddha or if they were not real dragons such a dialogue would have never taken place. The Black Dragon keeps his jewels under his jaw, but they can plucked out by those with real ability.

We should know that Seppō wished to look into the hermit's heart and the hermit wanted to see through Seppō. One spoke, one did not; one shaved and one was shaved. Therefore, that is why good friends who have attained the Way can naturally understand each other. Such people who can express themselves without speaking are like old friends. This type of mutual practice and study is the actualization of attaining and speaking about the Way.

This was written on October 5, 1242, at Kannondōri-Kōshōhōnrinji. Recopied on November 2, of the same year by Ejō.

[39]

"BUKKYO"

"The Buddhist teaching"

THE actualization of the Way of all the Buddhas is the Buddhist teaching. Since this is done by Buddhas and Patriarchs for the Buddhas and Patriarchs their teaching is rightly transmitted as the Buddhist teaching. This is the turning of the wheel of the Law. This turning of the wheel of the Law within enlightened vision is the actualization of all the Buddhas and Patriarchs and their nirvana. All the Buddhas and Patriarchs surely emerge in a speck of dust; one speck of dust in nirvana. The entire world emerges, the entire world of nirvana. One instant emerges, endless time emerges.

However, one speck of dust and one instant are without any lack of virture. The entire world and endless time are not compensations for a lack of virture or some other insufficiency. Therefore, all the Buddhas who have attained the Way in the morning and entered nirvana in the evening also do not lack any virture.

If you think one day lacks sufficient virtue, then even a life of eighty years is not enough [for you]. An eighty-year life compared to ten or twenty kalpas is the same as one day compared to eighty years. It is very difficult to understand the difference between this Buddha and that Buddha. When we compare the virtue of an eighty-year life with one of endless time, there can be no doubt that there is no basic difference between them. Therefore, the Buddhist teaching is to teach; it is the total virtue of all the Buddhas and Patriarchs. Buddhas are high and vast, and the Dharma teaching is not narrow and small.

Truly, we should know that when Buddha is great, the teaching is great. When Buddha is small the teaching is small. Consequently, Buddha and his teaching cannot be measured by large and small, is not bound by designations of good, bad, or neuter, and is not limited to the teaching of self or others.

Some have said, "Shakyamuni transmitted a special teaching to Mahākāśyapa that was separate from the teachings and sermons in the sūtras. That teaching was the supreme vehicle of one mind which has been transmitted from generation to generation. Other teachings and discourses are used as expedients and mind is the real nature of truth. The transmission of one mind is a special transmission outside the scriptures. The three vehicles and the twelve teachings are not equal to the right transmission of one mind. The supreme vehicle of one mind is 'direct pointing to the heart of man, looking into one's nature and becoming Buddha.'"

Such a statement shows a lack of understanding of the Buddhist Dharma and inadequate utilization and dignity. Those who think like that, regardless if they are called elders or not, have not clarified or mastered the Buddhist Dharma or Buddhist Way. Why? Because they do not know the meaning of Buddha, teaching, mind, inside, or outside. They do not know about such things because they have not heard the Buddhist Dharma. They are called Buddhas but they do not know Buddha's essence. They have not properly studied the meaning of coming and going and therefore cannot be called disciples of Buddha. People think that only "one mind" has been rightly transmitted because they do not know the Buddhist Dharma. Those who do not know or have not heard the one mind of the Buddhist teaching say that there is some other Buddhist teaching beside one mind because their minds are not part of "one mind". Further, if someone says that there is "one mind" outside the Buddhist teaching it means that his Buddhist teaching is not the real Buddhist teaching. Such people transmit an erroneous version of "a special transmission outside the scriptures" since they do not know the meaning of "outside" or "inside"; consequently, their principles do not fit with their words. How is it possible for Buddhas and Patriarchs who individually transmit Buddha's Eye and Treasury of the True Law fail to transmit the Buddhist teaching? Moreover, why would Shakyamuni formulate Dharma teaching that cannot be used as a basis for all Buddhist followers? Shakyamuni has formulated the basis of Dharma teaching through individual transmission so how can there be a Buddha or Patriarch who does not follow it? The supreme vehicle of one mind is nothing more than the three vehicles and twelve teachings, i.e., all the sūtras of the Mahayana and Hinayana.

We must know that the Buddha-mind is the enlightened vision of Buddhas. It is a broken ladle, all dharmas, and the three worlds, i.e., mountains, oceans, earth, sun, moon, and stars. The Buddhist teaching is all the phenomenal world before us. "Outside" means "inside" and "coming inside."

Since right transmission is the right transmission from self to self, there is a self within right transmission. Since one mind is rightly transmitted to one mind, there is one mind in the right transmission. The supreme vehicle of one mind is earth, stones, and sand. Since earth, stones and sand are one mind earth, stones, and sand are earth, stones, and sand. If we think like that concerning the supreme vehicle of one mind we are on the right track.

However, people who have a mistaken view of "a special transmission outside the scriptures" can never get the central point. Therefore, to believe that there is "a special transmission outside the scriptures" is to misinterpret the Buddhist teaching. That is a bad mistake. Anyone who talks like that should ask themselves if it is possible to say that there is a special transmisson outside the mind? If we say "a special transmission outside the mind" it is just senseless words; such words can never make a transmission occur. If we cannot say that there is "a special transmission outside the mind" then surely we cannot say there is "a special transmission outside the scriptures."

Mahākāśyapa is the Dharma-heir of Shakyamuni and master teacher of the Dharma; he transmitted The Eye and Treasury of the True Law and maintained the Buddhist Way. Anyone who thinks that the Buddhist Way was not transmitted like that has a prejudiced view of the Buddhist Way. Even if only one verse is transmitted, still the Dharma is transmitted. If one verse is rightly transmitted, mountains and rivers are rightly transmitted. This principle holds true in all cases.

Shakyamuni's Eye and Treasury of the True Law and supreme enlightenment was only rightly transmitted to Mahākāśyapa, and no one else. The right transmission surely passed to Mahākāśyapa. Therefore, anyone who wishes to study the truth of the Buddhist Dharma in the past and present and wants to determine the correct teaching must study and practice under the Buddhas and Patriarchs. They should not go anywhere else. If someone lacks the correct standards of the Buddhas and Patriarchs it means that he lacks any kind of correct standards. Anyone who wishes to determine if a teaching is correct or not should use the standards of the Buddhas and Patriarchs. They are the true masters of the wheel of the Law whom we should consult. Only Buddhas and Patriarchs can clarify "existence," "non-existence," "emptiness," "form," and transmit them correctly. Therefore, make use of both ancient and present Buddhas.

Once a monk asked Haryō, "The spirit of the Patriarchs and spirit of the sūtras: Are they the same or different?" The master said, "When a chicken is cold it climbs a tree; when a duck is cold it goes into the water."

We must study this saying, looking for the Patriarch's interpretation of the

Buddhist Way by seeing and listening to the Buddhist teaching. The monk's question concerns the difference between the spirit of the Patriarchs and the spirit of the sūtras. Haryō's answer "when a chicken is cold it climbs a tree; when a duck is cold it goes into the water" seems to indicate a difference; however this "difference" is not the usual "difference" of most people. Therefore, that is why we should be aware of the special difference between them even though we realize it goes beyond limited views of same or difference. Consequently, we should not ask such questions about "same or different."

Once a monk asked Gensha, "Are the three vehicles and twelve teachings unnecessary? And what about the meaning of the first Patriarch's coming from the west?" Gensha replied, "The three vehicles and twelve teachings are all unnecessary". The monks question, "Are the three vehicles and twelve teachings unnecessary? And what about the first Patriarch's coming from the west?" is based on the common assumption that the three vehicles and twelve teachings each represent a different aspect of the Buddhist teaching while the first Patriarch's coming from the west has a separate, deeper meaning. Those two things are not considered to be equal to one another. Therefore, how could the monk know that the 84,000 gates to the Dharma are equal to the first Patriarch's coming from the west? We must look into this more closely.

Why are the three vehicles and twelve teachings unnecessary? When they are necessary what kind of principle is behind it? If the three vehicles and twelve teachings are unnecessary is proper study of the meaning of the first Patriarch's coming from the west actualized? The monk's question was not a mischievous one.

Gensha said, "The three vehicles and twelve teachings are all unnecessary." This saying is the wheel of the Law. Where this wheel turns we find the Buddhist teaching. The point here is that the three vehicles and twelve teachings are the wheel of the Law of the Buddhas and Patriarchs and turn both where the Buddhas exist and where they do not; they turn both before and after the Patriarchs existed. There is great virtue in the turning of the Buddhas and Patriarchs. When the meaning of the first Patriarch's coming from the west appears all the wheels of the Dharma become "unnecessary." "All unnecessary" does not mean "not usable" or "broken."

This wheel of the Dharma only turns as the wheel of "all unnecessary." Do not say that the three vehicles or twelve teachings do not exist, just look for the occasion of "all unnecessary." "All unnecessary" becomes the three vehicles and twelve teachings. Since the three vehicles and twelve teachings [include everything] they are not simply three vehicles and twelve teachings. Therefore, the three vehicles and twelve teachings are "all unnecessary." Now let us outline the three vehicles and twelve teachings.

The three vehicles:

1) The śrāvaka vehicle. This is the vehicle of those who have attained the Way through the Four Noble Truths. The Four Noble Truths are: 1) all things are suffering; 2) the cause of suffering 3) the destruction of suffering; and 4) the Eightfold Path. To hear those truths leads to their practice and the transcending of birth, old age, sickness, and death and culminates in nirvana. When the Four Noble Truths are practiced suffering and the cause of suffering belong to the world while cessation and the Eightfold Path become the first principle. That is the view of abhidharma scholars. If practice is based on the Buddhist Dharma, the Four Noble Truths are transmitted from Buddha to Buddha and comprise one's individual status of enlightenment. Together the Four Noble Truths are the form of reality and Buddha-nature. Therefore, it is not necessary to mention concepts of "unborn" or "uncreated" etc., since the four truths are also "all unnecessary."

2) The pratyekabuddha vehicle. This is the vehicle of those who have attained nirvana through the twelve linked chain of dependent origin. The chain of dependent origin consists of: 1) ignorance; 2) action; 3) consciousness; 4) name and form; 5) creation of the six sense organs; 6) contacts; 7) perception; 8) desire; 9) attachment; 10) existence; 11) birth; and 12) old age and death.

The practice of this chain of dependent origin is based on the relationship of cause and effect in the past, present, and future and the distinction between observer and observed. However, if we study the relationship between cause and effect carefully we can see that both samsara and causality are "all unnecessary." We must know that if ignorance overtakes the mind, then action, consciousness, etc. will also overtake it. If ignorance is destroyed then action, consciousness, etc., will be destroyed. If ignorance becomes nirvana, then action, consciousness, etc., will also become nirvana. When [the wheel of] life is destroyed, we can say such things. Ignorance is one aspect of this truth, and the other links are exactly like it. We must know that the relationship between ignorance, action, etc., is like [Seigen telling Sekitō]. "I have an ax [i.e., the Buddhist Dharma] and I'll give it to you so that you can live in the mountains" and [Sekitō's reply] "I was about to leave and my teacher kindly gave me his ax which I gratefully received."

3) The Bodhisattva vehicle. This is the vehicle of those who attained the Way through the teaching, practice, and enlightenment of the six pāramitās and it is the actualization of supreme and perfect enlightenment. That actualization is

not intentional nor unintentional, not originally existent, not newly or previously attained, not original action or non-action. It is nothing but the actualization of supreme and perfect enlightenment. The pāramitās are: 1) giving; 2) precepts; 3) observance; 4) effort; 5) contemplation; and 6) wisdom. These are all supreme enlightenment and not concepts like "unborn" or "uncreated." Giving is not necessarily first nor is wisdom necessarily last. It says in the sūtras, "A clever Bodhisattva knows that wisdom is first and giving last, while a foolish Bodhisattva thinks that giving is first and wisdom last." However, effort or meditation can just as easily be put first. Altogether there are thirty-six possible permutations of the six pāramitās; they are all interrelated and inseparable.

"Pāramitā" means "gone to the other shore." The other shore is not originally characterized by coming and going. "Gone" means "actualized," truth without error. Do not think that we arrive at the other shore after practice. We have practice on the other shore and therefore arrive there. That practice surely possesses the power to be actualized throughout the entire world of relativity.

The twelve teachings:

1) Sūtras (kaikyo), these contain the Tathāgata's explanations of the relative and absolute aspects of the objective and subjective worlds.

2) Geya (jūju), four to nine-word verses based on the sūtras.

3) Vyākarana (juki), contain predictions of the attainment of Buddhahood by all sentient beings, even pigeons and swallows.

4) Gathās (geju), independent verses praising the Buddhist teaching.

5) Udāna (mumon jisetsu), are explanations not prompted by questions from his disciples.

6) Nidana (innen), are historical narratives illustrating the consequences of bad deeds and also deal with various precepts and prohibitions.

7) Avadāna (hiyu), allegories describing the world.

8) Itivrttaka (honji), contain the past lives of the Buddhas.

9) Jātaka (honshō), are concerned with the past lives of Shakyamuni Buddha.

10) Vaipulya (hōkō), are sūtras which deal with vast subjects.

11) Adbhutadharma (mizou), describe the miraculous workings of the world.

12) Upadeśa (ronji), are discussions of doctrine.

These twelve teachings are forms of instruction for this world and given to help save all sentient beings.

It is not easy to hear the names of all the twelve teachings. We can only hear about these classifications when the Buddhist Dharma is widespread. If the Buddhist Dharma is not widespread, or almost extinct, such teachings cannot be heard. Only those who have seen the Buddha and have a long history of good karma can hear the twelve teachings. Once those teachings are heard supreme and perfect enlightenment will soon follow.

Each of the twelve may be called "sūtras" or classified as teachings. Each of the twelve contain all the others; consequently, we have 144 types of teaching. Since all the teachings involve all the others each one can be considered complete in itself. Nevertheless, it does not depend on amount or quantity. Each one of them are the enlightened vision, bones and marrow, everyday actions, divine light, adornment, and land of the Buddhas and Patriarchs. When you see the twelve teachings you see the Buddhas and Patriarchs; when you grasp the essence of the Buddhas and Patriarchs you can comprehend all the twelve types of teaching.

Therefore, that is why both Seigen's dialogue with Sekitō and Nansen's "resemblance does not always mean similar" are the twelve teachings. Also Gensha's "all unnecessary" is just like that. Ultimately, they all reduce to the Buddhas and Patriarchs, no one or nothing else; they existed before existence. At that time what was it? We should say "all unnecessary."

There is another form of classification called the nine teachings. They are: 1) sūtras; 2) gathas; 3) itvrttaka; 4) jātaka; 5) adbhutadharma; 6) nidana; 7) avadāna; 8) geya; and 9) upadeśa. These nine divisions possess nine interchangable possibilities giving altogether eight-one divisions. These nine divisions are each complete within themselves. If even one of the nine divisions lacks the virtue to be reduced to one division then there cannot be nine divisions. If each division has the virtue to be reduced to one division then each is complete. Therefore, we have eighty-one divisions. This division, my division, a fly whisk division, a staff division, and an Eye and Treasury of The True Law division.

Shakyamuni Buddha said, "I proclaimed the nine divisions of the Law corresponding to the ability of sentient beings. The divisions are the basis of entering the Great Vehicle and that is why those sūtras were proclaimed."

We must know that "I" is the Tathāgata. This is the emergence of his original face and body and mind. "I" is the nine divisions of the Law and vice versa. This verse also contains the nine divisions of the Law. Here Shakyamuni proclaims according to ability of sentient beings. Therefore, that is why the life, death, and daily activities of all sentient beings appear, and those sūtras were proclaimed. All sentient beings are transformed and enter the Buddhist Way. That is why the sūtras were proclaimed. Sentient beings correspond to Shakyamuni's nine divisions of the Law. "Correspond" means corresponding to others, to oneself, to sentient beings, to life, to "I," to "those." Sentient beings are surely "I," and therefore each of the nine divisions.

"The basis of entering the Great Vehicle" is to enlighten, practice, hear, and proclaim the Great Vehicle. We cannot say that sentient beings naturally attain the Way; that is only one part of it. "Enter" is the "basis"; "basis" means correct from head to tail. Buddha proclaims the Dharma, the Dharma proclaims Buddha. The Dharma is proclaimed by Buddha, Buddha is proclaimed by Buddha. Fire is proclaimed by the Buddha and Dharma; Buddha and Dharma proclaim fire.

The reason for proclamation is already present with "those sūtras"; that is why they are proclaimed. It is impossible not to proclaim those sūtras—that is how they are proclaimed. "Proclaimed" means the entire universe, and the entire universe proclaims. This Buddha, that Buddha, both call those divisions "sūtras." This world and other worlds also proclaim those sūtras.

Therefore, "Those sūtras were proclaimed." Those sūtras are the Buddhist teaching. We must know that the vast and unlimited Buddhist teaching is not separate from a *shippei* or fly whisk. The vastness of the Buddhist teaching is revealed in a staff and fist.

We must know that the three vehicles and twelve teachings are the enlightened vision of the Buddhas and Patriarchs. If we have yet to open our eyes how can we be called descendants of the Buddhas and Patriarchs? How can we transmit the True Eye of the Buddhas and Patriarchs? If we have not mastered the Eye and Treasury of the True Law, we cannot be Dharma-heirs of the seven Buddhas.

This was delivered to a large assembly at Kōshō monastery on November 14, 1241, and redelivered at the same place on November 7, 1242.

[40]

ARAKAN

"The arhat"

ALL evil thoughts are consumed, passions are cut off, the merit of enlightenment is possessed, illusion is dispersed, and complete freedom of mind emerges. This is the Way of a great arhat. It is the ultimate state of those who learn the Buddhist Way, and the fourth stage of Hinayana practice—that is the Buddhist arhat.

"All evil" is like the broken handle of a ladle. Even though evil has been done for a long time, it is consumed and a real ladle appears in its original form instead. "The merit of enlightenment is possessed" is the appearance of the most important thing. "Illusion is dispersed" and not hidden anywhere in the ten directions of the universe. "Complete freedom of mind emerges" should be studied as "high is of itself high, low is of itself low." Therefore, we have "walls, tiles, and stones." "Complete freedom" is the total activity of mind. "Passions are cut off" means that originally there are no defilements. Defilements obstruct defilements and cannot occur.

The spiritual power, wisdom, meditation, proclaiming of the Law, instruction, radiance, etc. of an arhat is far beyond comparison to the action of non-believers or demons. The sūtras say that arhats can see a hundred Buddha worlds. Such things cannot be seen by ordinary people. It is the principle behind "I thought foreigners had red beards, but now I know men who have red beards are foreigners."[1] To enter nirvana is to enter our clenched fist [i.e., the actions of everyday life] and carry on our natural life. Therefore, it can be said that the serene mind of nirvana is impossible to avoid. To find the essence of the arhat is to become an arhat; if we have not yet found the arhat's essence we cannot be true arhats ourselves.

---

[1] See the chapter *Daishugyō* in vol. I, p. 141.

An old sūtra says, "Today we have become true arhats. With the voice of the Buddhist Way we will proclaim the Law so that all beings will hear it." The meaning of "all beings will hear it" is that all our actions should be the voice of Buddha. This is not just limited to Buddhas and their disciples. Anyone who possesses consciousness, intelligence, skin, flesh, bones, and marrow can make "all beings hear." Consciousness and intelligence is said to extend to countries, land, grass, trees, walls, tiles, and stones. The falling leaves and blooming flowers, and the coming and going of life and death can also make others hear Buddha's voice. "All beings will hear it" shows us that we should not just listen to words through our ears.

Shakyamuni Buddha said, "If my disciples call themselves arhats or pratyekabuddhas, yet have not heard or learned what the Buddhas have only taught the Bodhisattvas, they are not my disciples, nor arhats, nor pratyekabuddhas."

"Taught to the Bodhisattvas" means "Only I and all the Buddhas of the universe know it" and "Only Buddha transmits Buddha." Master this and then give instruction based on *shobō jissō* and supreme and perfect enlightenment. Therefore, what the Bodhisattvas and the Buddhas say is equal to what arhats and patyekabuddhas say. The reason for this is that they hear and have learned that the Buddhas and Tathāgatas only instruct Bodhisattvas.

An old sūtra says, "In the sūtras of the śrāvakas there are those who are called arhats and have arrived at the level of Buddhas." This saying is the certification of the Buddhist Way. It is not just the explanation of abhidharma scholars, but rather a rule of the Buddhist Way. We must study the principle of "Those who are called arhats have reached Buddha's level" and "Those who have reached Buddha's level are called arhats." Outside the stage of an arhat nothing else exists. Furthermore, is there supreme enlightenment? Outside of supreme and perfect enlightenment nothing extra exists. Are there four kinds of practice and their effects? When an arhat accomplishes all dharmas it is the time for the unlimited Buddhist Way—it is "not mind, not Buddha, not things." Even the eye of Buddha cannot see it. It cannot be described as some certain time among innumerable kalpas. We must learn the power that enables us to see with enlightened vision. Then we will see that even the smallest thing contains all things.

Shakyamuni Buddha said, "Some bhikkhus and bhikkhunis think they have already attained arhathood, reached their final incarnation, and obtained the goal of nirvana, and therefore do not seek supreme and perfect enlightenment. Such people are arrogant, and if they do not believe in supreme and perfect enlightenment there is no basis for calling them arhats."

That is, if one believes in supreme and perfect enlightenment he can be called an arhat, and the Dharma can be transmitted. This direct transmission is the practice and enlightenment of the Dharma. Truly, attaining the stage of arhathood is not simply being in one's final incarnation and entering into final nirvana. Seeking supreme and perfect enlightenment is the seeking of enlightened vision, zazen facing a wall, and the opening of our eyes. Although the world is limitless, total and free activity emerges. Time is unchanging, yet uninhibited dialogues between masters and disciples appear. This is "seeking supreme and perfect enlightenment"—that is, seeking an arhat. That seeking is total perfection.

Zen Master Kassan Engo said, "After the people of ancient times attained enlightenment they entered the deepest part of the mountains, chose a cave covered with shrubs and bushes, and cooked their meals with mended utensils. They lived like that for ten or twenty years. They completely forgot the world of men and were happy to have left its dust far behind. People nowadays do not expect to lead such a life. They simply wish to remain anonymous, keep themselves hidden, and not do any more than necessary. They become old, little more than skin and bones. They live an enlightened life by themselves according to their individual ability. Old karma is cut off and ancient habits melt away. If they have some special power they try to pass it on to others, and work to establish relationships based on karma. They train themselves further, bearing much fruit.

"For example, it is like plucking one blade of grass in a wild field [finding just one person who seeks the Way]. Together [with that person] they have knowledge and attain liberation from life and death, living fruitful lives with gratitude toward the Buddhas and Patriarchs. However, such attainment cannot be kept to ourselves, even if we try. It is like the autumn frost which enables the spring fruit to grow. That practice benefits society and is utilized by those who seek it; it cultivates the world yet is not captivated by desires. How could someone with that kind of practice possibly become a worldly monk, clinging to rich people? If he did, his actions would offend both lay people and saints and by seeking wealth and fame his karma would lead him to hell. Those who keep the right practice will be able to lead a desireless life even if they are in powerful positions; also, even though they may not accomplish great deeds, their lives are those of true arhats."

Therefore, that is why the monks described above are real arhats who have left the dust of the world behind. If you want to know the real form of an arhat you must understand this point. Do not listen to the mistaken teachings of

Indian abhidharma scholars. Zen Master Engo of China is a Buddha and Patriarch and the Dharma-heir of the right transmission.

Zen Master Daichi of Mt. Hyakujō in Koshū said, "The six sense organs—eye, ear, nose, tongue, body, and consciousness—are each undefiled by all existent and non-existent dharmas."This is called possessing a four-verse gatha[2] or the fourth stage of practice. When the six sense organs function and transcend self and others, the total dimensions of their merit cannot be measured. Therefore, the entire body is undefiled and all existent and non-existent dharmas are undefiled. Possessing a four-verse gatha means that each organ is undefiled. This is also called the "fourth stage"; that is, the stage of an arhat.

Therefore, the present actualization of the six sense organs is the arhat. To formulate and maintain this principle is to transcend defilement. This breaking through the barrier, and possessing a four-verse gatha is the fourth stage. From top to bottom the entire body is actualized and nothing remains.

We can express it this way: "When an arhat stays with ordinary people his entire teaching becomes obstructed by them. When he stays with saints his entire teaching becomes liberated. We must know that in every circumstance, arhats and all dharmas co-exist. If we certify arhathood, it covers everywhere." That is the fist which existed before Kūō Buddha [the Buddha who existed before time].

This was delivered at Kannondōri-Kōshōhōrinji in Uji on May 15, 1242. Recopied on June 16, 1275, by Ejō.

---

[2] For example, the famous "All things are impermanent,
All dharmas are without self,
All things are full of suffering
Within the bliss of nirvana."

[41]

SHUNJŪ

"Spring and fall"

ONE day a monk asked Great Master Tōzan Gohon, "How can we avoid hot and cold?" Tōzan said, "Why don't you go somewhere that is neither hot nor cold?" "Where is a place that is neither hot nor cold?" Tōzan replied, "When it is cold, be completely cold; when it is hot, be completely hot!"

This story has been studied by many people in the past and we should also take it up in the present time. Buddhas and Patriarchs surely study it; those who study it are Buddhas and Patriarchs. All the Buddhas and Patriarchs of the past and present, in India and China, have actualized the original face of this study. That actualization is the koan of the Buddhas and Patriarchs.

We must clarify the monk's question, "How can we avoid hot and cold?" We should examine closely the meaning of "hot" and "cold." "Hot" is completely hot; "cold" is full of coldness. Hot and cold are only themselves; since they are only themselves, they arrive from the head and are actualized from the eye [i.e., the root and essence] of hot and cold. Above the head and within the eye is the place where there is no hot and cold.

Tōzan said, "When it is cold, be completely cold; when it is hot, be completely hot!" This is to confront the essence of hot and cold. That is, when hot and cold arrive we must "kill" them; yet there is a place where they cannot be killed—cold is completely cold, hot is completely hot. Even if we try a million ways to avoid hot and cold, it is still hot and cold from top to bottom. Cold is the lively enlightened vision of the Patriarchs; hot is the warm skin and flesh of our predecessors.

Zen Master Jōin Koboku (also known as Priest Hōjō), the Dharma-heir of Priest Fuyo (Dōkai), said, "Some monks were discussing Tōzan's answer and one of them said, 'That monk's question was given from a relative level and Tōzan's answer was given from an absolute level. However, the monk knew the sound of Tōzan's words and somehow entered Tōzan's level; consequently, Tōzan's answer had to stand on a relative level.' If we understand in this way, we slander our holy predecessors and sink into falsehood. Haven't you ever heard [Kassan Zen'ne's] saying, 'When we listen to the understanding of sentient beings, discrimination arises in our consciousness. It is like beauty gradually turning into ugliness right in front of our eyes.' Generally, high-minded pilgrim monks who wish to clarify this must study the Eye and Treasury of the True Law of Tōzan. Do other Buddhas and Patriarchs teach the same thing? Do their words possess the same value? Now I will ask all of you, 'Where is the place that is not hot or cold?' Do you understand? Male and female birds nest in the castle tower and are kept in the golden hall."

Jōin was in the line of Tōzan and a great master even among Patriarchs. He warned monks not to prostrate themselves before Tōzan because they would be discriminating between the relative and the absolute. If the Buddhist Dharma had been transmitted from a relative standpoint, how could it have been handed down to the present day? People who are as immature as wild kittens or coolies have not studied the essence of Tōzan's teaching. They misunderstand the heart of the Buddhist Law and mistakenly believe that Tōzan taught the five stages of the absolute and the relative.[1] This is totally inadequate and should not be listened to. The only thing we should concentrate on is Tōzan's Eye and Treasury of the True Law.

Zen Master Wanshi (Shōkaku) of Mt. Tendō in Keigenfu, (Dharma-heir of Tanka Shijun), said, "If we discuss Tōzan's story it is like two people playing a game of *go*. If one challenges the other's stone, his opponent will try to capture his stone. If he tries to avoid capture, his opponent will attack. If you understand this, you can understand Tōzan's saying. However, I'd like to add something to the story. If we look deeply there is no hot or cold. The ocean drains away and dries up; then it is easy to catch a giant sea turtle. Why do you use a fishing pole? That is very comical."

What is the meaning of "two people playing *go*"? If we say "two people are playing *go*" it means we are a third party not actually playing. If we say such things then we must stop talking and directly face our opponent. Also we must understand that Wanshi's "tries to avoid capture" means "you are not me." "His opponent will attack" means there is no separation between them. There is mud within the mud. If even a small part gets muddy we have to wash the

---

[1] 1) The absolute within the relative; 2) the relative within the absolute; 3) the absolute alone; 4) the relative alone; and 5) the absolute as relative, the relative as absolute.

entire thing. There is a jewel within the jewel. It illuminates others and illuminates ourselves.

Zen Master Engo (Kokugan) of Mt. Kassan (Dharma-heir of the fifth Patriarch Hōen) said, "A tray rolls across the jewels, jewels roll across the tray; the relative is in the absolute, the absolute is within the relative. No trace of the antelope's horns can be seen as it hides in the woods, and the bloodhound vainly runs across the forest."

"The tray rolls across the jewels" is quite an unusual expression, never used before, although it is similar to the old saying, "Jewels do not roll across a tray in any special place. The antelope's horns are now visible and the forest runs around the bloodhound."

Zen Master Myōkaku (Juken) of Shishōji temple on Mt. Secchō in Keigen-fu was in the line of Priest Chimon Kōso of Hokuto. He once said, "Tōzan's teaching is like a steep slope. Why is it necessary to discuss it from a relative or an absolute standpoint? A bright moon shines over the emerald palace, and Kanro's bark[2] reaches the sky."

Secchō was in the third generation descended from Ummon. We may say that his practice was sufficient. Although "Tōzan's teaching is like a steep slope" seems to refer to some exalted level of teaching, actually it does not. This story about Tōzan and the monk is not based on direct or indirect teaching, or the emergence or non-emergence of Buddha, so why is it necessary to use expressions like "absolute" and "relative"? If we think we must use "relative" and "absolute" to solve this problem, we have not arrived at Tōzan's level or seen the main point of the Buddhist Dharma. We should put on a pair of straw sandals and start on a pilgrimage; abandon the notion of Tōzan's true teaching being the five ranks.

Zen Master Chōrei (Priest Shitaku) of Ten'ne in Tonkin said, "The absolute is within the relative, the relative is within the absolute. Transmigrating as a human for thousands of years, I wish to return [to a state of non-transmigration i.e., nirvana] but cannot make it. Rather, wild grass continues to grow and grow in front of the temple gate."

This also uses the expressions "relative" and "absolute" but still manages to bring out the main point. We cannot say there is no main point; therefore, what is within the relative?

Priest Busshō (Hotei) of Tanshū, who was in the line of Engo, said, "Tōzan attempted to show us the place where there is no hot or cold. Flowers bloom

---

[2] The dog Kanro is famous in Chinese literature for its diligence and patience.

once again on a withered tree. [Those who do not understand this point] are as ridiculous as someone who tries to use his boat to mark the place where he dropped his sword. Such people are living among cold ashes [i.e., they have no understanding]."

This interpretation reveals a certain capability of being able to understand Tōzan's koan.

Zen Master Tandō Monjun of Rokutan said, "When hot, be completely hot; when cold be completely cold. Basically, hot and cold are not related. Master the entire world of hot and cold, then it will be like a boar-skin crown on the head of an old lord."

Let us ask, "What is the meaning of 'not related'?" Answer quickly, quickly!

Zen Master Kassan Butto (Priest Shujun), Dharma-heir of Zen Master Taihei Bukkan Ego, said, "Many Zen people have lost the location of Tōzan's 'place where there is no hot or cold.' When it is cold, face the fire; when it is hot, go outside to cool off. Then we will be able to avoid hot and cold in our life."

Although Shujun was in the line of the fifth Patriarch Hōen, his words are those of a child. However, "Then we will be able to avoid hot and cold in our life" contains a kernel of understanding. Namely, one life covers all lives, and avoiding hot and cold is the dropping off of body and mind.

We have quoted a number of interpretations of Tōzan's koan from various masters of different eras, but none of them are even close to Tōzan's level. Since most of them do not know what hot and cold means in the Buddhas' and Patriarchs' everyday life, all they have is "going outside to cool off" and "facing the fire." This is a great pity. We should ask ourselves, "How should we study hot and cold when we live with an old Zen master?" It is shameful that the Way of the Buddhas and Patriarchs has been lost. Students should learn the real meaning and actual time of hot and cold, and then make their own interpretations and commentaries. If you cannot arrive at such a stage, you must look for your inadequacies. Worldly people can understand the sun and moon, and know about the phenomenal world. Saints, sages, and fools are so named because of their respective understanding. Never think that the hot and cold of the Buddhist Way is the same as the hot and cold of fools. That is what we must earnestly study.

This was delivered on two different occasions during 1244 as a memorial and exposition of Tōzan's wonderful teaching. A Patriarch said, "Many animals have horns, but one horn of a kirin [a magical beast] is sufficient."

[42]

KATTŌ[1]

"Spiritual entanglement"

ONLY Mahākaśyapa transmitted the Eye and Treasury of the True Law and the Supreme Enlightenment of Shakyamuni Buddha on Vulture Peak. It was continually transmitted to the twenty-eighth Patriarch Bodhidharma. Bodhidharma came to China as the first Patriarch and transmitted the Eye and Treasury of the True Law and Supreme Enlightenment to the Great Teacher Shōshū Fukaku [Eka], who became the second Patriarch.

The twenty-eighth Patriarch came to the east as the first Patriarch of China, and the twenty-ninth Patriarch is the second Chinese Patriarch. This is the Chinese method of reckoning. The first Patriarch practiced under Prajñātāra from whom he learned the Buddhist Teaching and essence of the Way, and received the transmission. He inherited the inner root of the Buddhist teaching and passed it on to his descendants.

Generally, saints study in order to cut off the root of their spiritual entanglements but do not use their entaglements to cut off entanglements. Do they know how to use entaglements to transmit entaglements? It is rare to find anyone who knows that entanglements [cannot be separated] from the transmission of the Dharma. Few have experienced it or even heard it. How can it be possible for many people to experience it?

My late master, an ancient Buddha, said, "A gourd is really a type of wisteria; its tangles make it a gourd."

Such a teaching cannot be found anywhere else in the past or present. My

---

[1] *Kattō*, "a tangled wisteria," usually is used as a derogatory word to mean complicated teachings or wordy Zen; it is a synonym for illusion. However, in this chapter Dōgen urges us to use *kattō* to cut off *kattō*; use illusion to cut off illusion. Also, *kattō* symbolizes the relationship between Buddha and Buddha, inextricably bound together through the Dharma transmission.

late master was the first to reveal such a teaching. The gourd's intertwined vines are like Buddhas and Patriarchs seeking out Buddhas and Patriarchs, or Buddhas and Patriarchs confronting the Buddhas and Patriarchs. It is mind to mind transmission.

The twenty-eighth Patriarch said to his disciples, "The time has come for you to tell me what you have attained." The disciple Dōfu said, "This is my viewpoint: Neither be attached nor not attached to words or letters. Utilize that condition freely." Bodhidharma said, "You possess my skin." Then the nun Sōji said, "This is my present understanding: After Ānanda saw the Buddha land of Akṣobhya once, he never looked at it again." Bodhidharma said, "You possess my flesh." The third disciple Dōiku said, "The four elements are empty and the five skandhas are non-existent. In my view there is not one thing to be gained." The Patriarch said, "You possess my bones." Finally, Eka made three prostrations and without speaking returned to his seat. Bodhidharma said, "You possess my marrow." Then Bodhidharma transmitted his Dharma and robe to Eka, designating him the second Patriarch.

We must study the first Patriarch's words "you possess my skin, flesh, bones, and marrow"—these are the words of a Patriarch. Each disciple had a certain understanding and possessed some good points. Each of those points are the skin, flesh, bones, and marrow of the liberated body and mind; i.e., the skin, flesh, bones, and marrow of the body and mind that has dropped off. We should not listen to or study any Patriarch's words with superficial understanding or discrimination. The Patriarch's words are not "this" or "that" trying to describe the whole.

Nevertheless, those who lack the right transmission think that there is a difference between the levels of understanding of the four disciples and that there is a distinction in the first Patriarch's "skin," "flesh," "bones," and "marrow." They think that the first Patriarch's skin and flesh is farther away than his bones and marrow. Also, they believe that the second Patriarch was given the marrow because his understanding was the best. If we say such things we have not studied the Buddhas and Patriarchs nor received the right transmission.

We should know that the Patriarch's skin, flesh, bones, and marrow have nothing to do with their relative depth. Even if there happens to be a difference in understanding, what the Patriarch said was, "You possess my...." This means that the teaching in both "you possess my marrow" and "you possess my bones" can be used to instruct and lead people—there is no thought of sufficiency or insufficiency. They are like the holding up of the flower [of

Mahākāśyapa] or the transmission of the robe [to Enō]. What the first Patriarch said was the same from the very beginning. Although what the Patriarch said was equal, the four interpretations are not necessarily equal. The four disciples' interpretations may differ, but the words of the Patriarch are still the words of a Patriarch.

Often, the speaker's intention and the listener's understanding do not coincide. For example, when Bodhidharma spoke to his four disciples he meant "you possess me through your 'skin'." If the second Patriarch has hundreds of thousands of disciples, there will also be hundreds of thousands of interpretations—there is no limit. In the present case there are only four disciples and therefore we tentatively have the four aspects of skin, flesh, bones, and marrow. If there had been someone else mentioned, there would have been yet another different interpretation.

When we speak to the second Patriarch we must be able to understand the meaning of "you possess my skin." Even if there is "you possess my skin," there still must be a transmission of the Eye and Treasury of the True Law of the second Patriarch, independent of possessing the skin, flesh, bones, or marrow.

In the case of Dōfu, Dōiku, and Sōji we must understand the meaning of "you possess my marrow." Even if we possess just the skin we still must possess the Dharma. The body and mind of Bodhidharma is his skin, flesh, bones, and marrow. But remember, it is not that his marrow is deep or that his skin is superficial.

If we are able to open the eye of study and receive the seal of "you possess my skin," we will have found the correct way to possess Bodhidharma. It is his entire skin, flesh, bones, and marrow, body and mind, body and body, mind and mind. He is a Patriarch who is completely a Patriarch; he is saying, "you possess my entire body." When this Patriarch appears and speaks to hundreds of thousands of disciples he will say, "You possess my skin." Every one of the disciples will probably make a distinction between the skin, flesh, bones, and marrow. If Bodhidharma had six or seven disciples studying under him he would have said "you possess my heart," "you possess my body," "you possess my Buddha," "you possess my enlightened eyes," "you possess my enlightenment," etc. "You" sometimes means Bodhidharma, sometimes Eka. We must study in detail the principle of "possess."

We must also be aware of the expressions "you possess me," "I possess you," "possessing me and you," "possessing you and me." If we look into the body and mind of the Patriarch and say his interior and exterior are not one and there is no unity in the entire body, we are not actualizing the land of the Buddhas and Patriarchs. If we possess the skin it means we possess the flesh, bones, and marrow. If we possess the bones and marrow it means we possess the original face of the skin and flesh.

The body of the entire universe is not only Bodhidharma's body; it is his skin, flesh, bones, and marrow. Therefore, we can say "you possess my robe" and "you possess my Law." Further, the words of both Bodhidharma and the disciples transcend universals and particulars; consequently, master and disciple learn together.

This mutual study and seeking of the Way between master and disciple is *kattō*, the spiritual and physical entwinement of the Buddhas and Patriarchs. This forms the life of the Buddhas and Patriarchs; skin, flesh, bones, and marrow form the smile of Mahākāśyapa.

We must study further that the seed of this entwinement has the ability to liberate us; it has branches, leaves, flowers, and fruit that wind together to form the plant. They are mutually bound to each other, although they seem independent; here Buddhas and Patriarchs are actualized and real form emerges.

Great Master Jōshū Shinsai said to an assembly of monks, "Mahākāśyapa transmitted the Law to Ānanda. To whom did Bodhidharma transmit the Dharma?" A monk said, "Everyone knows that the second Patriarch possessed the marrow of Bodhidharma's teaching. Why do you ask such a question?" The master said, "Don't slander the second Patriarch like that!" Then he said, "Bodhidharma stated that those on the outside get the skin and those on the inside get the bones. What do those who are in the innermost part get?" The monk asked, "What is the principle of attaining the marrow?" The master said, "You possess only the skin and this old monk does not depend on the marrow." The monk asked, "What is this marrow?" The master replied, "If you ask a question like that you won't even be able to get the skin."

Therefore, we should see that if we are not able to get the skin we cannot get the marrow. If we can get the skin we can get the marrow. We must clarify the principle of "If you talk like that you cannot even get the skin." In reply to the question "What is the principle of attaining the marrow," the master said, "You possess only the skin and this old monk does not depend on the marrow." Where we find the skin and do not depend on the marrow is the principle behind attaining the marrow. Therefore, we have a question like: "Everyone knows that the second Patriarch possessed the marrow of Bodhidharma's teaching. Why do you ask such a question?" When we look at Mahākāśyapa's transmission to Ānanda, we see that Ānanda's entire body was absorbed by Mahākāśyapa; they became one. However, at the time of transmission the face, eyes, skin, flesh, bones, and marrow cannot avoid being changed somewhat. Hence, Jōshū asked, "To whom did Bodhidharma transmit the Dharma?" When Bodhidharma decided to transmit the Law he was already the real Bodhidharma, and when the second Patriarch possessed the marrow he had already become Bodhidharma. This is the principle behind the intact transmission of the Buddhist Law up to the present age. If such a principle had not been present the Buddhist Dharma could not have been transmitted. We should study this principle carefully, comprehend it ourselves, and teach it to others.

"Those on the outside get the skin, those on the inside get the bones. What do those who are in the innermost part get?" Here "outside" and "inside" directly indicate the essence. When we say outside it means the skin, flesh, bones, and marrow are outside. When we say inside it means the skin, flesh, bones, and marrow are inside.

Therefore, that is why the four disciples of Bodhidharma studied the development of myriad kinds of skin, flesh, bones, and marrow. Do not think that there is no other development outside of the marrow. Other developments do exist.

The ancient Buddha Jōshū's address to the monks is the real Buddhist Way. Others such as Rinzai, Tokusan, Dai'e, Ummon, and others do not surpass him; on the contrary, they cannot even dream of his level. How can they begin to talk about it? Elders of the present age who lack understanding of the Dharma, also know nothing about it and if they hear such talk they will be totally surprised.

Zen Master Secchō Myōkaku said, "Jōshū and Bōkūshu are both ancient Buddhas." Therefore, the Way of ancient Buddhas is the experience of enlightenment in the Buddhist Dharma, and the understanding of one's own essence. Great Master Seppō Shinkaku said, "Jōshū is an ancient Buddha." Both of these Buddhist Patriarchs praised the ancient Buddha Jōshū. Now we know that ancient Buddhas transcend the development of past and present.

The principle of mutual entwinement of skin, flesh, bones, and marrow is the standard of ancient Buddhas' use of the expression "you possess me." We must study and clarify this standard.

"The first Patriarch returned to the west." That is a mistaken interpetation. According to Sōun he met Bodhidharma on the way back to India, but how can that be true? How could he see Bodhidharma's actions? It is correct to say that after he entered parinirvana Bodhidharma's ashes were interred on Mt. Uji in China.

This was delivered to the monks on July 7, 1242 at Kannondōri-Kōshōhōrinji, Yamashiro, Uji-gun. Transcribed on March 3, 1243, at the chief disciple's quarters of Kippōji, Yoshida-gun, by Ejō.

[43]

HAKUJUSHI

"The oak tree"

GREAT Master Jōshū Shinsai was the thirty-seventh Patriarch descended from Shakyamuni, the Tathāgata. He first developed the resolve to seek the Way at the age of sixty-one, left his home and began to study the Way. At that time he said, "If I meet a hundred-year-old man who is inferior to me, I will teach him; if I meet a seven-year-old child who is superior to me, I will ask him about the Way." He made this vow and then left for the south to begin his pilgrimage.

One day he arrived at Nansen's and went to pay his respects. Jōshū entered the room to give his greeting and saw Nansen lying down. Nansen asked him, "Where are you from?" Jōshū replied, "Zuizo-in [the name of Nansen's temple]." Nansen said, "Have you seen the zuizo [i.e., the glorious image of Buddha]?" Jōshū said, "No, I haven't seen it, but I see a reclining Buddha." Nansen sat up and asked, "Are you a master-less novice or not?" Jōshū said, "I have a master." Nansen asked, "Who is he?" Jōshū said, "It's early spring and still chilly but you look fine, honorable priest." Nansen called the director of monks and said, "Take special care of this novice."

That is how he came to study under Nansen. After that he did not go anywhere else for more than thirty years and diligently practiced the Way. He never wasted his time or did useless things. After he received the transmission of the Way he became abbot of Kannon-in of Jōshū and lived there another thirty years. As abbot he was very different from the typical priests of the time.

One day Jōshū said, "Smoke drifts only from the neighboring kitchens and I haven't eaten a *manju* or *dango*[1] since last year. The monks think little about

---

[1] Kinds of sweet cakes.

their practice but complain much. There are no good people left in the town. When they visit the temple the first thing they ask for is tea; if there is no tea they get angry and leave."

It is a great pity that no smoke rises from Jōshū's kitchen and there is little food. There has been no food since last year. People only come from the village for tea; if they do not want tea they do not come. None of them bring tea as an offering. The monks want to see a sage, but no one wants to be one.

Another time, Jōshū said, "Out of all those who have renounced the world is there anyone who lives the way I do? I sleep on the earthen floor on a torn mat without a cover and with only a wooden pillow. No incense is offered before the Buddha-image; instead, there is the smell of manure chips."

We can see from the above illustrations how poor Jōshū's life was. We should all follow his example. Yet he had fewer than twenty monks studying under him since few can lead such a difficult life. The monastery was small and lacked proper facilities such as seats and washstands. There was no light at night and no charcoal for winter. It was a very severe life, especially for someone of advanced age. Nevertheless, all of the ancient Buddhas lived like Jōshū.

Once one of the temple officers wanted to replace a leg on a platform that had been broken some time before and had been patched with a piece of scrap wood, but Jōshū would not permit it. This is a very unusual anecdote.

Often there was not even a single grain of rice for the morning gruel, just light pouring through the window, and dust blowing through the cracks. Sometimes Jōshū himself picked nuts and berries to use for the monks' food. All his descendants praise his austere life, and even though they cannot follow in his footsteps they long for such a life.

Another time, Jōshū told the monks, "I lived for thirty years in the south, doing nothing but zazen. All of you should concentrate on zazen in order to solve the great matter of life and death. If after three, five, twenty, or thirty years of practice you cannot gain the Way, cut off my head and use it for a lavatory basin." He uttered such hard sayings as this. Truly, the practice of zazen is the direct road to the Buddhist Way; look into zazen for the truth. Later on, many people said that Jōshū was an ancient Buddha.

Once, a monk asked the Great Master Jōshū, "Why did the first Patriarch come from the west?" Jōshū said, "The oak tree in the front garden." The monk said, "O Priest, you shouldn't give such an objective answer." Jōshū replied, "I didn't." The monk asked again, "Why did the first Patriarch come from the west?" Jōshū said, "The oak tree in the front garden."

Although this koan originated with Jōshū, it was created by the entire body of all the Buddhas. Who is the master of this koan? We should know that the principle of "the oak tree in the front garden" and "Why did the first Patriarch come from the west" does not belong to the objective world. Furthermore, the oak tree is not the objective "self." Because we have "O Priest, you shouldn't give such a concrete answer," there is the reply, "I didn't"; how can the priest become attached to the priest? If he is not attached he becomes "I." How can "I" be attached to "I"? If he is attached he becomes a human being. What stage of objectivity can be obstructed by "come from the west" since "come from the west" occurs in the objective world? However, do not consciously wait for an objective state of "come from the west" since it is not necessarily the Eye and Treasury of the True Law and Serene Mind—it is not mind, not Buddha, not things.

This "Why did the first Patriarch come from the west" is not a question nor does it indicate that both the monk and Jōshū shared the same viewpoint. When this question is given, not one person is seen, nor can the questioner gain anything. The deeper we look into this question the more unfathomable it is. Therefore, our answer is incomplete, mistake after mistake piles up, and our speech is like an empty echo, is it not? Since there is no objectivity or subjectivity in "the oak tree in the front garden," it is rooted in complete freedom.

We are not speaking in an objective sense, so therefore, this oak tree is not a usual type. Yet even if it is considered from an objective standpoint, Jōshū did not give an objective answer. That oak tree is not like the one that grows near the emperor's tomb. Since our oak tree is not like that one [which cannot be cut down], it can turn to dust. Even when it becomes dust it cannot obstruct our thoughts or practice, and consequently, Jōshū said, "I didn't give an objective answer." How can it be shown to other people, since we ourselves are like the oak tree [without discrimination of objectivity or subjectivity].

A monk once asked Jōshū, "Does an oak tree have Buddha-nature or not?" Jōshū replied, "It has." Then the monk asked, "When does the oak tree become Buddha?" Jōshū said, "It waits for the sky to fall to earth." The monk asked, "When does it fall to earth?" Jōshū said, "It waits for the oak tree to become Buddha."

We should pay attention to both the monk's question and the Great Master's answer. Jōshū's "when the sky falls to earth" and "when the oak tree becomes Buddha" do not express an idea of mutual waiting. The monk was asking about "oak tree," "Buddha-nature," "becoming Buddha," "time," "sky," and "falling to earth." When Jōshū answered, "It has," it means the oak tree possesses Buddha-nature. In order to master this we must take the lifeblood of the

Buddhas and Patriarchs. "An oak tree possesses Buddha-nature" is not usually said. Since it has been said, however, we should clarify it. Does the oak tree that possesses Buddha-nature have a high or low status? We should find out if it has a long or short life, how high it is, and to what genus and family it belongs. Are a hundred thousand trees the same or different? Is there an oak tree that becomes Buddha, an oak tree that practices, or an oak tree with an awakened mind? Do the sky and oak tree have a special relationship? The oak tree waits for the sky to fall to become Buddha; does this mean that the oak tree becomes the sky? Is the oak tree on the first or last step in the sky? We must study this in detail.

Now, let us question Jōshū. "Since you are one with an old oak tree, you can talk like that, can't you?"

Generally speaking, "The oak tree possesses Buddha-nature" is not the outlook of non-believers or Hinayanists, nor the standpoint of scholars of the sūtras or abhidharma. Furthermore, how can such dry, lifeless people even express it? Only people like Jōshū can study and clarify it. Jōshū's "the oak tree possesses Buddha-nature" is concerned with whether or not oak trees obstruct oak trees, or whether Buddha-nature obstructs Buddha-nature. This expression is not mastered by just one or two Buddhas, and it is not necessary to have the appearance of Buddha in order to master it. Among the Buddhas some might give such an expression, but others might not. "Waiting for the sky to fall to earth" does not mean that such an event does not occur. Every time the oak tree becomes Buddha, the sky falls to earth. The roar when the sky falls to earth surpasses a hundred thousand peals of thunder. When the oak tree becomes Buddha, the hours of the day are turned upside down. The sky that falls to earth is not the sky seen by ordinary people or saints; there is another kind of sky only seen by Jōshū. "Earth" is not the earth possessed by ordinary people or saints; it is a different kind of earth. Shade or light cannot go there, only Jōshū. The sun, moon, mountains, and rivers also wait for the sky to fall to earth.

Anyone who can talk about Buddha-nature surely becomes Buddha. Buddha-nature is the adornment of becoming Buddha. Furthermore, Buddha-nature co-exists simultaneously with becoming Buddha.

Therefore, that is why the oak tree and Buddha-nature are not a different sound or the same pitch. Yet no matter how we attempt to express it, it cannot be done. All of you must clarify this problem.

This was delivered to the monks at Kannondōri-Kōshōhōrinji, Uji-kun, on May 21, 1242. Transcribed on July 3, 1243, in the master's quarters by Ejō.

[44]

SANGAI YUISHIN

"The three worlds are only mind"

THE Great Teacher Shakyamuni said, "The three worlds are only mind; outside the mind nothing exists. Mind, Buddha, and sentient beings are not three different things."

This verse contains the teaching of Shakyamuni's entire life. Those words were spoken intentionally; they had to be expressed. Therefore, the Tathāgata's "The three worlds are only mind" is the actualization of the entire Tathāgata. The entire life of the Tathāgata is expressed in one complete verse. "Three worlds" are the entire universe. Yet we should not say that the three worlds are "mind" since the three worlds clearly show themselves in all directions, yet remain three worlds.

We may mistakenly believe that the three worlds do not exist; nevertheless, we cannot separate ourselves from them. Inside, outside, center, beginning, middle and end are all three worlds. The "three worlds" is the world seen as three worlds. If someone thinks the three worlds do not exist he is mistaken. Some may think the three worlds represent an old viewpoint [illusion] or a new viewpoint [enlightenment]. The three worlds are seen both as illusion and enlightenment.

Therefore, Shakyamuni the Great Teacher said, "The three worlds I see are not like the three worlds of ordinary people." This is the correct viewpoint. The three worlds should be seen like that. The three worlds are not original or present existence, not newly made nor formed by karma, not beginning, middle, or end. There are three worlds detached from the world of suffering; these are the present three worlds. There is a meeting of the function of detachment and the function caused to be detached. Practice develops practice. The present three worlds are the three worlds we see. "Seeing" is seeing the three worlds. Seeing the three worlds is seeing the actualization of the three worlds, and the actualization of the three worlds seen—this is the actualization of reality. Through the three worlds resolve, practice, enlightenment, and nirvana arise.

This is "all things are my possessions." That is why Shakyamuni said, "In the present three worlds all things are my possessions; all sentient beings within the three worlds are my children."

Since the present three worlds are the possessions of Shakyamuni the entire universe is the three worlds, the three worlds are the entire universe. The present three worlds cover past, present, and future. The actualization of past, present, and future does not obstruct the present world. The actualization of this present world does not obstruct past, present, or future. "My possessions" means that the true body of man covers the entire ten quarters of the universe. "The entire universe is in the eye of a monk." "Sentient beings" are the true body of the entire universe. Each sentient being exists as "being"; consequently, taken together they make up all sentient beings.

"All my children" is the principle of the emergence of the total activity of children. Surely, "my children" have received their bodies, hair, and skin from their compassionate father. Consequently, they should not harm themselves by separating themselves from the Dharma, or develop any insufficiencies. Then they can be actualized as children. Here, it is not father first, child second, nor child first, father second, nor is it simultaneous birth—this is the principle of "my children." The father does not give the child life; he receives it himself as a child. The child does not take its life from the father, but simply receives it. It is not a case of father leaving and child emerging; it is not a measure of great or small, nor a comparison of old and young.

The relationship between old and young should be thought of as the relationship between Buddha and Patriarch. The father is young and the child is old, the father is old and the child is young, the father and child are old, the father and child are young. It is not that the child has learned that his father is old, and we cannot say that the father was not young once. We must carefully study the meaning of "old" and "young" in father and child. We must not be flippant. There is a father and child that emerge and disappear simultaneously as father and child, and a father and child that do not. Neither father nor child create any obstructions; therefore, both child and compassionate father appear. There are sentient beings with mind, and there are sentient beings without mind. There are children with mind and children without. Like this, "my children" and "children as me" become Dharma-heirs of the compassionate father, Shakyamuni. All sentient beings of the past, present, and future throughout the entire universe are all the Buddhas of the past, present, and future throughout the entire universe. The children of all the Buddhas are sentient beings; sentient beings are the compassionate father of all the Buddhas.

Therefore, that is why the flowers and fruits of a hundred grasses, and large and small rocks are the possessions of all the Buddhas. That is also why the forests and fields are places of peace, free from all suffering. We may talk about this, but the essence of this saying of Buddha concerns "my children." He did not say "my father." We must study this.

Shakyamuni Buddha said, "Buddha's Dharma-body, bliss-body, and nirvana-body are never separated from the three worlds. There are no sentient beings outside the three worlds. Where else can Buddhas teach? Therefore I say, 'Anyone who says there is a world of sentient beings outside the three worlds is quoting the writings of non-believers, and not the teaching of the seven Buddhas.'"

We must clarify that the Dharma-, bliss-, and nirvana-bodies of all the Buddhas form the three worlds. There is nothing outside the three worlds. There is nothing outside Buddha, nothing outside fence and walls. Just as there is nothing outside the three worlds, there is nothing outside sentient beings. If there are no sentient beings, how can Buddha teach? Where the Buddhas teach, surely there are sentient beings.

We should know that only in the writings of non-believers is there a world of sentient beings outside the three worlds; it is not in the sūtras of the seven Buddhas. "Only mind" is not just "one" or "two," not the three worlds, nor has it emerged from the three worlds. It contains nothing false and is both the possession and non-possession of thought, knowledge, cognition, and awakening. It is wall, tiles, and stones, mountains, rivers and earth. "Mind" is skin, flesh, bones, and marrow, Buddha's holding up of the flower, and Mahākāśyapa's smile. "Mind" is existent, non-existent, with a body, bodiless, existing before the body appears, and after it disappears. There are several kinds of bodily births: live, egg, by moisture, and spontaneous. Mind is also born in the same ways. Mind is blue, yellow, red, white; width, length, and form; the coming and going of life and death; years, months, days, and minutes; dreams, illusions, and empty flowers; mist and shimmering air; spring flowers and the autumn moon; and all the actions of our daily lives. None of those things can be abandoned or thrown away. The reality of all forms is mind; only Buddhas transmit Buddha.

Great Master Gensha-in Soitsu once asked Great Master Jizō-in Shinō, "What is your understanding of 'the three worlds are only mind'?" Shinō pointed at a chair and said, "What do you call this?" Gensha said, "A chair." Shinō said,

"Then you don't know anything about 'the three worlds are only mind'." Gensha said, "I call this a bamboo tree. What do you call it?" Shinō answered, "I also call it a bamboo tree." Then Gensha said, "Everywhere throughout the great earth it is impossible to find anyone who has attained the Buddhist Dharma."

The point of Gensha's "What is your understanding of 'the three worlds are only mind'?" is that whether you understand it or not, it is still the same 'three worlds are only mind.' In either case we can say that the three worlds are only mind. Shinō pointed at a chair and said, "What do you call this?" We must know that Gensha's "What is your understanding?" is the same as Shinō's "What do you call it?"

Is Gensha's "chair" a word used in the three worlds or not? Is it related to words used in the three worlds or not? Did the chair say it, or did Gensha say it? We should look into such questions and derive some insight from them.

Shinō said, "Then you don't know anything about 'the three worlds are only mind'." This saying is an example of Jōshū's eastern and southern gates which also can be western or northern gates. In addition, there are the eastern and western gates of Jōshū Province. Even if we understand that the three worlds are only one mind, we must also clarify "do not understand." The three worlds are only mind since there is a "three worlds are only mind" that transcends understanding or non-understanding.

Gensha said, "I call it a bamboo tree." This shows us a wordless word and timeless time. "I call it a bamboo tree." What else can it be called? Originally, everything is beautiful from all sides from the beginning, middle and end like the bamboo tree. Here, is "I call it a bamboo tree" concerned with "the three worlds are only mind" or not? If we grasp the meaning of "the three worlds are only mind" in the morning, it becomes a "chair," "only mind," or "the three worlds." If we grasp its meaning in the evening, it becomes "I call it a bamboo tree."

Shinō said, "I also call it a bamboo tree." We must know that this dialogue between master and disciple involves complete, mutual, and correct understanding. Nevertheless, we must determine whether Gensha's "I call it a bamboo" and Shinō's "I also call it a bamboo tree" are the same or different, right or wrong.

Gensha said, "Everywhere throughout the entire world it is impossible to find anyone who has attained the Buddhist Dharma." We must carefully digest this point. Gensha said, "I call it a bamboo tree" and Shinō said, "I also call it a bamboo tree." It is not clear whether or not either of them understood the meaning of "the three worlds are only mind."

However that might be, let us question Gensha. You said, "Everywhere throughout the great earth it is impossible to find anyone who has attained the Buddhist Dharma." What do you mean by "the great earth"? This is what we must clarify and practice.

This was delivered to the monks at the peak of Zenjihō, Echizen, on July 1, 1243. Transcribed on July 25, the same year, in the abbot's quarters by Ejō.

SESSHIN SESSHŌ

"Explaining mind, explaining nature"

WHEN Zen Master Shinsan Somitsu was on a pilgrimage with Great Master Tōzan Gohon, he pointed at a temple and said, "Inside that temple there is someone explaining mind and explaining nature." Somitsu asked, "Who is it?" Tōzan said, "If you ask such a question you will go directly to your death." Somitsu asked again, "But who is explain-mind and explaining nature?" Tōzan said, "Life is found in the midst of death."

Explaining mind and explaining nature is the root of the Buddhist Way. Buddhas and Patriarchs are actualized from it. If there is no explaining of mind and nature, there is no turning of the wheel of the Law, no awakening or practice, no simultaneous attainment of the Way by all beings, and no Buddha-nature in sentient beings. The holding up of a flower and blinking the eye, Mahākāśyapa's smile, Eka's prostrations, Bodhidharma's entering China, and Enō's reception of the kesa at midnight are all explaining mind and explaining nature. Holding a staff or putting the fly whisk down is also explaining mind and explaining nature.

In general, all the virtues of the Buddhas and Patriarchs are contained in explaining mind and explaining nature. Their everyday life is explaining mind and explaining nature; wall, tiles, and stones are explaining mind and explaining nature. It is the actualization of the saying: "When mind appears, all phenomena appear; when mind perishes, all phenomena perish." This is the time of explanation of the mind and the time for explanation of nature. However, those who do not go into mind and nature are in the dark about explaining mind and explaining nature. They cannot fathom its profound and marvelous nature and therefore teach that it is not the Way of the Buddhas and Patriarchs. They think that explaining mind and explaining nature is nothing more than a normal discourse on mind and nature, since they have not tried to critically understand the meaning and character of the great Way.

Later on, Dai'e Shuko of Kinzan said, "People nowadays like explanations of mind and nature to be profound and marvelous, so it takes them a long time to gain the Way. If we abandon both mind and nature, and forget about profound and marvelous speech, when the time comes those two subjective views will not arise and we will attain enlightenment."

Such an understanding came about because Dai'e lacked the abundance and serenity of the Buddhas and Patriarchs. He thought that "mind" is just a faculty of discrimination; he did not know that such discriminatory thoughts are also contained in "mind." That is why he talked like that. He did not know that "nature" is pure, deep, and serene and was unaware of existence and nonexistence, and Buddha- and Dharma-nature; he could not even dream about the nature of suchness. Consequently, his view of the Buddhist Dharma was very one-sided. The mind obtained through the Way of the Buddhas and Patriarchs is their skin flesh, bones, and marrow. The nature possessed by the Buddhas and Patriarchs is a *shippei* and staff. Their profound enlightenment is a round pillar and stone lantern. Their marvelous Way is their field of knowledge and comprehension.

Becoming a Buddha and Patriarch, based on the truth of Buddhas and Patriarchs, occurs first through hearing the words "mind" and "nature" and then through explanation; it is attained through practice and enlightenment. We must strive to maintain and learn more about this profound study. If we study in this way we may be said to be true students and descendants of the Buddhas and Patriarchs. If we do not, it is not proper study of the Way.

Therefore, when we think we have attained the Way we have not; and we cannot say there is no attainment when we have not consciously attained the Way. In both of these cases misunderstandings arise. Even if we talk like Dai'e and say "forget about mind and nature," we are still using one of the millions of ways to explain mind. "Abandon profound and marvelous speech" is just another form of profound and marvelous speech. If we lack proper study of this point and foolishly forget it, it will fly out of our hands and flee from our body.

How can those who are not liberated from narrow-minded Hinayanist thinking possibly arrive at the heart of the Mahayana? Furthermore, how can they make any progress on the Way? These people have never shared a meal with the Buddhas and Patriarchs. The meaning of study and practice under a master is the experience of the body and mind of "explaining mind and explaining nature." We must also study it before and after we obtain a body. There is nothing else besides this.

Once, the first Patriarch Bodhidharma said to the second Patriarch, Eka, "Cut off your analysis of the external world and stop the working of your mind. Keep your mind like fences and walls; then you can enter the Way." The second Patriarch had heard many different explanations of mind and nature but had never attained enlightenment. One day he accidentally stumbled across the meaning of his master's words and told Bodhidharma, "For the first time, your disciple has cut off all the karma that bound him." The first Patriarch had already perceived that Eka had truly attained enlightenment and did not question him further. Later on, Bodhidharma said, "Aren't you attached to your detachment?" Eka said, "No!" Bodhidharma said, "Tell me what it's like." Eka said, "I'm just using my everyday mind and no words can describe it." Then Bodhidharma said, "That is the essence of mind transmitted by all the Buddhas and Patriarchs. Now that you have attained it preserve it well."

Some people discredit this story, while others praise it. This is just one of the many stories concerning the first and second Patriarchs. In the beginning, the second Patriarch explained mind and nature, but it did not mesh with the explanation of the first Patriarch. After a time he acquired merit which enabled him to attain the Way of the first Patriarch. Foolish people think that the second Patriarch was unable to gain enlightenment because he was attached to his explanations of mind and nature, and that after he abandoned his explanations he finally attained enlightenment. Such people have never studied the saying: "Keep your mind like fences and walls; then you can enter the Way." That is why they think like that, and are unable to distinguish between various methods of study.

Such things happen because people seek ascetic practice, rather than the enlightenment-seeking mind and practice of the Buddhist Way; therefore, their practice is completely worthless. Instead, they should follow a virtuous master or the sūtras, and then they can make progress.

In order to master one aspect of the Buddhist teaching in the present, we have to build on all the failures accumulated in the past. After many failures we finally become skillful. Hearing the teaching, practicing the Way, and attaining enlightenment occurs in this way. We may have failed hundreds of times in the past to master explaining mind and nature, but we can turn it into mastery in the present. Often when people first begin to practice the Buddhist Way they feel it is too difficult; then they abandon it and seek a different path. If we do that we will never be able to attain the Buddhist Way. We must completely understand the real meaning of Buddhist practice from start to finish. The principle behind failure and eventual success is difficult to understand.

In Buddhism, both the initial resolve for enlightenment and attainment of perfect enlightenment are the Buddhist Way—it exists throughout the beginning, middle, and end of our practice. For example, when someone walks ten thousand *ri*, one step includes one thousand *ri*, just as a thousand steps include one thousand *ri*. Although there is a difference between the first step and the one thousandth step, they both are contained within one thousand *ri* and are the same.

However, very foolish people think that when we study Buddhism we do not arrive at the Buddhist Way until our study is completed. This occurs because such people do not know that proclaiming, practicing, and enlightening the Buddhist Way are all complete within themselves and contain all aspects of the Way. They say that only those who are lost in illusion need to practice the Buddhist Way and attain great enlightenment. They do not know that even those who are not in illusion practice the Buddhist Way diligently and attain great enlightenment.

Although explaining mind and explaining nature prior to attaining enlightenment also contains the Buddhist Way, enlightenment is manifested through explaining mind and explaining nature. We should not study enlightenment as something that occurs only when unenlightened people are awakened to great enlightenment. Both people in illusion and enlightened people have great enlightenment: unenlightened people and those who are not in illusion also have great enlightenment.

Hence, explaining mind and explaining nature is the direct path to the Buddhist Way. Since Dai'e Shūkō failed to master this, he said that explanations of mind and nature should not occur. This is not the principle of the Buddhist Dharma. Yet, in present Great Sung Dynasty China, he is considered to be an unsurpassed example.

The Great Teacher Tōzan Gohon was a Patriarch among Patriarchs who mastered the principle of explaining mind and explaining nature just as it is, and nothing else. All the Patriarchs in every direction who have not attained this principle and have never heard such a dialogue cannot understand Tōzan's "Inside that temple someone is explaining mind and explaining nature," spoken when he and Somitsu were on a pilgrimage.

The story has been carefully transmitted by the descendants of Tōzan as an example of his special method of teaching. People from other schools cannot dream of seeing or hearing it, much less understand it. Only Tōzan's descendants rightly transmit it. If we do not have the right transmission of this principle, how can we arrive at the root of the Buddhist Way? The principles of "inside," "outside," "someone," and "there is" all point toward explaining mind and explaining nature. "Inside" and "outside" are explaining mind and explaining nature. We must clarify and practice this principle. There is no explaining without nature, and no mind without explaining. "Buddha-nature" is the explaining of the whole; yet "no Buddha-nature" is also explanation of the whole.

When we study "Buddha-nature" we must study both aspects of possessing and non-possessing Buddha-nature; otherwise, it will not be total study of the Way. If we study the nature of "explaining," and then believe and accept it, we become descendants of the Buddhas and Patriarchs. However, if we think that the mind moves and nature remains stable, or that nature remains pure and still while form changes, it is the view of non-believers. Studying, practicing, and clarifying mind, and nature in the Buddhist Way differs from the methods of non-believers.

In the Buddhist Way, explaining mind and explaining nature exists whether or not there is man, and whether or not there is mind and nature. We may explain mind and nature, but actually there is no explanation of mind or nature. We must study the explanation of mind and nature where there is or is not a man; if we do not, it means we have not arrived at the place of explanation of the mind. We should study explaining the mind with no man, no man explaining the mind, explaining the mind with a man, and with this man explaining the mind.

Rinzai insisted that there was a "true man of no rank," but he did not say that there is a "true man with rank." Real study and understanding has not been actualized here; it is still incomplete. Explaining mind and explaining nature is the explanation of the Buddhas and Patriarchs and therefore, it can be met through the ear and eye. Previously, Somitsu said, "Who is it?" In order to actualize this understanding he used such an expression. "Who is it?" is the inner essence of explaining mind and explaining nature. Hence, how we use the expression "Who is it?" shows our understanding of explaining mind and explaining nature. This kind of explaining mind and explaining nature is not known by those in other places because they not only mistake the "son for the burgler," but also the "burgler for the son."

Tōzan said, "If you ask such a question you will go directly to your death." Students in other branches who hear this think that someone was explaining mind and explaining nature, that Somitsu asked, "Who is it?" and that because of his question he will go directly to his death. "Who is it?" means I have not seen or had direct knowledge of that man; consequently, anything I say about him will be nothing but a dead expression. However, this is not true. Few people know about the real explaining mind and explaining nature.

Tōzan said, "Life is found in the midst of death." "In the midst of death" is not the "death" of "go directly to your death," nor is it the "who" in "Who is it?" "Who" is the man said to be explaining mind and nature. We should learn that it is not necessary to expect total death. Tōzan's saying, "Life is found in the midst of death" means there is someone who is explaining mind and explaining nature. Furthermore, this is only one part of total death. Life is total life, but there is no manifestation of changing into life. There is nothing but total and complete dropping off of life.

Generally, among Buddhas and Patriarchs such explanations of mind and nature occur and we must study them carefully. Also, through the death of "total death" the actualization and attainment of life can emerge.

We must know that from the T'ang Dynasty to the present there are many who have not clarified the Buddhist Way of explaining mind and explaining nature, who do not know its teaching, practice, or enlightenment, and who have distorted ideas and opinions. Such people must be led to the truth in both the past and future. We must say to them, "Explaining mind and explaining nature is the essence of the seven Buddhas and all the Patriarchs."

This was delivered to the monks of Kippōji, Echizen, Japan, during 1243. Transcribed January 11, 1244, in the chief disciple's quarters by Ejō.

[46]

MITSUGO

"Secret teaching"

The Great Way which is preserved and maintained by all the Buddhas is actualized in the koan, "You are like that, I am like that and each of us preserves the virtue and shares in the enlightenment of our predecessors."

Once an official made a donation to Great Master Kōkaku of Mt. Ungo and asked, "Shakyamuni possessed a secret teaching but Mahākāśyapa did not conceal it. What was the secret teaching of Buddha?" Ungo said, "Shōsho [the man's name]!" "Yes, "replied the official. Ungo then said, "Do you understand?" "No," said the official. Ungo said, "If you don't understand, that is Shakyamuni's secret teaching, if you do understand it is Mahākāsyapa's not concealing it."

Ungo was the fifth generation Dharma-heir of Seigen. Ungo was a teacher of men and gods and one of the world's greatest and most virtuous masters. He instructed both animate and inanimate worlds. As the forty-sixth Buddha descended from Shakyamuni he proclaimed the Dharma for all Buddhas and Patriarchs. It is said that when he lived at Sambō-an he received his meals from the celestials; however, after he transmitted the Dharma and attained the Way he went beyond such manifestations of holiness.

"Shakyamuni possessed a secret teaching but Mahākāśyapa did not conceal it." This is the transmission and original face of the forty-sixth Patriarch. It was not gained from another person and did not come from outside. Yet it was not possessed originally nor newly acquired.

This secret teaching is not only possessed by Shakyamuni but by all the Buddhas and Patriarchs. Therefore, anyone who is a teacher to the world must surely possess a secret teaching. And if there is a secret teaching "Mahākāśyapa did not conceal it." We must study the principle that if there are a hundred thousand teachers of the world there must a hundred thousand Mahākāśyapas. When you study do not try to comprehend everything at once; consider everything in detail over and over, hundreds or thousands of times, just as you would when cutting a very hard material. Do not think that it is easy to gain under- after listening to an explanation.

Now Ungo himself is honored as a Buddha and has both Shakyamuni's secret teaching and Mahākāśyapa's not concealing it. Shōsho was called and answered standing "Yes" but do not think that that is the "secret teaching."

Ungo said to Shōsho, "If you don't understand, that is Shakyamuni's secret teaching; if you do understand it is Mahākāśyapa's not concerning it." Such an understanding must be developed by continuous practice and study of the Way. "If you do not understand, that is the secret teaching of Shakyamuni." After hearing this, Shōsho stood there silently but it does not necessarily mean that he could not understand. We should not say that he did not understand "not knowing." We must study the principle behind "if you don't understand" and try to discern its central point. We must practice diligently. Furthermore, "if you understand" does not necessarily mean "understanding."

There are many ways to study the Buddhist Dharma; the two key expressions, however, are "understanding the Buddhist Dharma" and "not understanding the Buddhist Dharma." If you have not met the right master you will not even know that there are such key expressions. People foolishly think that there is a secret teaching that cannot be perceived by the faculties of seeing or hearing. Since we have "if you understand" we should not say "Mahākāśyapa did not conceal it" because there is also a "if you don't understand" that "Mahākāśyapa did not conceal." "Not conceal" does not mean that everyone can see or hear it. We should rather study the "not concealed" that we already have—that is, the proper time when there is no place that is not concealed.

Therefore, we have not studied the secret teaching as something related to a world not known through the senses. Even at the time when we do not understand the Buddhist Dharma, it is still one part of the secret teaching. This is surely possessed by, and possesses Shakyamuni.

However, those who have neither heard nor learned the teaching of a right master will not be able to even dream of this principle even through they may be lecturing as an abbot of a large temple. Such people say, without any basis, that Shakyamuni had a secret teaching i.e., the holding up of the flower and winking before the great assembly on Vulture Peak. Therefore, using words to describe the Buddhist teaching is very superficial—they only express letters or forms. "Without speaking he held up the flower" is the occasion of Buddha's secret teaching, yet millions could not understand it [that day on Vulture Peak] and it became a "secret teaching" hidden from them. The meaning of "Mahākāśyapa did not conceal it" is his smile. When Shakyamuni held up the udumbara flower it was not hidden by Mahākāśyapa. This is the real secret teaching which has been directly transmitted from master to disciple. People who think like that when they hear such an explanation are many and they exist throughout China. That is a great pity, and it has caused the way of the Buddhas and Patriarchs to decline. Those with real insight should closely examine such misunderstandings.

If we think that Buddha's teaching with words is superficial, then "holding up the flower and blinking the eye" is also superficial. If we think that Shakyamuni's words only contain letters and forms, then we are not students of the Buddhist Dharma. Those who think they know that words are just names and forms, do not know that Shakyamuni's words are not bound by letters or forms. Those people are not liberated from the body and mind of ordinary people. The Buddhas and Patriarchs, who have totally cast off body and mind, use words to proclaim the Dharma and turn the wheel of the Law and many benefit from seeing and hearing it. Those who have faith and follow the Dharma will be influenced by both the spoken and wordless Buddhist teaching.

Sentient beings see "holding up the flower and blinking" as just "holding up the flower and blinking," do they not? They should not be different from Mahākāśyapa, and must be on the same level as Shakyamuni. All sentient beings should be the same [as Mahākāśyapa]—they all begin with the same awakening of the mind, they walk the same path, and live in the same country. They see the same Buddha and hear the same Dharma, albeit with or without Buddhist wisdom. After one Buddha is seen, progressively more and more Buddhas are seen. In each community of the Buddhas there are billions of sentient beings. Each of the Buddhas penetrate "the holding up of a flower and blinking of the eye" on the same level. What they see is bright, what they hear is clear. There is an eye of the mind and eye of body, and there is an ear of the mind and an ear of the body.

How should we understand Mahākāśyapa's smile and what should we say about it? If it is like what we said above, it is the "secret teaching." However, this "secret teaching" is not hidden so the whole matter is quite foolish.

Later on, Shakyamuni Buddha said, "I possess the Eye and Treasury of the True Law and the Serene Mind of Nirvana. I now bestow it to Mahākāśyapa." Does this expression use words or is it wordless? If Shakyamuni disliked words and liked to hold up flowers, then the words should have preceded the holding up of the flower. Mahākāśyapa surely understood Shakyamuni's words and all the sentient beings surely heard it. If they had not, then we would not be able to use it now.

In general, we can say that Shakyamuni has a secret teaching, a secret practice and a secret enlightenment. However, foolish people think that others cannot know someone's secret or that a secret is only known by a few people. In India and China, there are many people in both the past and present who think like that because they lack proper study of the Buddhist Way. Such people say that those who do not study many different things have secrets while those who do have no secrets. Why do they say that people with wide experience lack many secrets? Then those with the eyes and ears of heaven, or the eyes and ears of the Dharma cannot have any secret teaching or secret mind, can they?

Secret teaching, secret mind, secret practice, etc., in the Buddhist Dharma differs from the above explanation. Whenever we meet someone we both hear and give a secret teaching. When we know ourselves we know our secret practice. Of course, the Buddhas and Patriarchs know much more about their own secret mind and secret teaching. We must know that when we become Buddhas and Patriarchs secret teaching and secret practice are suddenly actualized.

"Secret" is the principle behind inner secrets, a relationship with no gaps—it covers the Buddhas and Patriarchs, it covers others, it covers oneself. It covers all our actions and all generations; it covers all merit and all secrets. When we meet a "secret man" with a secret teaching we cannot see him with the Buddha Eye. Secret practice is not conscious of distinctions between self and others. One alone knows his own secrets, and others cannot understand others' secrets. Rather, we should know that the secret is right in front of us. Secrets are everywhere, nothing is hidden.

That is the principle we must study and clarify. Anyone who studies diligently will surely receive a secret teaching. This is the right transmission of the Buddhas and Patriarchs. At a certain time we have a secret, others have a secret, Buddhas and Patriarchs have a secret, everyone has a secret. Hence, secrets become the secret that transcends all secrets. This kind of teaching, practice, and enlightenment becomes the Buddhas and Patriarchs; therefore, secrets transcend the Buddhas and Patriarchs.

Secchō said to an assembly of monks, "Shakyamuni possessed a secret teaching but Mahākāśyapa did not conceal it. One night the rain blew away all the blossoms and fragrant water streams throughout the castle."

Secchō's "One night the rain blew all the blossoms and fragrant water streams throughout the castle" is the inner secret. This tells us to investigate the enlightened eyes and nostrils of the Buddhas and Patriarchs. Rinzai and Tōzan did not surpass Secchō's level. We should open the nostril within the enlightened eye and sharpen our ears and nose. The essence of the ear, nose and enlightened vision is not old or new; it is simply the function of the entire body and mind. This is the principle of the rain blowing and the world emerging.

Secchō's "fragrant water flows throughout the castle" means that the body is hidden and shadows appear. Because of this, in the everyday life of the Buddhas and Patriarchs there is both earnest study and dropping off of "Shakyamuni possessed a secret teaching, but Mahākāśyapa did not conceal it." The seven Buddhas, all the other Buddhas, Mahākāśyapa, and Shakyamuni study and practice like that.

This was delivered to the monks on September 20, 1243 at Kippōji, Esshū, Yoshida-ken. Transcribed on October 16, the same year, in the chief disciple's quarters by Ejō.

HOSSHŌ

"Dharmatā, the real nature of phenomena"

WHEN we study sometimes we follow the teaching of the sūtras, sometimes we follow the teaching of a master; ultimately, however, it comes down to self-enlightenment without a teacher. Self-enlightenment without a teacher occurs through dharmatā, the real nature of the phenomenal world. Even if we possess such knowledge innately it is still necessary to visit masters and seek the Way. If we think we lack such innate knowledge we must study and practice harder. There is no one who does not possess innate knowledge. We must follow the teaching of the sūtras or masters until we achieve Buddhist enlightenment.

We must know that we enter the world of *hosshō samādhi* when we look at the sūtras or meet a master. To enter and obtain *dharmatā samādhi* is called innate knowledge. Thus, we obtain knowledge of our previous existences and *sammyo*, the three types of knowledge.[1] This is the certification of supreme enlightenment. We learn innate knowledge by meeting innate knowledge. We correctly transmit wisdom not obtained from a teacher and natural wisdom by meeting wisdom not obtained from a teacher and natural wisdom. If we do not possess innate knowledge, even if we meet sūtras or masters we will not be able to hear or enlighten dharmatā.

When we drink water we know if it is hot or cold. The principle of the Great Way is not like that. All Buddhas, Mahasattvas, and sentient beings clarify the Great Way of dharmatā through the power of innate knowledge. Following the sūtras or masters and clarifying the Great Way of dharmatā is the illumination of one's own dharmatā. The sūtras are dharmatā, i.e., they are one's self. Masters

---

[1] The rememberance of former births, insight into the future destiny of beings and recognition of the origin of misery and the way to its removal.

are also dharmatā, i.e., one's self. Dharmatā is masters, dharmatā is our self. Since dharmatā is one's self, it is not the "self" of non-believers or demons. In dharmatā there are no non-believers or demons; there is nothing more than to eat the gruel when it is served, take the rice when given, and drink tea when it is offered.

There are some who claim to have had twenty or thirty years of study yet when they are confronted with a discussion of dharmatā they are dumbstruck and all their efforts are wasted. Others have spent years in a monastery and now occupy seats of honor but are totally confounded by the voice and form of dharmatā. Their understanding is that dharmatā only emerges after the entire universe and the three worlds are destroyed, and dharmatā is not seen in the present world. The principle of dharmatā is not like that. It completely goes beyond ideas of difference and indentity, separation and unity between this phenomenal world and dharmatā. Since it is not past, present, or future, not temporary nor eternal, and not form, perception, mental conceptions, volition, or consciousness it becomes dharmatā.

Zen Master Baso Daijaku of Kosei in Koshū said, "Sentient beings have never left the state of *dharmatā samādhi* throughout myriads of kalpas. They are always in a state of *dharmatā samādhi*, putting on their clothes, eating rice, greeting their visitors, and using their six sense organs. All their actions are the function of dharmatā."

Baso's "dharmatā" is dharmatā's dharmatā. If we study under Baso, we are studying dharmatā. Baso understands dharmatā and therefore cannot fail to express it. Dharmatā is riding Baso ["Ba" means horse]. Human beings eat rice, rice eats human beings. Dharmatā emerges as dharmatā, it has never left *dharmatā samādhi*. Both before and after its manifestation dharmatā has never left anything. Dharmatā and myriad kalpas are *dharmatā samādhi*; dharmatā is "myriad kalpas."

Therefore, all things in the present are dharmatā, dharmatā is all things in the present. "Wearing clothes and eating rice" is the wearing and eating of *dharmatā samādhi*. It is the actualization of the dharmatā of wearing, eating, clothes, and rice. If we do not wear clothes and eat rice, do not give a greeting, do not use the six sense organs, and do not do anything, it is not *dharmatā samādhi* and we cannot enter dharmatā.

The present actualization of the Way was transmitted by all the Buddhas to Shakyamuni Buddha and all the Patriarchs rightly transmitted it to Baso. Each Buddha and Patriarch mutually receives and transmits *dharmatā samādhi*. Buddhas and Patriarchs make dharmatā lively and active through their detachment.

Teachers of doctrine may talk about dharmatā, but it is not the dharmatā of Baso's sentient beings who have never left dharmatā. Even if they doubt this dharmatā, they still will be able to gain something. That is, such a thought is just a different form of dharmatā. They may think they lack dharmatā, but they still give greetings and act and this is dharmatā. Unlimited kalpas flow by and dharmatā passes. The present and future are exactly like that.

We may think that the measure of body and mind is limited to what we can weigh and it differs from dharmatā, but even such an idea is still dharmatā. The converse is also true. "Thought" and "non-thought" together form dharmatā. "Tā" (shō) means nature but we should not take it as something permanent like water that does not flow, or a tree that neither grows nor perishes. That is the opinion of non-believers.

Shakyamuni Buddha said, "Suchness is form, suchness is [all] nature." Hence, blooming flowers and falling leaves are "suchness is [all] nature." Foolish people, however, think that there are no blooming flowers or falling leaves in the world of dharmatā. Let us stop questioning others for a while and ask ourselves the same questions. Try to pick up others' questions and study them yourself repeatedly. Then you should be able to solve those questions. Your previous ideas were not evil or misintented, just inadequate. And even when you clarify the above problems such inadequate ideas will remain somewhere. Blooming flowers and falling leaves are of themselves blooming flowers and falling leaves. Even the thought that there are no blooming flowers and falling leaves is dharmatā. "Thought" is the dropping off of all doubt, the thought of dharmatā as it is. The sum total of all our thoughts of dharmatā is our original face.

Baso's "everything is dharmatā" is 80 or 90 percent of the truth, but he still left much unsaid. For example, he did not say: "dharmatā does not leave dharmatā," "dharmatā is all dharmatā," "sentient beings cannot leave sentient beings," "sentient beings are only a small part of dharmatā," "sentient beings are only a small part of sentient beings," "dharmatā is half of sentient beings," "half of sentient beings are half of dharmatā," "no sentient beings are dharmatā," "dharmatā is not sentient beings," "dharmatā leaves dharmatā," "sentient beings leaves sentient beings."

He only said that sentient beings do not leave *dharmatā samādhi*. He did not say that dharmatā does not leave sentient being samādhi, nor that *dharmatā samādhi* leaves and enters sentient being samādhi. Furthermore, we did not hear: "dharmatā becomes Buddha," "sentient beings enlighten dharmatā," "dharmatā enlightens dharmatā," "inanimate things do not leave dharmatā."

Let us ask Baso, "What do you call sentient beings?" If we call sentient beings "dharmatā" where do they come from? If we call sentient beings "sentient beings" it means "not even one thing can be explained." Answer quickly, quickly!

This was delivered to the monks at Kippōji in the beginning of winter, 1243.

[48]

DHARANI

"The mystic formula"

WHEN the eye of study is clear, the eye of the True Law is clear. Since the eye of the True Law is clear, we obtain the clear eye of study. The most important aspect of right transmission is accomplished through the power of respecting great and excellent teachers. This is great karma and the great dharani. "Great and excellent teachers" are the Buddhas and Patriarchs. We must serve them always.

Therefore, that is why making and serving tea is the actualization of the mind's essence and spiritual power. It is also found in bringing a water pitcher, pouring it out, bringing the water without moving the pitcher, and studying with one's teacher. It is not only the study of the mind's essence of the Buddhas and Patriarchs; it is also seeing the Buddhas and Patriarchs through meeting the Buddhas and Patriarchs. We must not just receive the spiritual power of the Buddhas and Patriarchs, but also penetrate the spiritual power of seven or eight specific Buddhas and Patriarchs.

Because of this, the spiritual power and mind's essence of all the Buddhas and Patriarchs is condensed into one dharani. When we respect and venerate the Buddhas and Patriarchs we offer heavenly flowers and incense; this is not bad, but it is better to offer the dharani of samādhi. This is what it is to be a descendant of the Buddhas and Patriarchs.

"Great dharani" means "the proper manner of veneration." Because the proper manner of veneration is great dharani it can be actualized and seen. The expression "proper manner of veneration" is Chinese and has been used in society for some time. It was not handed down from Brahma or Indra; rather, it is only transmitted by Buddhas and Patriarchs. It is not the conscious world of voice and form, nor is it something that should be discussed as that which existed before or after Kūō Buddha, who was present at the beginning of the world.

The proper manner of veneration is to offer incense and make prostrations. There is a real teacher of renunciation and a real teacher of the transmission of the Law. The teacher of renunciation is a teacher of the right transmission and vice versa. Veneration for those teachers is the right dharani of study. Do not waste time; venerate them immediately.

At the beginning and end of training periods, at the winter solstice, and at the beginning and end of each month offer incense and make prostrations to those true masters. We can do this either before or after the morning meal. Straighten up and go stand in front of the master's room. "Straighten up" means put on your kesa, take your *zagu*,[1] arrange your footwear, and prepare incense. Stand before the master and greet him with a bow. The attendant monks should have already cleaned the incense burner and taken care of the candles. Offer incense immediately, regardless of whether the master is sitting in his chair, behind the curtain, lying down, or eating. If he is standing ask him to sit down and rest after you make your prostrations. There are many possibilities.

After the master sits down, give a bow in the correct manner and then walk over to the incense burner stand and make your offering. You may keep the incense on your collar, inside your kimono, or in your sleeve. It depends on the person. After making a bow, if the incense is wrapped in paper, turn it to the left, hold it from underneath, take it in both hands and open it. Place it on the burner making sure it is standing straight. After placing it upright, place your hands over your chest, walk toward the right until you are standing directly before the master; bow to him in the prescribed manner, place your *zagu* on the floor and make either nine or twelve prostrations depending on the situation. After making those prostrations fold the *zagu* and bow again.

In some cases, the monk makes three prostrations and gives a seasonal greeting. However, in the above case no greeting is given, only prostrations in sets of three. This custom has been handed down from the seven Buddhas. Since it has been rightly transmitted, it can be utilized by us. These prostrations have never undergone any modification in any era. Also, whenever we receive some teaching or special guidance we should follow the above procedure. For example, the second Patriarch used three prostrations to communicate with Bodhidharma. Whenever we talk about the level of the Eye and Treasury of the True Law we must make three prostrations. We must know that prostrations are the Eye

---

[1] A special cloth used for sitting on or making prostrations.

and Treasury of the True Law and that the Eye and Treasury of the True Law is the great dharani.

Lately, it has been the custom to make only one prostration when we request instruction from a master, but this is not the traditional custom. It is not absolutely necessary to offer nine or twelve prostrations to show our gratitude. Sometimes three prostrations are given, sometimes one prostration in which the head touches the ground is given, and occasionally six prostrations are given. Actually, all of these prostrations should be given with the forehead touching the ground. In India, such prostrations are considered to be the highest form of prostration. In each of the above prostrations—one, three, or six—you should touch your forehead to the ground. In the case of six prostrations, you should pound your head into the ground almost until it bleeds. You should use your *zagu*. Prostrations are also done in worldly society. There are basically nine kinds used there.

When we receive a master's teachings we should make countless prostrations. Prostrations should be non-stop, done hundreds of thousands of times. They are constantly used in the community of the Buddhas and Patriarchs.

In general, such prostrations should be done under the direction of a master and his instructions should be followed closely. Generally speaking, when prostrations are done in society, the Buddhist teaching exists there. If such prostrations are missing, then the Buddhist Law will disappear.

Prostrations before a true teacher who transmits the Dharma should be made without regard to the season or place. For example, even if he is lying down, eating, or going to the lavatory we should still make a prostration. Even if we are separated by walls, fences, mountains, or rivers we should make our prostrations from a distance. Even if we are separated by countless eons, by the coming and going of life and death, or by enlightenment and nirvana we should make our prostrations.

Novices and disciples must know many types of prostrations, but a true master need not give such prostrations in return. Usually, he only gives a gassho, and returns his disciple's third prostration. When we make our prostrations we must face north, directly across from the teacher who is facing south. This is the correct and proper manner. The right transmission holds that if we have right belief all our prostrations, from the very beginning, will be made facing north.

Therefore, when Shakyamuni was still present in this world, all those people, gods, and dragons who had taken refuge in Buddha, faced north and showed their veneration by making prostrations. After he attained the Way his former companions, Ajñātakauṇḍinya, Aśvajit, Bhadrika, Mahanaman, and Daśabala-kāsýapa, stood up across from the Tathāgata, faced north and made prostrations. Non-believers and demons who abandoned their evil minds and took refuge in the Buddha, also faced the north and made prostrations without any prodding. In each of the communities of the twenty-eight Indian Patriarchs who followed Shakyamuni and of the Chinese Patriarchs, all the believers in the True Law naturally faced the north and made prostrations. This is the natural form of the true Dharma, and there is nothing forced or unnatural between a master and disciple. This relationship is the great dharani.

There is a great dharani named "perfect enlightenment," one named "proper manner of veneration," one named "actualization of prostration," one named "kesa," one named "Eye and Treasury of the True Law." By chanting this dharani we can protect the entire earth, all time, every Buddhaland, and the inside and outside of our hermitage. We should study and clarify that great dharani. All dharanis are based on this dharani. As relatives of this dharani all dharanis are actualized. All the Buddhas and Patriarchs derive their resolve, practice, enlightenment, and turning of the wheel of the Law from this dharani.

Therefore, since we are the descendants of the Buddhas and Patriarchs we must study and clarify this dharani in detail. "If we put on the robe of Shakyamuni we put on the robe of all the Buddhas and Patriarchs of the entire world." "Put on the robe" means wear a kesa. The kesa is a special symbol of Buddhists. It is difficult to have the opportunity to wear a kesa.

Even someone who is born in a remote country, and is also foolish, can still ultimately find the Dharma of Shakyamuni through the actualization of a dharani chanted earlier and through the power of merit. Within the various forms of phenomena, when we make a prostration to the Buddhas and Patriarchs, regardless of whether it was done under our own or another's initiative, it is the same as Shakyamuni Buddha's attainment and practice of the Way. This is the miraculous power of dharanis.

When we make a prostration to all the Buddhas of the past and present innumerable kalpas it is the occasion of putting on the robe of Shakyamuni Buddha. When we cover our body with a kesa it is the attainment of Shakyamuni Buddha's body, flesh, hands, feet, head, eye, marrow, and brain. It is also the Divine Light of turning the wheel of the Law. We should wear our kesa in that spirit. This is the actualization of the kesa's merit. We should maintain and venerate it, protecting it always, and wearing it when we venerate Shakyamuni Buddha. That is how we can complete the practice of innumerable kalpas.

Making prostrations and venerating Shakyamuni Buddha means making prostrations and venerating a true teacher who has transmitted the Dharma, given you the precepts, and shaved your head. This is to see and venerate Shakyamuni through the power of the Dharma and dharanis.

My late master, the ancient Buddha Tendō, said, "There is a prostration like Eka's in the snow, and one in the rice hut like Enō. This is an excellent precedent and example of great dharani."

This was delivered to the monks at Kippōji in 1242. Transcribed on January 13, 1244, in the chief disciple's quarters by Ejō.

SANJUSHICHIHON-BODAI-BUMPŌ

"The thirty-seven conditions favorable to enlightenment"

THERE is a koan of the ancient Buddhas concerning the teaching, practice, and enlightenment of the thirty-seven conditions favorable to enlightenment. Both the advancement toward enlightenment and the return to the world to save sentient beings are inextricably bound together; this bond is the basis of the koan and actualizes all the Buddhas and Patriarchs.

First of all, there are the four types of meditation which eliminate false views (*shinenjo*): 1) observation that the body is impure; 2) observation that perception leads to suffering; 3) observation that the mind is impermanent; and 4) observation that all things are devoid of self.

"Observation that the body is impure" is observing that the body is a bag of skin that covers the entire universe of the ten directions. This becomes the true body and therefore transcends pure and impure. If there is no detachment there can be no attainment of this observation. If there is no body there can be no attainment of practice, teaching, or observation of the body's impurity. Yet the attainment of this observation has already been actualized, so we should know that it is gained through detachment. The attainment of this observation appears in such daily activities as sweeping the grounds and wiping the zazen platform. If we practice like this for months and years it will become an absolute act, covering the great earth in its total suchness.

Observing the body is the "body observing," i.e., not the observation of other things. Right observation occurs like that. When "body observing" is actualized, "mind observing" is involved and cannot be actualized. Therefore, "observation of the body's impurity" becomes both diamond samādhi and

---

[1] Samādhis based on the teachings found in the *Diamond Sūtra* and *Sūramgama Sūtra*. Diamond samādhi (*vajra-samādhi*) is extremely sharp and clear; sūrangama samādhi is all powerful, destroying all illusions.

sūramgama samādhi.¹ The principle behind Shakyamuni's sighting of the morning star is called "observing the body's impurity." It cannot be compared to pure or impure. Yet physical bodies and one's actual body are "impure." Studying in such a manner, we see that demons become Buddhas when Buddhas take the form of demons and bring them to Buddhahood. Buddhas become Buddhas when Buddhas take the form of Buddhas and Buddha emerges. Human beings become Buddhas when they have the form of ordinary people, set themselves aright, and become Buddhas. Truly, we must study the principle behind such transformations.

For example, consider the method of washing a robe. Water removes the dirt from the robe, and the robe becomes wet. Although this water is used several times and changed several times, water is still is being used and the robe is being washed. More than one or two washings are necessary and we should not rest until it is clean. When the water is used up we put more water in. We wash the clean robe again to make it cleaner. After all kinds of water have been used, the kesa will be clean. That there is a fish in dirty water is the principle we must clarify. There are many different kinds of robes and different ways of washing them. Practicing like that, we actualize enlightenment in the washing of a robe. However, we must possess this purity in ourselves. That is why it is not always necessary to put the robe in water or for water to wet the robe. When dirty water is used to wash a robe, it is still possible to find a way to clean it. There is a method of cleaning a robe and other things with fire, wind, earth, water, and air; there is a way to clean earth, water, fire, wind, and air with earth, water, fire, wind, and air.

The essence of observation of the body's impurity is exactly like that. Body is nothing but body, observation is only observation, impurity is just impurity; this is being born wearing a kesa like the third Indian Patriarch Sāṇavāsa. If there had been no kesa when he was born then none of the Buddhas or Patriarchs could transmit a kesa. But why was only Sāṇavāsa born wearing a kesa? We must earnestly clarify this principle.

The "observation that perception leads to suffering" means suffering is perception. It is not self-perception nor the perception of others; neither is it existent nor non-existent perception. Perception and suffering co-exist in our living body. It is like a sweet melon clinging to a bitter gourd. Skin, flesh, bones, and marrow become bitter (i.e., suffer, *ku*); mind and no-mind, etc. also become bitter. This is the practice and enlightenment of individual miraculous powers. These powers are detached from the sweetness of melon stem and the bitterness of lotus root. Like this, the suffering of sentient beings emerges and exists.

Sentient beings include not only ourselves and not only others; they exist as suffering and we cannot deny it. A sweet melon is sweet to the stem, and the lotus root is bitter to the core. Since we are unable to comprehend suffering, we must question ourselves further to find what suffering is.

Concerning the "observation that the mind is impermanent," Sōkei [Enō] the ancient Buddha said, "Impermanence is the Buddha-nature." Impermanence has many interpretations but they ultimately are reduced to the fact that it is the Buddha-nature. Great Master Yōka Shingaku said, "All things are impermanent, everything is empty—this is the Tathāgata's Great and Perfect Enlightenment." Observation of the mind's impermanence is the Tathāgata's Great and Perfect Enlightenment, i.e., the Great and Perfectly Enlightened Tathāgata. If the mind does not have this observation it falls into subjectivity. If there is mind there must also be this observation.

The actualization of supreme and total enlightenment is the impermanence and the observation of the mind. Mind is not necessarily permanent, nor is it separated from various pluralistic forms; even wall, tiles, stones, and large and small rocks are mind. This is impermanence, i.e., observation. "Observation that all things are devoid of self" is that long things are long, short things are short, in themselves. Actualization and function exist and therefore, there is "no self." The dog has no Buddha-nature, the dog has Buddha-nature, all sentient beings have no Buddha-nature, Buddha-nature has no sentient beings, Buddhas have no sentient beings, Buddhas have no Buddhas, Buddha-nature has no Buddha-nature, sentient beings have no sentient beings. Like this, all dharmas are no dharmas—all things are without self. If we grasp this we can attain freedom from perplexity and doubt.

Shakyamuni Buddha said, "All the Buddhas and Patriarchs practice this law [the four types of meditation] and it forms their sacred essence." That is, all the Buddhas and Bodhisattvas keep the four types of meditation as their sacred essence. We must know that they are the sacred essence of perfect and and marvelous enlightenment. Consequently, Shakyamuni Buddha used the expression "all the Buddhas and Bodhisattvas," and even those Buddhas who have not yet realized marvelous enlightenment have it as their sacred essence as well as Bodhisattvas who have gone beyond perfect and marvelous enlightenment. Truly, the skin, flesh, bones, and marrow of all the Buddhas and Patriarchs take the four types of meditation as their sacred essence.

There are four right efforts: 1) to prevent future evil from arising; 2) to destroy present evil; 3) to produce merit; and 4) to increase the present good.

"Prevent future evil from arising." "Evil" does not have an exact definition, but due to certain influences and circumstances evil actions occur. Nonetheless, we must try to prevent evil before it arises. This is the Buddhist Dharma which has been transmitted to the present day. In the teaching of non-believers there is the concept of a pre-existent self, but such a notion is not found in the Buddhist Dharma. Where does evil exist if it has not occured yet? If we say there is evil in the future this is called *danmetsuken*, an idea of the non-believers [which omits the law of cause and effect]. Even if future evil is manifested in the present, that is still not part of the Buddhist teaching. That kind of thinking is nothing but confusion about the three aspects of time. If we are confused about the three aspects of time, we will be confused about the Dharma; if we are confused about the Dharma, we will be confused about the actual form of reality; if we are confused about the actual form of reality, we will be confused about "only Buddha transmits Buddha." Do not say that the future comes after the present. Furthermore, we should ask, "What is future evil?" Is there anyone who can comprehend it? Even if it can be comprehended, there are occasions when future evil does not occur or when it is not in the future. If that is so, then it cannot be called future evil—it is extinguished evil. Instead of studying the doctrines of non-believers, Hinayanists, śrāvakas, etc., study the doctrine of preventing future evil from arising. Accumulating evil throughout the world is future evil which has not yet arisen. "Not arisen" means that yesterday's definition is final, but today's is not.

"Destroy present evil." "Present" means all life in the present. In other words, all life is half-life; half-life is this life. This life obstructs nothing; it transcends evil. In order to destroy evil we must consider the story of Devadatta who fell into hell still living, but it was predicted that he would attain Buddhahood some day. A living person can become a donkey or a Buddha. After we study this principle we will find its essence—destruction must be destroyed, and there is nothing left but destruction.

"To produce merit" is to realize our original face that existed before our parents were born; then the real nature of human beings appears from the unlimited past; it is the understanding that preceded Kūō Buddha.

"To increase the present good" should not be confused with "to produce merit." Remember it says "increase." Shakyamuni was enlightened upon seeing the morning star, began to teach others to see what he saw, and helped others attain enlightened vision. [Baso Dōitsu] practiced for thirty years, and never lacked rice or salt [i.e., his merit increased]. This is the meaning of increase. The valley is deep and the ladle handle is long and can they continually increase their capacity.

There are four steps to supernatural power: 1) resolve; 2) mindfulness; 3) diligence; and 4) deep analysis.

"Resolve" is the determination to become the body and mind of Buddha and awaken from the sleep of illusion. The limited self makes a prostration to [the great self]. Resolve is not related to the body and mind formed by karma—it works freely like the birds flying in the vast sky and fish swimming in shallow water.

"Mindfulness" is wall, tiles, stones, mountains, rivers, and earth; it is each of the three worlds; a chair, bamboo, wood. Each reveals its own function and therefore possesses the mind of Buddhas and Patriarchs, the mind of fools and saints, the mind of grass and trees, the mind of demons and ghosts. All the minds are "mindfulness."

"Diligence" is the one step off the top of a hundred-foot pole. Where is the top of this hundred-foot pole? If there is no progress nothing can be gained; we must step ahead with no wobbling. In that step we move towards enlightenment, sometimes advancing, sometimes retreating. When we increase our diligence it covers the entire universe and then true diligence emerges.

"Deep analysis" is the liberated cognition of all the Buddhas and Patriarchs, and settles nowhere. There is an analysis of the body, of the mind, of consciousness, of straw sandals, and of the self that existed before time. These are called the bases of spiritual power, and there is no hesitation or reticence here.

Shakyamuni Buddha said, "Without taking a step we arrive at our destination." This is called the four steps to supernatural power. It is like a hole made by an auger and a sharpened chisel [i.e., any act can be accomplished through these supernatural powers].

There are five faculties leading to proper conduct: 1) faith; 2) diligence; 3) thought; 4) concentration (samādhi); and 5) wisdom.

We should know that "faith"[2] does not depend on oneself nor others. It cannot be created by oneself, nor be forced upon others. Since it cannot be developed, based on one's own tenets, it is the hidden transmission of the east and west. Faith is the faith of the entire body and mind. Surely Buddhahood bears fruit in oneself and others. If no such fruit is born, faith can never be actualized. Consequently, it is said, "The Buddhist Dharma is like the Great

---

[2] *Shinkon*, "faith" or "belief." Actually, the meaning of this word is closer to the English word "confidence"; that is, confidence in the enlightenment of Buddha and the truth of the Buddhist Dharma, rather than belief in some supernatural or abstract principle. It is a totally rational concept with no emotionalism or mysticism involved.

Ocean and can be entered only through faith." Where faith exists, Buddhas and Patriarchs are actualized.

"Diligence" is *shikantaza*, single-minded sitting in zazen. This means if we want to stop or rest we do not. Do not stop what should continue on and on. This faculty transcends diligence and neglect and is not limited to any special time.

Shakyamuni Buddha said, "I practice diligence continually and thereby attain Supreme and Perfect Enlightenment." "Continually practice" covers the past, present, and future from beginning to end. "I practice diligence continually" is the attainment of his enlightenment. Because he attained Supreme and Perfect Enlightenment he is continually diligent. If that was not so, how could he have been continually practicing? Or how could he have attained his enlightenment? Scholars of the abhidharma and sūtras cannot find this essential point. That is why they are unable to have true study.

"Thought" is the body of a withered tree. The "body" of a withered tree means a withered tree is "thought" i.e., the physical body of a withered tree possesses the life of Buddha. Thought is one's reflections. There is thought in the physical body and thought in no-mind. There is thought in the existent mind and thought in the non-existent body. The life of the entire body of the universe is thought. The life of all the Buddhas in the ten directions is also thought. One thought, countless people; one person, many thoughts. Nevertheless, there are people with thought and without. People do not necessarily possess thought, and thought does not always depend on human beings. Nonetheless, this faculty of thought possesses great merit.

"Samādhi" has the two aspects of *sekishubimo* [i.e., *jijiyū samādhi*, the samādhi of self-realization] and *sakkibimo* [*tajiyū samādhi*, to encourage the samādhi of others]. In other words, "karma never stops" and "karma ceases." Sometimes we become a donkey, sometimes a horse. A piece of jade may be surrounded by stones, but all the stones are not jade. The earth contains many mountains, but the earth is not only mountains. We must ultimately transcend all oppositions and harmonize them.

"Wisdom" is not completely understood by all the Buddhas of the three worlds, yet even raccoons and white oxen possess knowledge of it. Wisdom cannot be explained with words—it is breathing through the nostrils, or the fingers of a fist. When a donkey looks into a well, donkey sees donkey, well sees well—they are unified and inseparable.

There are five powers of the five faculties: 1) the power of faith; 2) the power of diligence; 3) the power of thought; 4) the power of concentration; and 5) the power of wisdom.

"The power of faith" is the power developed from the practice of faith that enables us to shatter all evil beliefs. From the time we are born until the time we die the power of faith is the essential force. That force is behind "seven times down, eight times up." There the power of faith is like pure water or a spotless pearl. The transmission of the Law and kesa is accomplished through faith—transmitted by Buddhas to Patriarchs.

The "power of diligence" is to teach with explanations when we cannot teach with actions, and to teach with actions when we cannot explain. That is why when we have sufficient explanation we do not need action, or when we have enough action we do not need any additional explanation. Strength comes from strength—this is the power of diligence.

The "power of thought" is [Seidō's] nose being yanked by his master. Actually, the master's nose was pulling [Seidō's]. Jade attracts jade, tile attracts tile. Even if you can grasp this, you still deserve thirty blows of the staff. This power can never be exhausted even if used by everyone.

The "power of samādhi" is like a child holding his mother, the mother holding the child, the child holding the child, the mother holding the mother. Nevertheless, the head cannot be called a face, money cannot buy money; this power is like a song continually increasing in volume becoming livelier and livelier.

The "power of wisdom" comes from deep in the distant past; it is like having a boat enabling us to cross over to the other shore. "We get a boat just when we need it" is an ancient proverb; it is absolutely necessary to have a boat when we need it. "Boat" means overcoming all obstacles in crossing over to the other side. This power gradually melts the spring ice.

There are seven ways to enlightenment: 1) discrimination of the true from the false; 2) diligence; 3) joy; 4) spiritual peace; 5) equanimity; 6) concentration; and 7) mindfulness.

If we make even the smallest mistake in "discriminating the true from the false," it creates a gulf like that between heaven and earth; discrimination is neither difficult nor easy, but we must investigate carefully with an attentive mind.

"Diligence" means not being like merchants who want to get something for nothing. Whatever we buy or sell we must know its price and value. This power enables us to put others first without having our own body broken. Even if we have not "sold" the one word of enlightenment, there is some merchant who has "bought" it [i.e., knows the mind of that one word]. Before the donkey's tail is finished, the horse's begins to grow.

"Joy" is heartfelt concern for others. Yet the thousand hands and eyes of Daihi (Kannon) are not enough to save all sentient beings. It is like plum blossoms blooming in the last snow of the season; spring has come but it is still bitterly cold. Nevertheless, we become vigorous and joyful.

"Spiritual peace" means stepping outside ourselves when we think about our inner nature, and stepping outside of others. When we are with them we can gain what others cannot. We spend our life in the midst of diversity and should remain in a state of spiritual peace.

"Equanimity" is Tōzan's saying "No matter what I say, don't accept it." A Chinese cannot learn about other countries by walking around China, nor can a Persian search for articles made from ivory other than those produced in his own country.

"Samādhi" is similar to anticipating things before they occur; that is, intuition. Use your own nostrils, not others'; completely control your own veins. Then we will be like the water buffalo on Mt. Issan.[3]

"Mindfulness" is walking through the air around a pillar in the Buddha Hall. The mouth resembles the wooden clapper used to announce various events in the monastery and the eyes become eyebrows [i.e., functionless functions]. It resembles sandalwood incense burning in the temple, or a lion roaring in his den.

The Eightfold Path (Eightfold Holy Path) consists of: 1) right vision; 2) right thought; 3) right speech; 4) right action; 5) right livelihood; 6) right effort; 7) right mindfulness; and 8) right samādhi.

"Right vision" is within the enlightened vision of our entire body. That is why we must possess the eye which existed before our body was born. This vision sees all things as they are in their true form—the actualization of enlightenment. We share that vision with the Buddhas and Patriarchs. If we do not have enlightened vision within our body we cannot be called Buddhas or Patriarchs.

When we have "right thought" all the Buddhas of the ten directions are actualized; when the ten directions emerge and the Buddhas appear it is the time of right thought. When we have right thought it is not ourselves, and not others. Although our thought occurs in the present, it should be like that of Shakyamuni at Benares. We should possess the same thought as Shakyamuni

---

[3] See *Shōbōgenzō* vol. I, p. 110.

at that time. An ancient Buddha said, "Think 'not-thinking.' How? By using 'non-thinking.' " This is right thought. Sitting until the cushion is worn away is also right thought.

"Right speech" is like a mute person thinking he is not mute. In the world of ordinary people a mute person does not speak; however, in their own world there are no mute people. We must study the proverb, "the mouth is hanging on all the walls—every mouth is on all the walls." That is, the silence of zazen is the actualization of right speech.

"Right action" is practicing the Way after renouncing the world, attaining enlightenment after entering the monastery. Shakyamuni Buddha said, "The thirty-seven conditions are the real actions of monks." The monks' actions should be neither Mahayana nor Hinayana. There are various kinds of monks —Buddha monks, Bodhisattva monks, śrāvaka monks, etc. If you have not yet renounced the world you will never be able to inherit or transmit the right action and great Way of the Buddhist Dharma. Recently, there are some lay people who are studying the Way, but none of them have mastered it. In order to master the Way, it is absolutely necessary to renounce the world and become a monk. If one lacks the determination to renounce the world, how can he ever hope to inherit the Buddhist Way?

However, there have been some Zen monks in Sung Dynasty China during the past two or three hundred years who claim that there is no difference between their study and that of lay people. These kind of people are worse than excrement-eating beasts. At times, some monks have said to kings and ministers that there is no distinction between a statesman's mind and that of the Buddha's and Patriarchs. Since kings and ministers do not know what the right teaching and right Law are, they are happy to bestow titles and honors to undeserving monks. Any monk who follows that path will become a Devadatta, a perverter of the Dharma. In order to get the praise of kings and ministers such monks tell childish and ridiculous stories. This is very pitiful. These monks are not the descendants of the seven Buddhas, but rather demons and beasts. They have not studied the Way through their body and mind, never learned anything, or attained liberation of body and mind. They lack knowledge of the evil side of court life and politics; consequently, they are unable even to dream of the Great Way of the Buddhas and Patriarchs.

Although the lay disciple Vimalakirti lived in the time of Shakyamuni, he was unable to master many things and had much to clarify. Hōon, another lay disciple, visited many Patriarchs but was unable to receive the transmission from Yakusan, or attain the stage of Kosei [Baso]. All that remains is his name.

His study bore little fruit. Other laymen such as Rifuba, Yūbunko, etc. studied a great deal but never ate a real rice cake [i.e., tasted the true teaching].[4] How then could they eat a painting of a rice cake or partake of the meal of the Buddhas and Patriarchs? The problem of receiving the mendicant bowl never even arises. It is very pitiful that they spent their lives as worthless skinbags. All beings, earthly and heavenly, and in the dragon kingdoms, should seek the Law of the Tathāgata, renounce the world, practice the Way, and then transmit the teaching of the Buddhas and Patriarchs.

We should not pay any attention to the words of inauthentic Zen masters. They do not know the body or mind [of Buddha]. That is why they talk like that. Such people lack compassion for sentient beings, and have no desire to protect the Buddhist Dharma; they only like the filthy offerings of laymen—they are like malicious dogs with human faces. Do not sit, talk with, or depend on them. They are beasts. If such monks possess filthy lucre, they think they are superior. Actually, these monks do not have anything equal to the filth of beasts. There is no evidence or principle anywhere in the five thousand volumes of the sūtras or in the two thousand year history of the Buddhist transmission that the mind of a layman and the mind of a monk are equal. None of the Buddhas and Patriarchs in fifty-four generations has ever said such a thing. Even a monk that has broken or does not keep any of the precepts, and lacks any Law or wisdom is still superior to a layman who keeps the precepts and possesses insight. This is because only a monk has the wisdom, enlightenment, and practice of the Way as the basis of his life. A layman may accumulate goodness and virtue, but he nevertheless lacks the root of virtue in body and mind.

Even during the lifetime of Shakyamuni, no layman attained the Way. A layman's house is not a dojo where the Buddhist Way can be studied; there are too many obstacles. Those who say that a layman's mind is the same as a Patriarch's mind do not possess the body and mind of the Dharma and have not transmitted the skin, flesh, bones, and marrow of the Buddhas and Patriarchs. This is very pitiful. Even though they live during the period of the propagation of the True Law they still fall into the realm of beasts.

Sōkei [Enō] the ancient Buddha left his parents and sought out a master; this is an example of right action. Prior to having his Buddha-seeking mind

---

[4] Hōkoji (Páng 740-803) was a lay disciple of Baso and also studied under Sekitō. Rifuba and Yubunko were Chinese court officials who studied Buddhism.

aroused by hearing a verse from the *Diamond Sūtra*, he was a woodcutter living in a hut. After he heard the *Diamond Sūtra* the fragrance of the Buddhist Law overcame him, and he abandoned his worldly concerns and became a monk. We should learn from this story that when we possess the Buddhist Dharma in our bodies and minds we cannot remain laymen. All the Buddhas and Patriarchs have experienced the same thing.

To think that it is not necessary to renounce the world is a graver sin than the five deadly sins, and such people are worse than Devadatta. We should have no traffic with such people because they are worse than the worst bhikkhus and bhikkhunis. Life is short and we have no time to waste talking to evil beasts. Nevertheless, these people have received a seed in their previous lives that enables them to hear the Buddhist Dharma and they have a place in the scheme of the Buddhist world. We should try to prevent them from falling into the realm of beasts. Do not forget the profound mercy of the Buddhas and Patriarchs, always preserve the virtue of the cream of the Law, and do not pay any attention to, or have anything to do with, the barking of malicious dogs.

The ancient Buddha Bodhidharma left the Buddhist country of India and came to the east; he transmitted the True Law of the Buddhas and Patriarchs for the first time. If he had not attained the Way by renouncing the world, such an event could never have occurred. Prior to the first Patriarch's coming to the east, the people of China neither saw nor heard the True Dharma. Therefore, we should know that the right transmission of the True Law is nothing other than the virtue contained in renouncing the world. The Great Teacher Shakyamuni did not take his father's crown, not because it was not noble, but because he wanted to inherit a more precious rank. His rank is the rank of one who has renounced the world. All sentient beings in the heavenly and earthly worlds venerate such a rank. How is it that human kings or dragon kings cannot share the same throne with Shakyamuni? Because his seat is the seat of a supreme enlightened one. One who has such a rank proclaims the Dharma and helps those in illusion; he appears radiant and bright. The actions of one who has renounced the world and attained such a rank are "right action." All the Buddhas, including the seven Buddhas of the past, have maintained this kind of action. This could not have occurred if Buddha had not searched for Buddha. People who have not yet renounced the world should venerate, respect, worship, and revere those who have renounced the world and show their sincerity with all their body and mind.

Shakyamuni Buddha said, "Renouncing the world and receiving the precepts is the seed of Buddhahood; such people are ordained monks." Therefore, we should know that ordination equals renunciation. People who have not yet renounced the world are just floating through life—this is a very sad and pitiful situation. In Shakyamuni's teaching there are many examples describing the virtue of renouncing the world. Shakyamuni taught the Dharma sincerely and all the Buddhas have certified it. Even if a monk breaks the precepts and does not practice, he can still attain the Way, but a layman can never do that. Emperors prostrate themselves before monks and nuns but they do not bow in return. The same thing occurs when celestials pay their respects to monks and nuns. Such things come about because of the superior virtue of renouncing the world. If monks and nuns who have renounced the world prostrate themselves before the celestials then palaces will crumble, Divine Light will lose its brilliance, and good fortune will end—all virtue will be lost.

Generally speaking, following the transmission of the Buddhist Dharma to the east, vast numbers of those who have renounced the world have attained the Way, but no laymen. This happens because if someone sees or hears the Buddhist Dharma he will quickly renounce the world. The lay world is not the place for the Buddhist Dharma. If someone maintains that a layman's body and mind is the same as the body and mind of the Buddhas and Patriarchs, he has not yet seen or heard the Buddhist Dharma. This is the mentality of criminals who have fallen into the darkest hell. Only fools who do not know what they are saying talk like that. Anyone who equates the layman's mind with the mind of the Buddhas and Patriarchs, and calls this the supreme Dharma, will make emperors overjoyed; however, the Buddhist Dharma is supreme only if the layman's mind is actually the same mind as that of the Buddhas and Patriarchs; then the body and mind of the Buddhas and Patriarchs becomes the body and mind of a layman—if that happens then the layman no longer exists. Zen masters who hold that both minds are the same have never learned the true meaning of the Buddhist Dharma; moreover, they cannot even dream of the mind of the Buddhas and Patriarchs.

In general, Brahma, Indra, human kings, dragon kings, etc. should not be attached to the law of retribution in the three worlds. Instead they should quickly renounce the world, receive the precepts, and practice the Way of all the Buddhas and Patriarchs. Throughout innumerable kalpas renunciation has the seed of Buddhahood. Upon reflection, we can see that if Vimalakirti had renounced the world and become a monk, as the bhikkhu Vimalakirti he would have been superior to the layman Vimalakirti.

Today we only see Sūbhuti, Śariputtra, Mañjuśri, and Maitreya [as Buddha's true disciples]. Vimalakirti does not have even half the stature of those monks.

Therefore, how can we see three, four, or five Vimalakirtis [i.e., his disciples and descendants]. If we cannot see three, four, or five Vimalakirtis we will not be able to see even one Vimalakirti who knows and possesses [the Buddhist Dharma]. If there is a Vimalakirti who does not possess [the Buddhist Dharma] we will not see the Buddha Vimalakirti. If there is no Buddha Vimalakirti there can be no Vimalakirti Mañjuśri, Vimalakirti Maitreya, Vimalkirti Śariputtra, etc. Moreover, how can there be a Vimalakirti of mountains, rivers, earth, or a Vimalakirti in grasses, trees, tiles, wind, rain, water, fire, etc. in the past, present, and future? Vimalakirti has not seen the virtuous Divine Light of those things because he has not renounced the world. If he had renounced the world he would be full of virtue.

Zen masters in the T'ang and Sung Dynasties failed to comprehend this principle; consequently, they think Vimalakirti has attained the Way. It is a great pity these people do not know what true teaching is in the Buddhist Dharma. Not only that, some even think that the Way of Shakyamuni and Vimalakirti is the same. These people have yet to learn the Buddhist Dharma, the Way of the Patriarchs, or about Vimalakirti—they have no idea of the differences between them.

Such people think that Vimalakirti's thundering silence as an answer to the Bodhisattvas is the same as the silent teaching of Buddha. That indicates they do not really know the Buddhist Dharma, and they lack the ability to learn the Way. Since the words of the Tathāgata are different from all others his silence, of course, is different from all other kinds. The silence of the Tathāgata and the silence of Vimalakirti cannot be compared in any way. If we evaluate those who maintain that the words are different but the silences are the same, we find that they have never advanced beyond the stage of a novice. It is a great pity that such people have never seen nor heard the voice or form of Buddha. How can they possess the Divine Light of the unsurpassed voice and form of Buddha? How can they find the real meaning of studying silence with silence? They know nothing about it. In general, things differ from one another, so how is it possible to compare the action and silence of Shakyamuni with others? They have not penetrated the depths of the Buddhas' and Patriarchs, teaching and therefore cannot make such comparisons.

Sometimes malicious people think that teaching and deeds are mere expedients and that silence and keeping quiet are the truth. To talk like that is not the Buddhist Dharma, it is closer to the teaching of Brahma and Shiva. How can that teaching be related to either the action or silence of the Buddhist Dharma? We must study in detail whether or not action and contemplation exist in the Buddhist Way and what their relationship is. Present day students should study this eagerly.

In present Sung Dynasty China almost no one studies the Great Way, probably not more than two or three. People there think Vimalakirti maintained his noble silence and that if we do not follow him we will be inferior. That is the goal of their Buddhist Dharma. Again, there are those who equate Vimalakirti's silence with that of Shakyamuni; consequently, they lack the Divine Light that enables one to distinguish between them. People who think like this have never studied, nor seen or heard the Buddhist Dharma. Just because they happen to be men of the Great Sung Dynasty it does not mean that they possess the Buddhist Dharma. This principle is easy to understand.

Right action should be a monk's work. Scholars of the abhidharma or the sūtras do not know this. The work of monks is to practice in the monastery, to make prostrations in the Buddha Hall, and wash the face in the lavatory. Making a gasshō, bowing, offering incense, and boiling water—this is right action. Not only does the head change into a tail, but the head changes to a head, the mind changes to mind, Buddha changes to Buddha, the Way changes to the Way—this is right action. If we have a mistaken understanding of the Buddhist Dharma, our eyebrows will fall off and our original face will be lost.

"Right life" is taking rice gruel in the morning, and eating lunch at noon. It is spiritual forging in the monastery, sitting in a chair and receiving instruction. Old Master Jōshū had less than twenty disciples because he actualized right life. Yakusan had less than ten, Fumyō[5] only seven or eight. This is the lifeblood and basis of right life, separated from all evil deeds.

Shakyamuni Buddha said, "None of the śrāvakas have attained right life yet." That is to say, the teaching, deeds, and enlightenment of śrāvakas is not right life. However, recently foolish people say that there should not be any distinctions between śrāvakas and Bodhisattvas; the hearing and observation of the precepts must be the same. From the standpoint of the Hinayana they criticize the actions of the Mahayana Bodhisattva.

Shakyamuni Buddha said, "Keeping the precepts of the śrāvakas is the same as breaking the precepts of the Bodhisattvas." Therefore, although the śrāvakas may think that they keep the precepts, when compared with those of the Bodhisattvas it is like breaking their own precepts. The same can be said for their respective practices of samādhi and wisdom. For example, the form of the precepts "Not to kill any living being," etc. seems to be the same for both

---

[5] Fumyō Zenshō d. 1024.

śrāvakas and Bodhisattvas, yet there is certainly a distinction—a difference greater than that between heaven and earth. How can we say that śrāvakas transmit the essence of the Buddhas and Patriarchs? There is not only right life, but pure life. Therefore, that is why study under the Buddhas and Patriarchs is the only right life. It is not necessary to use the interpretations of abhidharma scholars since they have not yet attained right life—their life is not a real one.

"Right effort" is practice with our entire body, the practice that strikes people in the face. It is like riding a horse upside down or whirling around the Buddha Hall one, two, three, four, or five times. Nine times nine even equals eighty-two; [that is, it transcends rational systems of counting]. Turn the head and many intersections can be seen; turn the face and more intersections appear. Entering your master's room and the master's lecturing in the Dharma Hall are right effort. Meeting at the Boshutei or Usekirin, in front of the monastery, or behind the altar in the Buddha Hall is like two mirrors facing each other and giving three reflections.

"Right mindfulness" is eighty or ninety percent deception. It is a mistake to think that wisdom develops from mindfulness; this is like the foolish boy who abandoned his father. Wisdom that develops within mindfulness is detached insight. People who say that no-mindfulness is right mindfulness are heretics. Again, do not think that the spirit of earth, water, fire, and wind is mindfulness, nor that it is some form of inverted consciousness. "You possess my skin, flesh, bones, and marrow" is right mindfulness.

"Right samādhi" is the dropping off of the Buddhas and Patriarchs; dropping off is right samādhi. Then we will have the ability to cut off the head and make nostrils [i.e., complete freedom of activity]. It is the holding up of an udumbara flower within the Eye and Treasury of the True Law. Within the udumbara flower there are a hundred smiling Mahākāśyapas. This dynamic, lively activity has been practiced for a long time, like a broken wooden ladle. Therefore, after six years of leaves falling and grasses fading, one night the flower bloomed. The universe was set afire, and all impurities were burned away.

These thirty-seven conditions favorable to enlightenment are the enlightened eyes, the nostrils, the skin, flesh, bones, marrow, hands, feet, and face of the Buddhas and Patriarchs. Moreover, enlightenment is the actualization of 1,369 [37×37] conditions. Practice zazen continually, and drop off body and mind.

This was delivered to the monks on February 24, 1243, at Kippōji, Echizen. Transcribed the same year on March 9, in the chief disciple's quarters by Ejō.

[50]

SENJŌ

"Rules for the lavatory"

THE Buddhas and Patriarchs maintain their practice and enlightenment through pure, undiluted action. Once the sixth Patriarch [Enō] asked Dai'e Ejō of Kannon-in on Mt. Nangaku, "Why do we seek practice and enlightenment?" Dai'e answered, "Practice and enlightenment are not 'not here' but they cannot be gained if there is any impurity." The sixth Patriarch then said, " 'No impurity' is what all the Buddhas preserve. You are like that. I am like that; indeed all the Patriarchs in India said the same thing."

In the *Daibikku Sanzen Iigi Sūtra*[1] it says: "In order to purify the body, eliminate all internal impurities and trim the nails." Even though our body and mind may be impure there is a method that can purify not only our own body but the entire world. Further, although the Buddhas and Patriarchs may reside in a country free of dust and dirt they work to maintain and increase their purity—even after attainment of the Way they neither relax nor abandon their practice. Their essence cannot be measured; their essence is their bearing and manner, and this manner is their attainment of the Way.

In the Jogyobon chapter of the *Avatamsaka Sūtra* it is written: "Entering the lavatory, vow to remove all dirt and cast off lust, anger, and stupidity. Purify yourself with water, vow to follow the supreme Way, and practice renunciation of the world. After the dirt is washed away, pray for all sentient beings, vow to maintain true equanimity and then no impurities or dirt will remain."

Originally, neither water nor our body is pure or impure. All things are like this. Also, neither water nor our body is originally animate or inanimate. All things, even the teaching of the World-honored One, are like this. Therefore,

---

[1] A work dealing with various monastic rules and giving explanations of all aspects of a monk's life.

water cannot purify our bodies. Maintaining the Buddhist Dharma and acting in a refined, true Buddhist manner purifies body and mind. Then the body and mind of the Buddhas and Patriarchs is transmitted as our own body and mind and we are able to see and hear the sayings of the Buddhas and Patriarchs. Such purification actualizes countless virtue. The proper time to enoble true practice of body and mind is when the eternal aspects of all real activity are manifest—then the essence of the practice of body and mind emerges.

We must trim the nails on the fingers of both hands and also trim our toenails. It says in the sūtras that if the length of the nails is more than one *bu* [3 mil.] it is a transgression. Therefore, do not let your nails grow like non-believers. Be careful about their proper length.

Among the monks in Great Sung Dynasty China there are some who lack the proper spirit for study and let their nails grow long. Some let them grow one or two *sun* [one *sun*=3 cm.] or even as long as three or four *sun*. This is against the precepts, and is not the body and mind of the Buddhist Dharma. Those priests do not understand Buddhism. A virtuous priest with a right-minded attitude is not like that. Some priests also let their hair grow even though that too is prohibited. Do not be misled into thinking that such attitudes represent the true Dharma just because those priests come from a great and powerful country.

My late master, an ancient Buddha, admonished those monks who let their hair or nails grow: "Those who fail to comprehend the significance of shaving the head are neither laymen nor monks—they are nothing but beasts. Among all the Buddhas and Patriarchs of the past there is not one who did not shave his head. If you fail to understand this you are simply an animal." After my master gave this reprimand many of the monks shaved their heads. In both his formal lectures and informal talks he sharply reprimanded errant monks. He told them that since they understood nothing they let their hair and nails grow. It was pitiful and although they had the body of a human being they had completely separated themselves from the Way. He said that in the past two or three hundred years the Way of the Patriarchs has been gradually fading away and the number of careless people increasing. Sometimes such people become heads of temples and receive special titles from the emperor, all the while pretending to be spiritual leaders. This is a scandal in both heaven and earth. In all of the mountain temples in the Great Sung Dynasty there is hardly anyone who possesses a Buddha-seeking mind; consequently, those who have attained the Way almost never appear. The monks only become more and more degenerate.

My master often spoke of this in informal talks yet the elders in various places ignored his reproaches. We must realize that monks with long hair are strongly reprimanded by all the Buddhas and Patriarchs, and that only non-believers have long nails. Descendants of the Buddhas and Patriarchs never do this—they remain pure in body and mind by trimming their nails and shaving their heads.

Do not be too lazy to wash your hands after using the lavatory. There is a story about Śariputtra converting a non-believer by observing this precept. At the time, neither Śariputtra nor the non-believer intended such a thing to occur. It came about through the power and dignity of the Buddhas and Patriarchs, which subjugates all malicious acts.

In the case when we are practicing outdoors or in the woods it is necessary to build a privy. Wash yourself with water and sand from a river or stream. After you remove your robe arrange seven balls of sand, the size of large soy beans, into two rows. Place the balls on top of stones or in some other convenient place. Put some stones aside to be used later for brushing. Then you may use it for a lavatory. After you finish use a spatula or paper. Go to the river and wash your hands. Take three of the mud balls; put the first one in the palm of your hand, mix it with a little water and wash off the genitals. Take the second ball, mix it with water and wash off the buttocks. Take the last ball and cleanse your hands.

After monks began to practice in temples it became necessary to construct a lavatory. It is called a *tosu*. In ancient times it was called a *shin (nigoru)* or *shi (kawaya)*. It is absolutely necessary to have a lavatory in the monastery. The proper method to follow in using the *tosu* is as follows:

Take a *shukin* [a kind of towel], fold it in two, and put it over the left shoulder. When you arrive at the *tosu*, place the *shukin* on the *jokan*, the bamboo pole next to the lavatory. If you are wearing either a *kujoe* or *shichijoe* [types of undergarment] place it next to the *shukin* on the pole, making sure it will not slip off. Never throw it over the pole in a careless way. Remember where your name is written on the pole. It should be written on a piece of paper the shape of a half-moon. Do not forget where you put your robe and do not get it mixed with others' robes, especially when there are many other monks.

If there are many monks, take your place in line, put your left fist inside your right hand, and give a slight bow to the others. In the *tosu*, also bow to one another, even if you are not wearing a robe. If you are not using your hands keep them against your chest; if you must use one hand, keep the other in a one-handed gassho, bending the fingers slightly inward as if you are going to cup water. All monks should follow this procedure.

The robe should be placed next to the *shukin* on the pole in the following manner: Remove the outer robe, put the arms together, fold them over the back, grasp the collar with your left hand, lift the robe up with your right, fold it down the middle and then in half so that the collar faces the pole and the back faces you. Then hang it over the pole. Wrap the *shukin* around the robe and tie it, being careful not to drop the robe. Then make a gassho.

After that take the *bansu* [string-like belt] and put it over your shoulders. Next go to the *joka*, the place for washing hands. Put water in the bucket, hold it in your right hand, and proceed to the *tosu*. Do not fill the bucket completely, only nine-tenths of the way. In front of the *tosu* change your slippers; put on the special straw slippers. This is called *kanzai*, changing slippers.

In the *Zenen Shingi* it says: "Do not wait to go to the *tosu*; make sure you have enough time to eliminate your internal impurities. Do not hurry. Put your kesa either on the self in the monks' quarters or on the bamboo pole outside the *tosu*." (*Zenen Shingi, Sanzen Igikyo Bunjinyu*)

Enter the *tosu* from the left hand side of the corridor, sprinkle water on the lavatory bowl, and put the bucket in the proper place. Purify the lavatory by snapping the thumb and index finger of the right hand together three times; make a fist with your left hand and put it on your waist.

Lift up the skirt of the kimono, pull up the sleeves close to your body, squat down and eliminate your impurities. Be careful not to get the front, back, or sides dirty. Keep silent. Do not talk with the person next door, do not sing to yourself or recite poems, do not drool or let your nose run, do not scatter anything, do not grunt and do not draw anything on the wall. Do not make any marks on the floor with the spatula. After you finish your business use either a spatula or paper. Be sure never to use old paper or paper with characters written on it. Be sure to distinguish between a used and an unused spatula. The spatula should be eight *sun* in length, triangularly shaped, and the thickness approximately equal to one thumb. It may be either lacquered or unlacquered. Put the used spatula in the spatula box and place a fresh one on the spatula stand in front of the lavatory bowl.

After using either paper or spatula purify yourself like this: Hold the water bucket in your right hand, cup water in your left, and wash off the genitals and buttocks three times. Follow this prescribed manner. Do not attempt to pour water into your hands and do not waste water by spilling it. After washing put the water bucket down. If you have used a spatula clean it off. Then clean the lavatory bowl. Take down your kimono and sleeves with your right hand. Again take the bucket with your right hand, change your slippers, and return to the hand washing stand. Put the bucket back in place. Wash your hands by putting ashes in your right hand and rubbing them on the top of the stones; then put some water on your fingers and wash your hands as if you are cleaning a rusty sword. Do this three times. Next mix sand and water together and clean your hands three times. Now take some cleaning powder and thoroughly wash off your hands and forearms in a small bucket, with total concentration. Three times with ashes, three times with sand, and once with cleaning powder—all together seven times, an appropriate number. Finally, put some water in a big bucket and wash one more time without using ashes, sand or any kind of powder. Change the water in both buckets and rinse both hands.

The *Avatamska Sūtra* says: "When you wash your hands in a basin of water pray for all sentient beings. With pure hands prostrate yourself before the Buddhist Law." Hold the ladle in your right hand and do not make any sounds while using the ladle or basin. Do not splash water or washing powder and do not make the surrounding area wet. Never leave any of the utensils in a random manner. Wipe your hands with the *shukin*. After you finish wiping your hands in front of the pole remove the strings that bind your robe and place them on the pole. Make a gassho, untie the *shukin* and put on your robe.

Take some bulb-shaped incense pellets, about one thumb thickness in width and four times that in length, and fan the incense smoke over your body. Then tie two incense pellets to a thin string about one foot in length and hang it over the pole. Place the incense between your palms and rub, thus putting the fragrance on your hands.

Make certain you do not mix your string with the others or leave it in a disorderly manner. To take such care is to adorn and purify the Buddha land. Do it wholeheartedly; do not be sloppy or lazy. Do not hurry. When you go to the *tosu* keep in mind the words of [Zen, Master Jōshū] "The Buddhist Law is not preaching to others; [everyday actions themselves constitute the Buddhist Law]."

Do not stare at the faces of the monks going to the *tosu*. In the corridor there is a place to rinse your hands. Since hot water sometimes causes intestinal problems it is better to use warm. There should be a kettle beside the *tosu* with which to warm water.

The *Zenen Shingi* says: "The monk in charge of the *tosu* directs the boiling of water and the preparation of a night lamp and he makes sure the monks have the proper attitude." Both hot and cold water is permitted. If the corridor becomes dirty seal off the entrance and place a sign giving notice. Also if the water bowl is accidentally knocked over, close the entrance. If there is a notice on the sign board do not enter the *tosu*. If someone announces his presence in the corridor by snapping his fingers you should leave in a short time.

The *Shingi* says: "If you do not purify yourself you cannot take your place in the zendō. You cannot make any prostrations to the three treasures nor receive the bows of others."

In the *Sanzen Igigyo* it says: "If you do not purify yourself after using the *tosu* you commit a transgression. Your prostrations are tainted even though the cushion on which you sit is pure. Your prostrations will never help you attain bliss and virtue." Therefore in the dojo you must strictly follow the above procedures. How can it be that we are unable to make prostrations to the three treasures and receive the bows of others?

The place where the Buddhas and Patriarchs practice the Way possesses such a manner [as outlined above]. Therefore, all monks must keep the same bearing; it must be done naturally without any prodding. Such is the everyday bearing of all the Buddhas and Patriarchs, and not only in this world; it is the activity of all the Buddhas in the ten quarters of the universe, both in the world of misery and in the Pure Land.

People who have insufficient understanding think that Buddhas have no special manner or method when they use the *tosu*. They also think that the method of Buddhas in this world differs from that of those in the Pure Land. Those who have learned the Buddhist Way do not think like that. Purity and impurity, hot and cold belong to the discrimination of ordinary people. We should know this. All the Buddhas use the proper method of using the *tosu*.

The fourteenth Vinaya precept says: "Once Rāhula was caught hiding in Shakyamuni's lavatory. [All the monks scolded him] but Buddha, even though he was aware of his errant behavior, patted Rāhula with his right hand and recited this verse:

> "You did not renounce the world because of poverty,
> Nor because of losing your position or riches.
> You renounced it to seek the Buddhist Way—
> Now you must endure all hardships and suffering."

Therefore, we can see that even in the *tosu* Buddhas practice the Way. Their manner in the *tosu* is that of purification (*senjō*). It has been transmitted from Patriarch to Patriarch. The Buddhas' manner is to joyfully follow all the precepts. By following the precepts we can find the true Buddhist Way which is difficult to locate. Furthermore, Shakyamuni instructed Rāhula in the *tosu* and now all of us are grateful for that teaching. The *tosu* is also a place to turn the wheel of the Law and practice the proper bearing of the Way; this is the right transmission of the Buddhas and Patriarchs.

In the *Makasogiritsu*,[2] chapter thirty-four, it says: "The *tosu* should not be placed in the east or north. It should be constructed in the south or west. The same holds for the urinal." We must follow this injunction. This is the way temples were constructed in India during Shakyamuni's time. This manner of construction was not only used in Shakyamuni's time but also by the seven other Buddhas of the past.

Every dojo and monastery where Buddhas practice is like this. Shakyamuni was not the first to begin this practice; it has been done by all the Buddhas. Do not construct any temples before you understand this; otherwise you will commit many mistakes and the Buddhist Way will not be attained, nor will the Buddhas' supreme enlightenment emerge. In order to construct a real dojo you must follow the established procedure which corresponds to the right transmission of the Buddhas and Patriarchs. Then the virtue of the Buddhas and Patriarchs gathers and increases. If you are not the Dharma-heir of the Buddhas and Patriarchs you will not know the body and mind of the Dharma. If you do not know the body and mind of the Dharma you cannot clarify the Buddhist Law of karma.

Now the Buddhist Law of the Great Teacher Shakyamuni Buddha which has been transmitted throughout the entire universe is actualized as his body and mind. The actualization of the body and mind of Buddha is the proper time for us to purify ourselves.

This was delivered to the monks on October 23, 1242, at Kannondōri-Kōshō-hōrinji, Yamashiro no Kuni, Uji-gun.

---

[2] A Chinese version of a Mahāsamghika vinaya text.

[51]

HENZAN

"Direct study under a master"

THE great Way of the Buddhas and Patriarchs is to experience the ultimate goal of study—no strings [of attachment] can get under our feet, only clouds emerge.[1] Although we may say this, still, when a flower blooms the entire world emerges, and we are always on the [Buddhist Way].[2] Similarly, even the skin of a melon is sweet, while a bitter gourd is bitter to the roots—sweet is sweet, bitter is bitter. That is what we must study.

Great Master Gensha Soitsu was once called by his master Seppō. Seppō asked, "Why don't you continue to visit other masters?" Gensha replied, "Bodhidharma didn't come to China and the second Patriarch didn't go to India." Seppō praised this answer. The principle behind the question of visiting other masters (*henzan*) differs from the meaning of the words, and [in Bodhidharma's words] it is nothing special; basically there is no difference in rank between various masters.

The first time Zen Master Nangaku Dai'e visited the ancient Buddha Sōkei [Enō], the ancient Buddha asked him, "Where are you from?" Dai'e could not answer and spent eight years seeking the answer to that question. Finally, after this practice under his master he made a prostration before the ancient Buddha and said, "When I first came here you asked where I came from. Now I know the real intent of your words." The ancient Buddha Sōkei said, "What did you clarify?" Dai'e said, "I can't explain in words. That's what I learned." This is the actualization of Dai'e's eight years of practice under a master. The

---

[1] This refers to the debate between Bodhidharma and the non-believer Shūshō. After Shūshō conceded his defeat clouds arose beneath Bodhidharma's feet and he floated away.

[2] A saying of Tōzan.

ancient Buddha Sōkei said, "Why do we seek practice and enlightenment?" Dai'e said, "Practice and enlightenment are not 'not here' but they cannot be gained if there is any impurity." Sōkei then said, "I am like that, you are like that, and all the Buddhas and Patriarchs are like that."

After this Nangaku continued his practice for eight more years, altogether more than fifteen years. Yet even his first meeting with Enō was *henzan*, "receiving direct instruction from a master." And "it cannot be attained in words" opens the gate to meeting all the Buddhas and Patriarchs, i.e., practicing under a Zen master. Entering a monastery [and practicing the Way] does not necessarily require countless aeons. Someone who has much free time, and frequently comes and goes will not attain true practice under a master. Not coming and going is the complete enlightened vision and total attainment of study under a master. Perceiving the master's original face is also *henzan*.

The essence of Seppō's question about visiting other masters is not originally concerned with visiting other mountains in the north or south. Gensha's "Bodhidharma didn't come to China, and the second Patriarch didn't go to India" elaborates on that question. Gensha's answer "Bodhidharma didn't come to China" is not related to "coming" or "not coming." This is the principle of the great immeasurable earth. The lifeblood of Bodhidharma fills everywhere. Even if everyone in China studied under him it still cannot be said that Bodhidharma "came" to the east or "went" to the west. Thus, "not coming to China" is to freely come. In the east, we can see the faces of the Buddhas and Patriarchs, but that does not mean that they "came" to China. Attain the mind of the Buddhas and Patriarchs [by "not coming"] but do not lose their essence [by "coming"].

Generally speaking, the earth has no east or west; there is no place where east and west exist. Since the second Patriarch did not go to the west it is not necessary for us to go there to study. If the second Patriarch had gone to India he would have lost his other arm [and the Buddhist Way would not have been transmitted]. That is why he did not go. Because he leaped into the enlightened vision of Bodhidharma he did not have to stay in the west. If he had not possessed the enlightened eye of his teacher, surely he would have had to stay in the west. *Henzan*, true study under a real master, is to pluck out the enlightened eye of Bodhidharma—it is not going to the west or coming to the east. Similarly, going to Mt. Tendai, Mt. Nangaku, or Mt. Godai is not *henzan*. If we do not transcend the world of the four oceans and five lakes, [i.e., the world of discrimination] we cannot have *henzan*. We lose the Way, take the wrong step, and miss *henzan*.

All things throughout the ten directions of the entire universe have a real form and true body; the study of that form and body is *henzan*. That is why we can find *henzan* in "Bodhidharma didn't come to China and the second Patriarch didn't go to India." *Henzan* means "a big stone is big, a small stone is small." Stone is "stone," nothing else; big is "big," small is "small." If you see a different stone each time you look at it, this is not *henzan*. To be able to accept one word, or even half a word, of a master is to clarify ourselves. This is the unlimited detachment which is *henzan*. For example, [Dachi, a disciple of Baso,] would hit the ground when asked any question—this is *henzan*. If the monk strikes the ground, then the air, and then in all directions it is not *henzan*. The monk Gutei visited Tenryū and was enlightened after the master held up one finger. This is true *henzan* and thereafter Gutei would always hold up one finger when asked a question.

Gensha once said to an assembly of monks, "Shakyamuni and I studied together." One monk asked, "That's a little strange, isn't it? Who was the master at that time?" Gensha said, "Shasaburo, [Gensha's secular name] the fisherman." This is how we can say Shakyamuni and Gensha studied together and vice versa. This is the principle of *henzan*. Since Shakyamuni and Gensha studied together they both may be called ancient Buddhas. Gensha studied with Shakyamuni and is therefore known as his descendant. We must clarify this principle in detail.

In addition, we must clarify the essence of "Shasaburo the fisherman." The main point here is that Shakyamuni and Gensha studied together at the same time. We must consider whether or not the [young] Shasaburo saw the old master Gensha or if the baldheaded Gensha saw Shasaburo on the fishing boat. We must clarify whether they saw each other or not. Gensha and Shakyamuni met each other and received *henzan*. Shasaburo and I saw and met each other; we must seek out the principle behind this and receive *henzan*.

Oneself meeting and seeing oneself is the principle of *henzan*; if this principle does not emerge we cannot see ourselves. If we do not see ourselves we are not capable of seeing others—both of these are insufficient. If we cannot see others we cannot see ourselves. Then we cannot direct others or possess enlightened vision. We cannot fish for ourselves or gain enlightenment.

To completely attain *henzan* we must be totally detached from it. "The ocean dries up and we cannot see the bottom"; "People die but the mind does not depart." "Dry up" means that the entire ocean completely dries up. However, we also cannot see the bottom of the ocean if the ocean does not dry up. "Depart" or "not depart" is independent of the human mind. When a person dies the mind does not depart. When death comes it is complete death; consequently, the entire person is mind, and the total mind is the person. Like this, we must clarify these relationships from every angle.

One day, my late master Tendō, the ancient Buddha, was asked to address a group of elders who had previously practiced under the same master. At that time he ascended the platform and said, "The Great Way has no gate. Yet you have come from all directions taking the road of universal emptiness to enter the heart of Seiryōji. Actually, we are welcoming a bunch of thieves and ruffians who follow Rinzai. This is like a gentle spring breeze that follows a tremendous, earth-shattering storm. Such a breeze amazes the apricot blossoms as their crimson petals float to earth."

This was given when my late master, the ancient Buddha, was staying at Seiryōji in Kenkoku at a meeting of elders who came from all directions. My late master was both host and guest for these elders. They sat together and practiced zazen. Many people had gathered and a number were capable of making an address but since they especially asked Nyojō we can see how greatly he was respected at that time. Perhaps, the *henzan* of my late master was different from that of the other elders. An ancient Buddha like my late master has not appeared for the past two or three hundred years in Great Sung China.

"The Great Way has no gate." In spring countless willows and cherries bloom everywhere and wind and string instruments are continually playing. There is no other way to leap over, with our entire body, the gateless gate. We must jump over the head and enter the nostril of the Buddhas and Patriarchs. This is the proper way to study. Those who have not liberated themselves or entered the nostril of the Buddhas and Patriarchs cannot be called true students or receive *henzan*. The essence of *henzan* can only be found by studying Gensha.

The fourth Patriarch [Dōshin] practiced under the third Patriarch [Sōzan] for nine years, Zen Master Nansen Fugan studied for thirty years on Mt. Nangaku in Chiyo without once leaving the place, Ungan and Dōgo studied for more than forty years under Yakusan. These all represent true *henzan*. The second Patriarch practiced under Bodhidharma for eight years on Mt. Sūzan and mastered the skin, flesh, bones and marrow of *henzan*.

Henzan is *shikantaza*, single-minded sitting, and the dropping off of body and mind. Hence, we can find our true self and actualize the Buddha mind. The entire body of *henzan* is the entire body of the great Way. This is free, unfettered samādhi and the actions of an enlightened one. Such study and practice is continually transmitted like an inseparable tangle of vines and gourds. This has been the basis of Buddhist dojo from ancient times. The life of the Tathāgatas is an endless thread and has never been severed. One gourd gives *henzan* to another. Even one blade of grass can give *henzan*.

This was delivered to an assembly of monks on November 27, 1243, at Hotori hermitage on Zenjihō. Transcribed the same year on December 27, in the chief disciple's quarters by Ejō.

GANZEI

"Enlightened vision"

THE study of the Way during the past countless aeons bears fruit in the present eighty-four thousand forms of enlightened vision.

One day, when my late master Tendō, an ancient Buddha, was staying at Zuiganji he entered the Dharma Hall and said to the monks, "The autumn breeze is pure and fresh, the autumn moon is clear and bright. With enlightened vision we can see the real form of the great earth, mountains and rivers. Staying at Zuiganji has renewed my vision. The sound of the stick and the shout of a *katsu* are again lively as we test each other."

Here, "testing each other" is testing each other's ancient Buddha vision. The important point is for everyone to mutually use the stick and the shout. This is *tenkatsu*, i.e., making one's vision anew. Such a manifestation of insight and activity is enlightened vision. The real form of mountains, rivers, and the great earth is rooted in enlightened vision and exists throughout innumerable kalpas. "The autumn breeze is pure and fresh" and "the autumn moon is clear and bright" are viewed beyond time. The freshness of the autumn moon cannot be compared to the four great oceans, and the brightness of the autumn moon is beyond comparison with a hundred thousand suns and moons. "Pure and fresh" and "bright and clear" are the enlightened vision of mountains, rivers and the earth. "Each other" means the Buddhas and Patriarchs. Do not expect great enlightenment, unenlightenment, or some previous enlightenment in the distant past—this is the enlightened vision of the Buddhas and Patriarchs. "Testing" is also rooted in enlightened vision; it is the actualization of renewed vision and the active eye of enlightenment. "Renewing our vision" is the same as "meeting," i.e., [Nyojō's] eye meets [Buddha's] eye. They meet like thunder and lightening. Do not think that the body is large and the eye is small. Even though there are some old people who think like that, they do so because their enlightened eye is not open completely.

Once when Great Master Tōzan Gohon was practicing under Ungan, he found Ungan making a pair of straw sandals. Tōzan said, "I came here to receive enlightened vision [yet all you do are things like making sandals]." Ungan replied, "You want to give it to someone and then leave?" Tōzan said, "I don't have any." Then Ungan said, "If you had it to whom would you give it?" Tōzan did not speak. Ungan said, "Is what you want really enlightened vision or not?" Tōzan said, "It is not enlightened vision." Ungan gave a loud shout.

We can see that the focal point of all study and practice is to seek enlightened vision. Practicing the Way in the zendō, studying in the Dharma Hall, sleeping in the monastery—all these are seeking enlightened vision. Working together and sharing the life of the monastery is also enlightened vision. This story clarifies the principle that enlightened vision is not ourselves and not others.

Tōzan was seeking enlightened vision from his master and ultimately gained it. The problem of oneself is independent of the problem of others, and one should not depend on others. That is why Ungan said, "You want to give it to someone and then leave?" i.e., to whom are you going to give your version of enlightened vision? When Tōzan said, "I don't have any," it indicated his personal understanding of enlightened vision. We should quietly reflect on this actualization of the Way. Ungan said, "If you had it to whom would you give it?" This concerns the real nature of enlightened vision and is both "don't have" and "have" of "I don't have any" and "if you had . . ." This is the proper way of understanding which we should study. "Tōzan did not speak." This does not mean he could not answer. Ungan asked, "Is what you want really enlightened vision or not?" This is renewed enlightened vision, that is, illusion is crushed and enlightened vision comes to life. The essence of Ungan's expression is that enlightened vision seeks enlightened vision, water follows water, mountains follow mountains. Different things work reciprocally, similar things live together.

Tōzan said, "It is not enlightened vision." This indicates our own vision is enlightened. "Not enlightened vision" means the body and mind of insight; it should be taken as the form of our active enlightened vision. All the Buddhas of the three worlds turn and proclaim the Great Wheel of the Dharma of enlightened vision. In order to penetrate the deepest aspect of our study we must leap into enlightened vision through resolve, practice, and great enlightenment. This enlightened vision is not ours and not others'. Therefore, it contains no obstacles or attachments.

An ancient Buddha [Roya Ekaku] said, "How wonderful! All the Buddhas of the ten quarters were originally flowers in the eye." That is, all the Buddhas are enlightened vision; flowers in the eye are all the Buddhas of the ten quarters. Moving forward or backward, practicing zazen or sleeping are all functions of enlightened vision without any attachment or clinging.

My late master the ancient Buddha said, "Pluck out the enlightened eye of Bodhidharma, make it into a mud ball and strike people with it." Then he shouted, "Jaku! The ocean dries up and waves billow to the sky!" He said this at the abbot's quarters of Seiryōji to a large group of monks. Those people who are "struck" are like those who are "made" [i.e., being taught]. "Strike" means that each person can find his original face. For example, through the enlightened vision of Bodhidharma each person can make and be made. The principle of throwing at people is like this. Everyone can be reborn by being struck with this enlightened vision. We have had examples of monks being struck with a fist in the monastery, hit with a staff in the Dharma Hall, or belted with a fly whisk or stick in the master's quarters—this is the enlightened vision of Bodhidharma. Making a mud ball from Bodhidharma's eye is like petitioning a master to be accepted as his disciple, greeting him, and practicing zazen under him. About this being "struck" the master said, "The ocean dries up, waves billow to the sky."

My late master the ancient Buddha entered the Dharma Hall and praised the Tathāgata's attainment of the Way, saying, "After six years of ascetic practice he became like a wild fox. He fled from the mountains, full of perplexity; he had completely lost the enlightened vision he was seeking. There was no place else to look. He was like a madman, yet when he saw the morning star he attained enlightenment." "Attaining enlightenment when seeing the morning star" seemed to occur too suddenly since just prior to that he had completely lost his enlightened vision. It was like other people telling him he was enlightened. He was full of perplexity, and therefore had to overcome it. Enlightenment does not appear only where we want it to appear; it is independent of any one attainment of the Way.

Once my late master the ancient Buddha said, "When Shakyamuni lost his ordinary sight and attained enlightened vision, one branch of a plum tree bloomed in the snow. But now small branches have appeared and the beautiful blossoms laugh at the spring wind blowing wildly." Buddha's enlightened vision cannot be tentatively expressed by one, two, or three [or any number]. What kind of vision is lost? Is there any kind of enlightened vision that can be lost? The plum branch that bloomed in the snow was the enlightened vision of Shakyamuni. It bloomed in spring and actualized the heart of spring.

My late master the ancient Buddha said, "[Shakyamuni's ascetic practice] was like continuous rain, day after day, but his enlightenment was like a beautiful clear day. Even the bullfrogs and worms were singing. Ancient Buddha mind transcends time, and diamond enlightened vision emerges. Tottsu! Entwinement causes more entwinement." "Diamond enlightened vision" is in both the continuous rain and the beautiful sky, and in the singing of bullfrogs and worms. People of the present age lack such an understanding. Since there is no past we can call it "ancient Buddha." The ancient Buddhas of the past live in the present time; it cannot be compared to the passing of non-ancient Buddhas.

My late master the ancient Buddha said, "Today is the winter solstice and the days will gradually get longer. Enlightened vision will shine and the breath becomes lively." For countless generations, day after day, the days have gotten longer. This is the detachment of enlightened vision. Enlightened vision will shine and the mountains will be seen in the sunshine. Like this there is enlightened vision in all aspects of life.

One day my late master spoke at Jōjiji in Rinan. He said, "This is the morning of February 1. The enlightened vision of a fly whisk is shining. Its brightness is like a mirror, and its darkness like black lacquer. Its brightness illuminates the entire universe. Why are all of you monks encircled by an impenetrable wall?" Smiling, he was silent for a while and then said, "The spring wind has the answer to this question," and left the platform. The meaning of "encircled by a wall" is enlightened vision. This "morning," "February," and "first day" are each aspects of enlightened vision, that is, the enlightened vision of a fly whisk. Since it transcends black lacquer [i.e., the discriminations of ordinary people], it becomes this morning's enlightened vision. It is the enlightened vision of February which illuminates the entire universe and it is the first day praised by my master. The activity and actualization of enlightened vision is like this.

This was delivered to an assembly of monks on December 17, 1242, at Zenjihō, Echizen. Transcribed the same month at the chief disciple's quarters of Kippōji by Ejō.

JISHŌZAMMAI

"Self-enlightened samādhi"

THE right transmission of all the Buddhas and Patriarchs from the time of the seven Buddhas to the present is the samādhi of practice and enlightenment; namely, following the right master and studying the sūtras. This is the enlightened vision of the Buddhas and Patriarchs. That is why the ancient Buddha Sōkei asked a monk, "Why do you seek practice and enlightenment?" The monk said, "Practice and enlightenment are not 'not here' but they cannot be gained if there is any impurity." Therefore, we should know that undefiled practice and enlightenment is the Buddhas and Patriarchs. The samādhi of the Buddhas and Patriarchs is frost and hail, wind and lightening.

When we follow the right master, sometimes we see half our face and body, but then other times we can see all our face and body. Sometimes we see half of ourselves, and half of others. Sometimes a master reveals himself with the face of a god covered with hair [enlightenment]. Sometimes as a devil with horns [practice]. Different types of behavior confront us and personalities change unexpectedly. We find ourselves experiencing this on countless occasions. Searching for the Dharma is carried out throughout kalpas. This is the real function of study under a master. We meet our real selves and true form—[Shakyamuni] blinked and [Mahākāśyapa] smiled; [Eka] received the marrow [of Bodhidharma's teaching] and made a prostration after severing his arm.

Generally speaking, from the time of the seven Buddhas until the sixth Patriarch, seeing ourselves while studying under a master was not limited to one or two instances; and seeing others is not only in the past, or only in the present.

When we study the sūtras we study our own skin, flesh, bones, and marrow. When we cast off our own skin, flesh, bones, and marrow, the enlightened vision of the peach blossoms will emerge and the sound of a tile striking the bamboo will enable us to clearly see and hear frost and hail.

When we study the sūtras their true meaning should emerge. This "sūtra" is the sūtra of the entire universe—mountains, rivers, earth, grass, trees, self, and others. It is the taking of meals and the wearing of clothes, the work of everyday life. When we study the Way based on those respective sūtras, countless sūtras are revealed. The letters of those sūtras are the real ones. We also find unwritten gathas everywhere. Possessing such understanding enables us to study with our body and mind and spend countless lives in innumerable kalpas—then surely we can arrive at the proper stage of understanding. Studying with our entire body and mind takes us beyond time and we will surely receive the fruits of our efforts.

About five thousand of the Indian texts written in Sanskrit have been translated into Chinese. They are comprised of the three vehicles, the five vehicles, the nine divisions, and the twelve divisions.[1] We must study these texts; since it is impossible for us to avoid following these sūtras, they will become our enlightened vision and marrow. Head to tail, everything is true and right. Sometimes you get it from others, sometimes you give it to others—it is the activity of enlightened vision that drops off self and others. Since enlightened vision and the marrow [of Buddhism] is not dependent on self and others, the right transmission of the Buddhas and Patriarchs has been passed down from ancient times to the present. There is a sūtra of the long staff which freely proclaims [detachment] and breaks down all discriminations between emptiness and existence. There is a fly whisk sūtra which purifies snow and frost. There is a zazen sūtra proclaimed in each zazen session; also a one-chapter kesa sūtra which contains ten volumes. All these are protected by the Buddhas and Patriarchs. By following the teachings of these sūtras we attain practice and enlightenment. Various faces appear—human, divine, sun-faced, moon-faced—as well as the meaning of following the teaching of the sūtras.

Nevertheless, following the right master and the teaching of the sūtras ultimately means following our own self. The sūtras themselves are our own self as a sūtra; right masters themselves are our own self as a right master.

---

[1] The three vehicles are those of the śrāvakas, pratyekabuddhas, and Bodhisattvas; the five vehicles are the above three plus the vehicles of men and gods. The nine divisions are sūtras, gathas, records of the lives of the Buddha's disciples, jataka tales, tales of miracles performed by Buddha, historical narratives, allegories, verses taken from the sūtras, and discussions of doctrine. The twelve divisions include the above and prophecies of future Buddhas, sūtras which deal with broad topics, and statements by the Buddha not prompted by questions from his disciples.

Therefore, study and practice under a right master is the study and practice of oneself. Holding up a hundred grasses or ten thousand trees is the holding up of ourselves. Clarify the fact that surely, we ourselves are the final object of our practice and study. In this study, self is cast off and original being emerges. That is why in the Great Way of the Buddhas and Patriarchs there is a method of self-practice and self-enlightenment; if there had not been a right transmission of the Buddhas and Patriarchs, the right Dharma could not have been handed down. There is a right transmission from master to disciple; if it is not the bones and marrow of the Buddhas and Patriarchs, it cannot be rightly transmitted. Studying like this, we can say "You possess my marrow" or "I possess the Eye and Treasury of the True Law and now bestow it to Mahākāśyapa." Proclaiming the Law is not dependent on self or others. Proclaiming it to others is proclaiming it to ourselves. Then the self [of others] and our own self listen together. One ear hears, one proclaims. One tongue proclaims, one hears. All of the six sense organs should be like that. Furthermore, through one body and mind we can practice and have enlightenment. The ear itself and the tongue itself hear their own proclaiming. Yesterday the law of impermanence was proclaimed for others; today it is proclaimed for ourselves.

Like this, the days and months pass. Proclaiming the Dharma for others and practicing it diligently is to hear, clarify, and enlighten the Dharma, life after life. When we proclaim the Dharma for others in this life with a sincere mind, it is easy for us to attain the Dharma ourselves. In addition, when we help others to hear the Dharma it increases our own merit when we study, both mentally and physically. If we disturb others when they are trying to listen to the Dharma we will just be preventing ourselves from hearing it. Hearing and proclaiming the Dharma, life after life, existence after existence, is to hear the Dharma, world after world.

We can hear in our present existence the Dharma which has been transmitted from the past up to the present. Within the Dharma there is creation and destruction; therefore, if we rightly transmit the Dharma throughout the entire universe of the ten quarters, we can hear it life after life and practice it existence after existence. Since the Dharma is actualized life after life, and manifested in existence after existence, a speck of dust and the entire field of existence together enlighten the Dharma. Nevertheless, even if we hear only one word [of the Dharma] in the east, we should proclaim it in the west, if only to a single person. Just one person can make use of such a device and proclaim the Dharma.

In either the east or west one can have the same practice and enlightenment. Try to bring the Buddhist Dharma and Way of the Patriarchs as close to your body and mind as possible. Then your life will be full of joy, hope, and determination. Start from this moment, from this day, from this year, from this life—this is your task. Take the life of the Buddha Dharma and concentrate on it. This is the meaning of not wasting your life.

However, you should not think that we cannot proclaim the Dharma because we have not completely clarified it. If we wait until there is total clarification, it will require innumerable kalpas. Further, even if we master the human Buddha, we must still clarify the universal Buddha. Even if we succeed in clarifying the mind of mountains, we must also clarify the mind of water. Even if we can grasp the living aspects of karma, we must also get the non-living aspects of karma. We may completely understand the circumstances of the Buddhas and Patriarchs, but we must also comprehend their progression. Therefore, if we think that we should completely clarify all these problems in one life before proclaiming the Dharma to others, it means we lack sufficient reflection, courage, and study. Those who study the Buddhas and Patriarchs by studying just one Dharma or one object should develop a strong determination and make an effort to help others. Then they are able to transcend self and proclaim to others. Further, it is possible to help others complete their study, even if we have not completed our own study. Obviously, if we can help others we can help ourselves complete our study. Although we may innately understand this point, it cannot be experienced until we meet the right master. That is why if we have not yet met the right master nor realized our innate knowledge we cannot understand the nature of unchanging knowledge nor the eternal knowledge beyond knowledge. Although it is possible to say we all possess innate knowledge, the Great Way of the Buddhas and Patriarchs cannot be known unless we study.

Experiencing and comprehending ourselves and others is the Great Way of the Buddhas and Patriarchs. The initial resolve to study occurs simultaneously between self and others. From this initial resolve, both self and others practice and attain the final stage together. Your practice and the practice of others must advance like this.

Nevertheless, when scatterbrained people hear about the way of "self-awakening," "self-enlightenment," etc. they think it is sufficient to study by themselves and not receive any transmission from a right master. This is a great mistake. If we perceive the nature of mind and discriminatory facilities and believe that it is not necessary to receive the transmission from a master, we are like the non-believers and naturalist philosophers of India. If we understand this properly, how can we consider such people to be men of the Buddhist Way? Furthermore, if we hear the expression "self-enlightenment" and evaluate it as something depending on the formation of the five skandhas it is almost the same as Hinayanist self-cultivation. Among those who make no distinction between the Mahayana and Hinayana, there are many who call themselves descendants of the Buddhas and Patriarchs. However, how can they deceive clear-minded people?

In the Shōkō period [1131–1162] of the Sung Dynasty there was a Zen master known as Dai'e Shūkō of Kinzan. Originally he was a student of the sūtras and abhidharma. He traveled all over the country and first studied the commentaries and verses of Ummon and Secchō under Zen Master Myōkyō Shōri of Senshū. Before he completed his study of Ummon's school he took up study under priest Dōchō of Tōzan. However, Shūkō was unable to receive Dōchō's inner teaching. Dōchō was the Dharma-heir of Fuyo [Dōkai], who was beyond compare to any other master of his time. Shūkō studied under Dōchō for a time but was not able to find Dōchō's skin, flesh, bones, and marrow. Furthermore, he was completely unable to have enlightened vision within a speck of dust.

One day Shūkō, who had merely heard about the two ways [*hikyō*, a formal ceremony and *shiso*, a seal of transmission] of Dharma transmission of the Buddhas and Patriarchs asked Dōchō to designate him as his Dharma-heir. However, Dōchō would not allow it and said, "In order to receive my seal of transmission you must not be in a hurry. Instead, study harder and practice more diligently. Receiving the transmission of the Buddhas and Patriarchs cannot be done so simply. I do not begrudgingly withold my seal, but you have not yet opened your mind." Shūkō protested, "I innately possess the True Eye of self-awakening and self-enlightenment, so why don't you give it to me?" Dōchō just smiled and said nothing.

Later on, Shūkō studied under priest Tandō. One day Tandō asked Shūkō, "Why do you have only one nostril [i.e., only half your true self] today?" Shūkō said, "I am the disciple of Hōbō!" [Hōbō was Tandō's master.] Tandō said, "O you miserable Zen monk!"

Another time, Shūkō was chanting and Tandō asked him, "What sūtra are you reciting?" Shūkō replied, "The *Diamond Sūtra*." Tandō said, "In the principle of equanimity there is no high or low. Then why is Mt. Ungo high and Mt. Hōbō low?" Shūkō answered, "In the principle of equanimity there is no high or low." Tandō said, "You are just mimicking me," and chased him away.

Again another day, Tandō saw somebody dressed up as Emma, the King of Hell. He asked Shūkō, "Who is that man?" Shūkō said, "Ryō." Tandō rubbed his head and said, "His name is the same as mine [Tandō's secular name was

Ryō], but I'm not wearing the same kind of hood." Shūkō said, "That's true. You have the form of a monk." Tandō said, "O what a blockhead you are!"

One time Tandō said to Shūkō, "Perhaps you have a tentative understanding of my Zen and might even be able to explain it. Maybe you could even compose commentaries and verses, and explain, give discourses or personal instruction about it. However, you lack complete knowledge of one thing. Do you know what it is?" Shūkō said, "I lack something?" Tandō said, "Yes, you do. I will explain it to you. When you are in my room Zen exists. When you leave it Zen disappears. It is the same as when you are awake Zen is there, but when you sleep it goes away. If your Zen is like that, how can you face the problem of life and death?" Shūkō said, "Yes, that is truly my main doubt."

Later, Tandō became ill and Shūkō said, "O priest, one hundred years from now, who can I depend on to solve my central problem?" Tandō replied harshly, "There is Engo Kokugon, but I don't know him. If you meet another master surely you will resolve your doubts. If you meet another master do not go anywhere else. After that you will no longer need to study Zen."

When we reflect upon this we can see why Tandō did not allow Shūkō to become his Dharma-heir. Often he tried to help Shūkō open his mind, but Shūkō could not shed his doubts; he could not find out what his problem was or attain liberation from it. Priest Dōchō did not give the seal of transmission to Shūkō, but rather, encouraged him by saying he was not complete. Dōchō's vision was clear and believable. Obviously, Shūkō lacked proper study, did not attain liberation, could not solve his problem, or satisfy his doubt. He often requested to be given a seal of transmission because his study was superficial, he had no mind for the Way, and lacked proper study and practice. This is lacking deep thought. Those who fail to accomplish the Buddhist Way because of inadequate study, or because of their love of fame or wealth, destroy the inner essence of the Buddhas and Patriarchs. It is a great pity not to know the words of the Buddhas and Patriarchs. Such people do not know practice is self-awakening and that visiting masters leads to self-enlightenment. Therefore, they have much misunderstanding and misinterpretation. Because of that none of Shūkō's disciples or descendants understood the truth even though they pretended to be real students. If we fail to meet and comprehend the Buddhist Dharma such things occur. Monks of the present age must study this in detail and never be lazy.

After Tandō's death, Shūkō obeyed his master's instructions and went to study under Engo at Tennenji monastery in the capital. One day Engo was in the Dharma Hall and Shūkō said to him, "I have to confess that I possess Zen enlightenment." Engo said, "Not yet, you don't. You haven't clarified the Great Dharma, no matter what you say."

Another time, Engo was in the Dharma Hall speaking on the fifth Patriarch Hōen's "Sometimes we use words, sometimes not." After hearing this, Shūkō said, "I have attained the Dharma of peace and bliss." Engo laughed and said, "I'm not deceiving you [you haven't attained enlightenment yet]."

This is how Shūkō came to study under Engo. Shūkō was permitted to enter Engo's community, but he was unable to make any progress. In neither his informal discourses nor in his lectures did Shūkō show any new insight.

We should know that although there are chronicles that claim Shūkō possessed Zen enlightenment and attained the Dharma of great peace and bliss, that did not actually happen. He was only a student, nothing more.

Zen Master Engo was an ancient Buddha, honored throughout the ten quarters of the universe. Since Ōbaku, such a great figure as Engo has not appeared. He is a very rare type of ancient Buddha, even in other worlds. However, he is not well known in this sorry world of ours. In light of Engo's admonishments to Shūkō, we can see that Shūkō did not surpass his master or even equal him. How could such a man possibly surpass his master? It cannot even be dreamed.

Therefore, we should know that Shūkō was unable to possess even half the virtue of his master. He simply memorized and then repeated mechanically the sayings of the *Avatamsaka* and *Suramgama-samādhi-nirdesa Sūtras*. He was unable to gain the bones and marrow of the Buddhas and Patriarchs. Shūkō thought that the Buddha Dharma meant that all religious seekers, great or small, can be influenced by the spirit of such natural objects as trees and grasses, and that insight can be gained from that spirit. That is why he could not clarify the Great Way of the Buddhas and Patriarchs. After he left Engo he did not visit any other masters, and without any real authority he became abbot of a large temple and instructed *unsuis*. No matter what he said, he did not even touch the edge of the Great Law.

However, those who do not really know about him think that Shūkō is at least equal to other masters of the past. People who do know about him, though, state clearly that he neither clarified nor understood the Great Dharma; he was just babbling incoherently. We can see that Priest Dōchō of Tōzan possessed the correct view without any error. Nevertheless, the disciples of Shūkō are jealous of Dōchō even to the present day. Dōchō refused Shūkō permission to receive the seal, and Tandō was even more severe. Every time Shūkō asked for the seal he revealed his spiritual immaturity. However, his descendants are not jealous of Tandō. Those who are jealous of Dōchō should be ashamed.

There are many self-styled descendants of the Buddhas and Patriarchs in the great Sung Dynasty, but few have had real study and fewer have realized the truth. This is clearly seen in the above story. The Shoko period was like that and the present age is much worse. Recently, people who do not know the Great Way of the Buddhas and Patriarchs have become teachers of *unsuis*.

We must know that the seal of transmission is rightly transmitted from Buddha to Buddha, Patriarch to Patriarch, throughout the east and west in the line of Seigen. From Seigen, it was passed to Tōzan. Others throughout the universe have no knowledge of this. Only the descendants of Tōzan have complete understanding. This is what *unsuis* should respect. Shūkō could not even understand the true meaning of self-awakening and self-enlightenment in his own lifetime. How then could he master any koans? Or how can any of his disciples understand self-awakening?

Therefore, we can say the Way of the Buddhas and Patriarchs for self and others is surely the body and mind and enlightened vision of the Buddhas and Patriarchs. It is their bones and marrow, and fools cannot even scratch the surface.

This was delivered to the monks of Kippōji in Echizen on February 29, 1244. Transcribed in the chief disciple's quarters on April 12 of the same year, by Ejō.

KEMBUTSU

"Seeing Buddha"

SHAKYAMUNI Buddha addressed a large assembly and said, "If all forms are seen as non-forms that is seeing the Tathāgata." Seeing "all forms" and "non-forms" is complete transcendence; that is why we can see the Tathāgata. Opening the eye of Buddha is to see Buddha; actively seeing with the eye of Buddha is to actualize the eye of Buddha.

When we see our own Buddha-form in others, or if we see our Buddha-form outside of the Buddha, it means we are confused like a tangled branch. That is why the study, analysis, transcendence, actualization, and possession of seeing Buddha is the observation of sun-faced and moon-faced Buddha. Seeing Buddha like this is to see his unlimited face, body, mind, hands and eyes. The resolve to seek the Way, study and practice, enlightenment and understanding—all these are inseparable from seeing Buddha with enlightened vision and vibrant, lively bones and marrow.

Therefore, our world and the world of others in the eternal past and present is nothing but the practice of seeing Buddha. The Way of the Tathāgata is "all forms seen as non-forms." Some confused people think that this means that all forms lack self-form but they do not know how to see the Tathāgata. They think "form" is the Tathāgata itself. Only narrow-minded people who are attached to one standpoint study like this. However, the Buddhist Way is not like this. Buddha's true function is to be able to observe all forms and non-forms. The word "Tathāgata" has both form and non-form.

Zen Master Daihōgen Bun'eki of Seiryōin said, "If all forms are seen as non-forms that is not seeing the Tathāgata." Here Daihōgen's "not seeing" is actually "seeing" the Tathāgata, i.e., Shakyamuni's "seeing" and Daihōgen's "not seeing" are the two sides of one coin. We can gain real understanding through this. Daihōgen's "not seeing" should be likened to hearing with the ear of Buddha and Shakyamuni's "seeing" is like opening the eye of Buddha. If you study this principle you can see that all forms are nothing but the form of the Tathāgata. Do not think "all forms" is a tentative substitute for "non-forms." If you think like that you will be the lost son [in the *Lotus Sūtra*] who was separated from his rich father and wandered around as a beggar.

All the Buddhas say that since "form" is the form of the Tathāgata all forms come into existence as the form of reality. All those who have experienced the teaching of the Mahayana can say this; it certifies them as Buddhas and Patriarchs. To study this principle is to believe in the teaching of the Buddhas and Patriarchs. However, we must not be flighty, easily blown to and fro by the wind. "Forms" are the form of the Tathāgata; they are not "non-forms." To clarify, believe, and see Buddha is to enlighten, confirm, and transmit [his form]. Chant the teaching of Buddha with your voice and work to help others find the teaching of Buddha.

Like this, study the Way with your eyes and ears, drop off your body, mind, bones, and marrow, and transcend the mountains and rivers of your world. This is the Buddhas' and Patriarchs' study and practice of the Way. People who say they are unenlightened should not think they cannot open the Buddha-eye. "One word of teaching" dispels all illusion, changes our vision to that of the Buddhas and Patriarchs, and gives the experience of body and mind cast off. And these are the everyday actions of the Buddhas and Patriarchs. Therefore, there is a direct path to proper study of the Way and seeing Buddha, i.e., "all forms are non-forms, non-forms are all forms." Since "non-form" is "all forms," "non-form" is truly "non-form" and nothing else. Regardless of what we call it—"form" or "non-form"—it is the form of the Tathāgata.

We should know that there are two methods of reading and studying the sūtras: 1) the study of seeing Buddha; and 2) the study of not seeing Buddha. This is active, enlivened study of the Buddhist Way. If you do not study these two methods thoroughly you cannot be said to have completed the eye of study. Further, if you have not completed the eye of study you can never see Buddha. [Seeing Buddha has two parts:] "all forms are all forms" and "non-forms are all forms." If we say "non-forms" [we are like Zen Master Nansen who said,] "I do not possess the Buddhist Law." Not seeing "all forms as all forms" and not seeing "non-forms as non-forms" are also two aspects of seeing Buddha. If you thoroughly study both aspects you will be able to grasp the Buddhist Law. One who can master eighty or ninety percent of Hōgen's words will be like this.

Nevertheless, the great matter [of seeing Buddha] has another important aspect: if we experience *shohō jissō*, the true state of all elements, we see the

Tathāgata. This is the beneficence of Shakyamuni Buddha. It is nothing but his original face and his skin, flesh, bones, and marrow.

Once Shakyamuni Buddha was staying on Vulture Peak. At that time Yakuō Bodhisattva said to the assembly, "If you practice under a Dharma-master you will attain the Way of Bodhisattva. If you follow this master you will meet Buddhas without limit."

Practicing and attaining the Way under a Dharma-master should be done like the second Patriarch's eight years of practice [under Bodhidharma]. After that he attained his master's marrow. Nangaku spent fifteen years under his master and also received his master's marrow. This is true study under a master. The Way of a Bodhisattva is to be yourself as yourself, others as others. Then we can actually experience the formation of the life of Buddhas and Patriarchs in ourselves—this is direct experience and total comprehension. This direct experience does not duplicate the development of past Buddhas, nor does it create new formations which will develop in the future, nor does it dwell in the fullness of the present. It is the liberation that comes from true study under a master. All real attainments come from that direct experience.

We should know that study under a master is not simply to follow him but also to study the masters of the past. When such an attitude is actualized it is the time to see Buddha. Here we find unlimited Buddhas. These unlimited Buddhas actualize full, free activity everywhere. However, we must not force ourselves to see these unlimited Buddhas. First of all we must find and study under a master—to study under the right master is to see Buddha.

Shakyamuni Buddha said to a large assembly who had attained enlightenment, "Enter profound samādhi and see the Buddhas of the ten directions." The entire world is profound because the ten quarters are contained in the Buddha land. This land is not wide, not large, not small, and not narrow. No matter what form it appears in—large, small, etc.—it contains all things. It cannot be measured as seven, eight, or ten feet. It covers everything; nothing is excluded. To enter that profundity is to enter samādhi; to enter that samādhi is to see the Buddhas of the ten directions. Entering profound samādhi is to see all the Buddhas of the ten directions just as they are. Whether you possess it or not there is nothing but the Buddhas of the ten directions. Entering that profound state transcends time and seeing all the Buddhas of the ten directions is nothing more than seeing a reclining Tathāgata [i.e., a living Buddha]. Samādhi emerges and all opposing ideas are severed. If we are not afraid of a real dragon, then we will not doubt or abandon the real truth when we see Buddha. From seeing Buddha to seeing Buddha goes from samādhi to samādhi. The principles of samādhi, seeing Buddha, entering profundity, etc. are absolute. This is difficult for ordinary people to grasp and has not been transmitted to the present day by idlers. Each and every reception of the transmission of the Way is a reception of the fruits of practice.

Shakyamuni Buddha said to Samantabhadra Bodhisattva, "Anyone who receives, keeps, reads, and chants this *Lotus Sūtra*, memorizes it correctly, practices it, and copies it should be considered one who is able to see me and hear the sūtra directly from my mouth."

In general, all the Buddhas see Shakyamuni Buddha; to become Shakyamuni Buddha is to attain the Way and become Buddha. Like this, the bearing of all the Buddhas has been from the beginning the practice of the seven actions of receiving, keeping, etc. Those who practice the seven actions come to know themselves as they truly are. Shakyamuni Buddha sees like this; one who follows his Way can be said to hear the sūtras from Buddha's mouth. Shakyamuni Buddha is Shakyamuni Buddha because he is seen as Shakyamuni Buddha. It therefore follows that when he spoke, his words covered the three thousand worlds. The mountains and oceans are Buddhist sūtras. One who copies [the *Lotus Sūtra*] will see Shakyamuni Buddha. Buddha's voice is being projected everywhere at all times; how can there be an occasion when it is not being spoken? Therefore, if we receive and preserve the [*Lotus Sūtra*] as mentioned above, surely we will see Shakyamuni Buddha. The virtue we derive from our sense organs—eye, ear, nose, etc.—is exactly like this. Likewise, the actions of our daily life—front, back, right, left—[also possess the same potential, to see Shakyamuni Buddha].

When we see the *Lotus Sūtra* we will be overjoyed to see Shakyamuni Buddha, will we not? This is the living dimension of Shakyamuni Buddha. Those who receive, keep, read, chant, memorize, practice and copy this *Lotus Sūtra* with all their body and mind will without fail see Shakyamuni Buddha. No one can deny Buddha's speech or hearing his living sermon, can they? Those who are in no hurry to devote themselves to this valuable sūtra are mere low-minded sentient beings with no wisdom. One who practices [the *Lotus Sūtra*] will see Shakyamuni Buddha.

Shakyamuni Buddha said to a large assembly: "If devoted laymen and women hear that my life is eternal and have deep faith and belief in it they will see that Buddha is always living on Vulture Peak proclaiming the Law surrounded by Bodhisattvas, Mahasattvas and śrāvakas. Those devoted people will see the troubled world we live in change into a world of peace full of shining gems and precious jade."

"Deep faith" is seeing this troubled world [as the mind and body of Buddha].

"Belief" is belief that must come freely, without compulsion. The words of Buddha are absolute truth—no one can doubt it. Even accidentally hearing or seeing this sūtra provides an excellent opportunity to develop belief in it. Put deep faith in this *Lotus Sūtra*. By having deep faith in the Tathāgata's eternal life we can be born in this world to save sentient beings. The Tathāgata's supernatural power, the strength of his compassion, and the power of his eternal life give belief to the mind of sentient beings, to the body of the entire world, to Buddhas and Patriarchs, to all dharmas, to all phenomena, to skin, flesh, bones and marrow, to life and death, coming and going—the belief of all those is seeing Buddha.

Therefore, we should know that to open the eye of deep faith and to possess the eye of belief is to see Buddha. That is not just seeing Buddha but to see Buddha living eternally on Vulture Peak; living on Vulture Peak and the Tathāgata's eternal life are the same. Therefore, seeing Buddha is to live eternally on Vulture Peak; the Tathāgata and Vulture Peak are eternal and inseparable. Therefore, Bodhisattvas and śrāvakas are also eternal; proclaiming the Law also exists eternally on Vulture Peak. Buddha saw this world of trouble as beautiful and peaceful. He did not attach ideas of high and low to the present world of reality. Do not look upon such a view with contempt. You should look at the world as if it is full of shining gems and precious jade. If we think that this world is not full of precious jade then Vulture Peak is not Vulture Peak and Shakyamuni Buddha is not Shakyamuni Buddha. To believe that this world is full of precious jade is the real form of "belief"—this is seeing Buddha.

Shakyamuni Buddha said to a large assembly, "When we desire to see Buddha with all our heart and have no resentment present in our bodies I together with all monks can ascend Vulture Peak." "All our heart" is not the heart of ordinary people, Hinayanists, etc.; it is the heart of seeing Buddha. Seeing Buddha with all one's heart is Vulture Peak and all monks. Each and every moment of the present is the imperceptible desire to see Buddha with the mind of Vulture Peak. Therefore, this one mind is Vulture Peak. Our body is actualized in this mind, and this mind emerges through our body. Body and mind are like this; eternal and transitory life are also like this. Therefore, have no resentment and simply entrust your life to the supreme Way of Vulture Peak—this is the proper understanding of seeing Buddha with all one's heart.

Shakyamuni Buddha said to a large assembly, "Anyone who proclaims this sūtra will see me, Prabhūtaratna Buddha, and all other manifestations of Buddhas." "Proclaiming this sūtra" means that Buddha is always present in the world possessing vast spiritual power but is not seen by sentient beings because of their perverted views. That spiritual power, seen or unseen, is the virtue of the Tathāgata we must respect.

Shakyamuni Buddha said to a large assembly, "Anyone who keeps this sūtra will see me, Prabhūtaratna Buddha, and all other replicas of me." It is difficult to keep this sūtra although the Tathāgata counsels us to always preserve it. Anyone who keeps this sūtra sees Buddha. Seeing Buddha is to hold this sūtra and vice versa. Therefore, listening to just a single verse of one gatha is to possess the vision of Shakyamuni Buddha, Prabhūtaratna Buddha, and all other replicas of Buddha—it is the transmission of the Buddha and Dharma and the attainment of Buddha's True Eye, the Buddha's life, the development of Buddha's insight and the enlightenment and essence of Buddha.

Unrai-onshuku-okechi[1] Buddha said to King Śubhavyūha, "O Great King, know this! A teacher has great influence as your leader and causes you to see Buddha and attain supreme and perfect enlightenment." In this great assembly [Unrai-onshuku-okechi Buddha] came from the distant past; although he represents all Buddhas of the past, present and future do not focus your attention on the three worlds of ordinary people. That is, the past is our mind, the present is our finger tips, the future our brain; [they are not separate but contained in one body]. Therefore, Unrai-onshuku-okechi Buddha is the actualization of seeing Buddha in our mind. "Seeing Buddha" always has this connotation. Following the *Lotus Sūtra* is to see Buddha, to see Buddha is to awaken the mind of supreme and perfect enlightenment. The resolve to be enlightened is the head and tail of seeing Buddha.

Shakyamuni Buddha said, "Anyone who practices all virtues and is tolerant, peaceful, upright and stable will see my body in this proclaimation of the Law." "All virtues" means getting dirty helping those stuck in the mire or getting wet saving those who are drowning. "I am like this, you are like this" is the practice of one who is tolerant, peaceful, upright and stable—this is seeing Buddha in the mud and waves. If you can grasp this you can comprehend the proclaiming of the Law.

However, recently in Great Sung Dynasty China there are many with the title "Zen Master." Such people have neither seen nor heard the true width and breadth of the Buddhist Dharma. They have simply memorized two or three sayings of Rinzai and Ummon and think this constitutes the entire Buddhist Dharma. If the Buddhist Law can be condensed into a few sayings of

---

[1] Jaladharagaritaghoṣasusvaranakṣatrarājasaṃkusumitābhijña.

Rinzai and Ummon it would never have been transmitted to the present day. We cannot even say that Rinzai and Ummon have completely mastered the Buddhist Dharma.

Moreover, present day masters by no means surpass Rinzai and Ummon. We should not even mention them because they are so stupid and indiscriminately slander the sūtras without studying them properly. We must count them among the non-believers, not the descendants of the Buddhas and Patriarchs. How can we say they have attained the stage of seeing Buddha? They have not even understood the essence of Confucius or Lao-tzu. True disciples of the Buddhas and Patriarchs have nothing to do with these so-called "Zen Masters." You must search only for experience of the enlightened eye that sees Buddha.

My late master Tendō, an ancient Buddha, said, "Once King Hashinoku asked the honorable Binzuru,[1] 'I have heard, O Honorable One, that you have seen Buddha. Is it true?' Binzuru lifted his eyebrows and opened his eyes wide." My late master then recited this gatha:

"Raising his eyebrows he answered the question;
That he once met and saw Buddha was not a lie.
His virtue is respected everywhere.
Spring is in the tip of a plum tree branch
 covered with freezing snow."

"Seeing Buddha" is not seeing our Buddha, nor others' Buddha but seeing [all] Buddhas. One plum branch sees one plum branch, i.e., the flower blooms [throughout the world]. The central point of King Hashinoku's question is whether Binzuru saw or became Buddha. When Binzuru raised his eyebrows it proved that he saw Buddha; it is a clear fact. The present respect he is given has continued unbroken from the past—his meeting with Buddha cannot be doubted. The three hundred million people [in the kingdom of Srāvasti in Buddha's time] who saw Buddha, truly saw him. They did not just see the thirty-two forms of Buddha. This principle of seeing Buddha is not generally understood by celestials, humans, śrāvakas and pratyekabuddhas. It is like many who hold a fly whisk [and pretend] to be leaders, although there are few true masters. Seeing Buddha is actualized from Buddha's side [not from our own subjective side]. Even if we attempt to conceal it seeing Buddha will emerge by itself. This is the principle of seeing Buddha. We should study in detail the

---

[1] Prasenajit, the King of Srāvasti in central India during Buddha's lifetime. He and his family were devout followers of Buddhism. Binzuru is Pindola-bhāradvāja. The first of the sixteen Arhats.

essence of "raising the eyebrows" as if we are investigating the body and mind of the unlimited sands of the Ganges. Even if you stay with Shakyamuni Buddha day and night for countless aeons but lack the power of raising your eyebrows you cannot "see" Buddha. Although we are living two thousand years later and one hundred thousand *li* from Shakyamuni if we have the power to raise our eyebrows we can still see the aspect of Shakyamuni Buddha that has no beginning. This is seeing one plum tree with spring in its branches. Truly meeting and seeing Buddha is three prostrations [before Buddha], a gassho and bow, the smile [of Mahākāśyapa], liberation and unification, and sitting in the lotus posture on a mat.

Binzuru was once invited to dine at the court of King Aśoka. The King offered incense and prostrated himself before Binzuru and said, "I have heard, O Honorable One, that you have seen Buddha. Is it true?" Binzuru raised his eyebrow and said, Do you understand?" The King replied, "No, I don't." Binzuru said, "Once the Dragon King Anavatapta invited Buddha for a meal and I was among the attendants." The essence of King Asoka's question is whether or not Binzuru is truly an honorable one. At that time the honorable Binzuru raised his eyebrows—this is the actualization of seeing Buddha throughout the entire world. He had become Buddha and saw him everywhere.

"Once the Dragon King Anavatapta invited Buddha for a meal and I was one of the attendants" means that many in that assembly received and transmitted Buddha. If Hinayanists were not permitted in that assembly, and even if they were, they could not be counted among the Buddhas. Binzuru attended that meal. His presence was a result of the virtue derived from seeing Buddha. Inviting Buddha is not just Shakyamuni Buddha but all the countless Buddhas of the three worlds and ten directions. All the Buddhas come together and meet and see all other Buddhas. Seeing Buddha, seeing a master, seeing oneself and seeing others is like that. The Dragon King Anavatapta is the same as the Dragon King of the Pond of Anokuda. This pond is without heat [i.e., clear and cool, free of illusion].[2]

Zen Master Honei Jinyū[3] composed this verse:
  Our Buddha saw Binzuru;
  Yet his eyebrows were long, his hair short, and his eyes wild.

---

[2] Anavalapta is the name of the Dragon King who lives in the imaginary pond of the same name said to be located north of the Himalayas.

[3] A disciple of Yōgi Hōe (both dates unknown).

King Aśoka doubted it and chanted this dharani:
Om mani śrisūrya. (Hail to the adamantine bliss of
belief in the true Law.)

While this verse does not toally cover the entire scope of the Buddhist Way it contains the root, so we mention it here.

Great Master Jōshū Shinsai was asked by a monk, "I heard, O priest, that you met Nansen. Is it true?" Jōshū said, "A huge radish grows in Jinshū." This is truly meeting Nansen and experiencing and certifying his Way—it does not depend on the meaning, or lack of meaning, of the words. The sayings of Zen masters, common speech, raising the eyebrows opening the eyes etc., means to raise the eyebrow and truly meet and see Buddha. Even if one is an excellent person but lacks a real meeting with Buddha he cannot speak like Nansen.

"A giant radish appears in Jinshū" dates from the period when Jōshū was a monk at Shinsai-in, Tōka-en, in Jinshū. Later on he was known as Great Master Shinsai. Like this he opened his eyes and saw Buddha and could therefore correctly transmit the Eye and Treasury of the True Law of the Buddhas and Patriarchs. When the Eye and Treasury of the True Law is transmitted correctly, the great value of seeing Buddha is actualized and seeing Buddha emerges everywhere.

This was delivered to the monks at Mt. Zenjihō on November 19, 1243. Recopied the following year at the chief disciple's quarters of Daibutsuji, Yoshida-ken, Echizen, on October 16, by Ejō.

[55]

HOTSUMUJŌSHIN

"Developing the supreme mind"

THE High Patriarch of India [Shakyamuni] said, "Great Nirvana is like the Himalayas." We can see that this is a very appropriate simile. Shakyamuni was able to say this because he was familiar with the mountains and knew them well. "Himalayas" were chosen because of their magnitude, severity and similarity to Great Nirvana.

The first Chinese Patriarch said, "Each mind is like a petrified tree." "Each mind" is "Mind," i.e., the mind that covers the great earth. Therefore, there is the mind of self and of others. The minds of all the people of the great earth, of all the Buddhas and Patriarchs of the entire universe, of all heavenly dragons etc. are all this petrified tree. There is no other mind besides this. This "petrified tree" is not existent nor non-existent, not emptiness nor form, etc. Through the mind of a petrified tree we develop the mind of resolve for practice and enlightenment. Because the mind is originally a petrified tree we can actualize the eternal condition of "thinking" through "non-thinking." If we study the voice of the wind of the petrified tree we can, for the first time, transcend the ideas of non-believers. Outside this there is no Buddhist Way.

The National Teacher Daishō said, "Walls, tiles, and stones are the ancient Buddha mind." We must study carefully where walls, tiles, and stones exist. You must question where and how such things are actualized. "Ancient Buddha mind" is not Kūō Buddha, who existed aeons ago. Rather, it is just the ordinary everyday life of human beings. In such kind of life we sit and find Buddha. This is called the mind of resolve for enlightenment.

In general, the working of *hotsubodaishin* (the Buddha-seeking mind) is developed from *hosshin* (the initial awakening of the mind, the resolve for enlightenment); other than this, there is nothing. Awakening the mind of enlightenment is to make Buddha by holding up one blade of grass, or to make the sūtras with a piece of wood. Offer sand and the water from rice gruel to the Buddha, and then offer one handful of rice for sentient beings and five flower stems for the Tathāgata. The Buddha-seeking mind is to assist others when asked; it also can release you from the grasp of demons. Not only that, you must find the house that is not a house, i.e., enter the mountains and practice the Way with faith and trust in the Dharma. Make the form of Buddha, build stūpas, chant the sūtras, recite Buddha's name, proclaim the Dharma for all beings, find the right master, practice zazen, take refuge in the Three Treasures—this is to praise Buddha.

Like this, the workings of the eighty thousand kinds of practice are surely contained in the initial awakening for enlightenment. We can attain the Way through *hosshin* even in the midst of this dream world while still drunk—in the blooming flowers, in the falling leaves, in the peach blossoms, in the sound of a tile striking the bamboo, in the heavens, and in the ocean. All these are the Buddha-seeking mind in the Buddha-seeking mind. *Hotsubodaishin* is within the body and mind, within the body and mind of all the Buddhas, and in the skin, flesh, bones, and marrow of the Buddhas and Patriarchs.

Therefore, building a stūpa or making a Buddha is the Buddha-seeking mind. It is the resolve for enlightenment that leads directly to becoming Buddha. Do not stop midway or get caught in forms. This is the virtue of *mu-i* (not created) and *musa* (not being produced by conditions). They represent the observation of the Tathāgata and the true nature of the Dharma. All the Buddhas concentrate on this as their samādhi. It is their dharani and their supreme and perfect enlightenment; it is the fruit of arhats and the actualization of Buddha. There is nothing else besides the dharmas of *mu-i* and *musa*.

Although foolish Hinayanists say that the purpose of making a statue or building a stūpa is to gain merit, put such an idea aside. Give up discriminatory thinking and concentrate your mind—this is *mu-i*. It is unborn and unconditioned reality, and the observation of the true form of all dharmas. This interpretation of *mu-i* is standard in east and west, both past and present. Some people try to expiate their sins or pernicious deeds by making a statue or building a stupa, while others try to escape the world of defilement by reciting the name of Buddha or chanting the sūtras. If we act like that, we will not only destroy the seed of our own humanity but also the Buddha-nature of the Tathāgata. It is truly a pity that although we live in the age of the Buddha, Dharma, and Sangha, we become their bitter enemy. Even if we climb the mountain or enter the ocean of the Three Treasures, we will come back empty handed. Even if we see thousands of Buddhas or Patriarchs we cannot attain their Way and we lose the right direction of the Buddha-seeking mind. This occurs because we neglect the sūtras and do not follow them with a high degree of knowledge. We only follow non-believers and malicious teachers. Yet it is better to abandon the idea that building a stūpa, etc. is not *hotsubodaishin* as soon as possible. Just purify your heart, body, ears, eyes and do not look at or listen to such observations. Follow the teachings in the Buddhist sūtras and choose masters of high attainment. Take refuge in the True Law and practice the Buddhist Dharma.

In the Great Way of the Buddhist Dharma countless sūtras and innumerable Buddhas can be seen in a speck of dust. One blade of grass or one tree together form one body and mind. If all dharmas were not created, then one mind could not have been created. If all dharmas have real form then one speck of dust has real form; therefore, one mind is all dharmas, all dharmas are one mind, and the entire body.

When a stūpa, etc. is built for some purpose, the fruit of Buddha's enlightenment and the Buddha-nature of suchness must also have some purpose. However, since the Buddha-nature of suchness cannot be made intentionally, making a statue or building a stūpa should not be done with some purpose or intention. The Buddha-seeking mind must arise without any ulterior motive; it is the virtue of purity and purposelessness. Yet we must firmly believe that making a statue or building a stūpa, etc. is the Buddha-seeking mind. All the actions and wishes of countless ages started from this point. The Buddha-seeking mind cannot be destroyed in innumerable kalpas. This is "seeing Buddha and hearing the Law."

We should know that gathering petrified wood, piling up mud, and collecting gold, silver, and the seven precious jewels to make a Buddha-image or stūpa is to do so with the concentration of one mind. Gather air to make a Buddha, hold up the mind to form Buddha; pile one stūpa after another to make a stūpa, actualize one Buddha after another to make a Buddha. As it says in the sūtras, "Think like this and all the Buddhas of the ten directions emerge." We must know that when we have a thought to become a Buddha all the Buddhas of the ten directions share the same thought. When one thing becomes Buddha all things become Buddha.

Shakyamuni Buddha said, "The morning star appeared and I attained the Way simultaneously with all living things." That is why resolve, practice, enlightenment, and nirvana simultaneously occur together. The body and mind of the Buddhist Way is grass, trees, tiles, stones, wind, rain, water, and fire. The resolve for enlightenment in those things of nature lead to the Buddhist Way. Making a Buddha-image or constructing a stūpa is held by universal emptiness and formed by scooping water from a valley stream. This is supreme and perfect enlightenment. If there is one mind of enlightenment there must be millions. This also holds for practice and enlightenment.

Therefore, do not think that awakening occurs only once, practice is open-ended, or that the fruits of enlightenment bear just once—this is not hearing, knowing, or meeting the Buddhist Dharma. Countless awakenings arise from the initial resolve to seek enlightenment. The resolve of innumerable persons started with one person's initial awakening. The initial awakening becomes countless awakenings. Practice, enlightenment, and turning the wheel of the Law work exactly like this.

If grasses, trees, etc. are not themselves, how can they possess a body and mind, and vice versa. That is why grasses, trees, etc. are complete within themselves. Practicing the Way through zazen is the Buddha-seeking mind. The initial awakening and zazen are not the same, not different, not this or that; they cannot be separated. Study like this. There must be no ulterior motive from the initial gathering of grasses, wood, and jewels to the final construction of a stūpa or Buddha-image; otherwise it will prevent us from attaining the Way, and the thirty-seven ways to enlightenment will be forced. Also the practice of body and mind of men and gods in the three worlds will become forced. Then our ultimate goal will be lost. Grasses, trees, tiles, stones, the four elements, and the five skandhas are all only one mind, and the true form [of suchness]. Throughout the entire world of the ten quarters, the Buddha-nature of suchness has absolute, immutable existence. Yet how do grasses and trees exist within the Buddha-nature of suchness? How do they become the Buddha-nature of suchness? All forms that are free of intention and non-created are true forms. True form is the true form of suchness; suchness is the body and mind of the eternal present. This body and mind emerges with *hosshin*, resolve; do not stop pumping the water wheel [of Tōzan] or pushing the grindstone [of Enō]. Hold up a blade of grass to make a six foot golden image of Buddha; hold up a speck of dust to construct a stūpa of an ancient Buddha. This is *hotsubodaishin*, the Buddha-seeking mind: seeing Buddha, hearing Buddha, seeing the Dharma, hearing the Dharma, becoming Buddha, and practicing Buddha.

Shakyamuni Buddha said, "Both lay men and women who have taken refuge in the Dharma and ordinary good men and women give their own flesh and that of their spouses and children as an offering to the Three Treasures. How can all bhikkhus who have received such an offering and the trust of lay people fail to practice diligently?"

We can see that offerings of food and drink, clothing, bedding, medicine, monastery buildings, fields and forests, etc. is like offering one's own flesh and the skin, flesh, bones, and marrow of one's wife and children. Then they can receive a great ocean of merit from the Three Treasures and become one with them. Becoming one with them means making an offering to the Three Treasures. The virtue of the Three Treasures is actualized in one's own flesh and the skin, flesh, bones, and marrow of one's wife and children—this is to practice the Way with diligent effort. Then the form and nature of Shakyamuni is made into our own and we find the skin, flesh, bones, and marrow of the Buddhist Way. Here, "trust" is the resolve for enlightenment. Therefore, how can those bhikkhus who have received that "trust" be lazy? [The resolve for enlightenment and attainment of the Way] must work reciprocally, from beginning to end.

That is why, even an awakening as small as a speck of dust will ultimately give us a right-mind. With such a mind we can fathom emptiness. In general, if people have resolve for enlightenment they can attain the seed of Buddha-nature, regardless of whether they have studied it or not. If we practice with a stainless mind and the four elements and five skandhas [i.e., with a body] we can attain the Way. Even grasses, trees, fences, and walls attain the Way if they practice with a stainless mind. The four elements, the five skandhas, grasses, trees, fences, and walls attain the Way simultaneously and share the same nature. Therefore, they share the same mind, life, body, and function.

Many of those who studied under the Buddhas and Patriarchs practiced the Way by holding up the mind of grasses and trees. This is form of the Buddha-seeking mind. The fifth Patriarch was once the gardener Saishodōsha, Rinzai planted cedar and pine trees on Mt. Ōbaku, and Tōzan learned how to care for pines from the old man Ryū. Each of them had the dignity and constancy of a conifer and plucked out the enlightened vision of the Buddhas and Patriarchs. The actualized energy of the Buddhas and Patriarchs becomes our own and opens our eyes. Building a stūpa or making a Buddha-image, etc. are the articles of enlightened vision that awaken and are awakened by our mind. If we do not attain the enlightened vision of building a stūpa, etc. we cannot attain the Way of the Buddhas and Patriarchs. To attain the enlightened vision of making a Buddha-image is to make the Buddhas and Patriarchs. Some think a stūpa, etc. will ultimately turn to dust and consequently does not possess real virtue, while practice, which is beyond life and death, is the only stable, undefiled element. However, this is not the Buddha teaching. If the stūpa turns to dust practice will also turn to dust. Conversely, if practice does not turn to dust neither will the stūpa. "After all, what is this world we live in? Talking about the creation of life and death (*yu-i*) or explaining nirvana (*mu-i*)."

It says in the *Avatamsaka Sūtra:* "When a Bodhisattva dwelling in the world of samsara first awakens the mind, he directly searches for enlightenment. His mind is stable and unmovable. The virtue of one thought is profound and vast, with no limit. The Tathāgata's analysis [of the world] is similarly inexhaustible." We should be able to see clearly that the awakening and resolve for enlightenment is inextricably bound up with the problem of life and death [samsara]. This is the meaning of "directly searching for enlightenment." One of his thoughts is the same as a blade of grass or one tree because there is only one life and one death. Nevertheless, its virtue is unlimitedly profound and vast. The Tathāgata may explain his analysis of the world for aeons but can never exhaust it. The ocean may dry up but there is still the ocean floor. Even though a man dies his mind still lingers—we never arrive at some final state. Just as one of the Bodhisattva's thoughts is unlimitedly profound and vast so is one blade of grass, one tree, one stone, or one tile. If one blade of grass or one stone is seven or eight feet then one of the Bodhisattva's thoughts is seven or eight feet, and the resolve for enlightenment is seven or eight feet.

Therefore, that is why entering the deep mountains to meditate on the Buddhist Way is easy; building a stūpa or making a Buddha-image is difficult. Both can be accomplished through diligent effort, but there is a difference between self-awakening and the awakening of others. To accomplish this kind of Buddha-seeking mind is to actualize the Buddhas and Patriarchs.

This was delivered to the monks at Kippōji, Yoshida-gun, Echizen, on February 14, 1244. Recopied at Eiheiji on March 10, 1279 by Ejō.

[56]

TASHINTSU

"Reading others' minds"

THE National Teacher Echū (Seikyō Kōtakuji) was a courageous man of Eshū. His family name was Zen. After he received the seal of mind-transmission he went to live in Tōshi valley near Mt. Hakugai in Nanyō. For more than forty years he never left the monastry gate. Word of his strict practice reached the capital and the Emperor Shukushū of the T'ang Dynasty dispatched a courier with an invitation to teach in Rakuyō, the capital. This occured in the second year of Jogen [761]. Accepting the invitation, he moved to Saizen-in, a sub-temple of Senpukuji. Later on, Daishū was crowned Emperor and Echū was asked to come to Kōtakuji, where he remained for over sixteen years, using *taiki-seppō*, teaching according to the ability and capacity of his students.

Once a scholar-monk called Daini [Great Ears] Sanzō from India came to the capital. This monk claimed the ability to read others' minds. The Emperor wanted to test him and brought him to see the National Teacher. Sanzō greeted Echū with a bow and then stood on Echū's right. Echū asked him," I've heard that you can read other people's minds." Sanzō said, "Only a little." Echū said, "Well then tell me where this old priest [Echū himself] is right now." Sanzō said, "O Priest, You are the National Teacher. Why are you at Seisen watching the annual boat races?" Echū asked again, "Please tell me where I am right now." Sanzō said, "You are the National Teacher. Why are you looking at the monkey grinder on the Tenshin Bridge?" Echū repeated the question a third time, "Where am I right now!" Sanzō thought for a while but did not answer. Then Echū said, "You wild fox. Where is your ability to read others' minds?" Sanzō remained silent.

Once a monk asked Jōshū, "Why didn't Daini Sanzō reply to the third question? Where was the National Teacher?" Jōshū said, "On top of Sanzō's nose." The same monk asked Gensha, "If the National Teacher is in Sanzō's nostril why can't Sanzō see him?" "Because he was too close to see," replied Gensha.

Another monk asked Gyōzan, "Why couldn't Daini Sanzō see the National Teacher the third time?" Gyōzan said, "The first two answers were concerned with the objective world. Sanzō lacked *jijiyū samādhi*, the self-enjoyment of one's awakening, and he couldn't see the National Teacher."

Kai'e Shitan said, "Why couldn't Sanzō see the National Teacher if he was on top of Sanzō's own nose? Because he didn't know that the National Teacher was aleady in his eye."

Gensha said, "Did you [Sanzō] really see the National Teacher the first two times?"

Zen Master Secchō Juken said about this, "Sanzō failed."

As we can see there are many commentaries and interpretations about the testing of Sanzō Daini by the National Teacher Echū. We have chosen five by different masters. However, none of these correctly indicate the essense of the story, nor grasp the condition of the National Teacher. Most people in both ancient and modern times think that Sanzō's first two answers were not mistaken and correctly gave the National Teachers' location. This is a great mistake, and we must clarify this point. We may consider the five commentaries from two aspects: 1) that Sanzō did not know the real meaning of the National Teacher's questions; and 2) Sanzō did not know the body and mind of the National Teacher.

In the first case we can say that the meaning of National Teacher's first question, "Where am I now?" was to test whether or not Sanzō possessed the enlightened vision that enabled him to see and hear the Buddhist Dharma, i.e., was Sanzō able to read others' minds through the Buddhist Dharma. If Sanzō had possessed the Buddhist Dharma at that time, he could have answered from his experience of Buddhism and made free use of it profitably. When the National Teacher asked, "Where am I now?" he was actually saying, "Who am I?", "What time is this?" or "What am I?" There is a reason Echū used the expression "old monk." He was not necessarily old at that time; an old monk is [one who possesses the original Buddha-mind].

Although Daini Sanzō came from India he did not understand the [Buddha] mind since he had not learned Buddhism properly only but studied the teaching of non-believers and Hinayanists. The National Teacher asked "Where am I now?" The second time Sanzō gave a useless answer and the third time he was silent. Then Echū scolded him saying, "You wild fox! Where is your ability to read others' minds?" Although he was scolded like that he still did not answer. There was no reply, and no solution.

However, our predecessors thought that Sanzō was scolded by the National Teacher only because he did not know the answer to the third question. This is a great mistake. Sanzō was scolded because he did not have the slightest idea where the Buddhist Dharma is. Do not think that Sanzō knew the answer to the first two questions. That is an error.

Sanzō did posses some self-proclaimed power to read others minds but lacked understanding of that power. That is why he was scolded. First of all, Echū wanted to test Sanzō by asking in essense, "Is there the power to read others' minds in the Buddhist Dharma." The reply was "[I know there is] a little." The National Teacher assumed he did, but he found that even if such power exists in the Buddhist Dharma if it does not become part of it we have people like Sanzō.

Even if Sanzō had replied to the third question in the some fashion as the first two his answer would have been useless. All of Sanzō's answers should be scolded. The National Teacher questioned a third time because he still had some hope that Sanzō might get his point.

In addition, it is said that ancient people did not know the body and mind of the National Teacher. Sanzō could neither easily see nor comprehend the National Teacher's body and mind. Since even the ten saints and three sages, Bodhisattvas and pratyekabuddhas are unable to clarify it how could such an ordinary scholar of the Tripitaka possibly know the entire body of the National Teacher?

We must clarify this principle. If we talk about the body and mind of the National Teacher to Tripitaka scholars we will be slandering the Buddhist Dharma. If scholars of the sūtras and abhidharma think that they are equal to the National Teacher it is pure insanity. Those who want the power to read others' minds should not think they have learned where the National Teacher is.

In India the power to read others' minds is a convention possessed by some people. However, this has nothing to do with the enlightenment seeking mind and is not the true insight of the Mahayana. There has never been a case where the Buddhist Dharma was revealed by the power of reading others' minds. And even if we happen to possess the ability to read others' minds we still are obligated to develop the ordinary mind of resolve and practice to gradually enlighten the Buddhist Way. If it were possible to perceive the Buddhist Way through the power of reading others' minds all the saints of the past should have possessed such an ability and immediately comprehended the efficacy of Buddhism. However, this has never occured among all the countless Buddhas and Patriarchs. If we do not know the Way of the Buddhas and Patriarchs what help can reading others' minds be? Such an ability is not necessary in the Buddhist

Way. This holds true for everyone regardless it they possess a power or are just ordinary people who do not. Both ordinary people and those with the power to read others' minds possess the same Buddha-nature. Those who study Buddhism should not think that those who possess the miraculous powers[1] of non-believers and Hinayanists are superior to ordinary people. Rather, those who simply possess a mind for the Way and study the Buddhist Dharma are superior to those who possess such miraculous powers. [The Buddhist Dharma] is like an egg of a *kalavinka* bird.[2] This bird produces a sound superior to all other birds. Furthermore, those people of India who use the power to read others' minds should be more accurately called those who read others' thoughts. The ability to pick up others superficial thoughts is a totally useless and laughable talent. "Mind" is not necessary "thought" and vice versa; even when they are, it is not possible to read others' minds.

Therefore, that is why the miraculous powers of India do not equal our own country's work of clearing the earth and making rice paddies. Miraculous powers are completely useless. That is why east of China such miraculous powers were not used. A one foot thick wall is useful, but miraculous powers are not. That wall is not precious, but even a small amount of time is very important. Consequently, how can someone who knows that even a short amount of time is important waste time trying to attain miraculous powers? We have carefully evaluated that the power to read others' minds does not surpass Buddhist wisdom.

Nevertheless, all the honorable monks quoted above thought that Sanzō's first two answers correctly gave the National Teacher's location, but this is a great mistake. The National Teacher is a Buddha and Patriarch and Sanzō is just an ordinary person so how could they see and have a meeting of minds with each other?

The National Teacher first said, "Where is this old priest right now?" Nothing is hidden in this question; indeed the answer is revealed in the question. Sanzō should not be blamed for not knowing [since he was an unenlightened person] but if the honorable priests above have no idea about the answer it is very bad. The National Teacher said, "Where is this old priest right now?"

---

[1] For example, walking without touching the earth, reading others' minds, seeing all, coming without being called, passing through rocks, etc.

[2] An Indian bird with a melodious voice found in the Himalayas.

not "Where is the mind?" or "Where is the thought?" of this "old priest." We must be very careful about this point.

However, the honorable priests mentioned above failed to find the essence of the National Teacher's question and therefore were unable to know his body and mind—they only knew his words. If the National Teacher did not say anything, they think that is all, there is nothing else. How can they know the body and mind of the National Teacher, if they cannot transcend large and small, self or others. It is like forgetting the face and nostrils of the National Teacher. Although the National Teacher practiced ceaselessly he did not try to become Buddha. Therefore, he had no purpose or desire to become a Buddha. The National Teacher already possesses the body and mind of the Buddhist Dharma; it cannot be measured by practice and enlightenment based on miraculous powers, cognition, or karma. It is beyond cognition or non-cognition. The National Teacher is not Buddha-nature, not not-Buddha-nature, not a universal body—the body and mind of the National Teacher cannot be found. Beside Seigen and Nangaku there is only one Buddha and Patriarch, National Teacher Daishō, who came after Sōkei [Enō]. The honorable priests mentioned above must clarify this same point.

Jōshū said that the National Teacher was on top of Sanzō's nose but Sanzō could not see him. This interpretation misses the point. How can the National Teacher be so close to Sanzō when Sanzō cannot even see his own nose [i.e., his own essense]? If Sanzō could see his own nose then the National Teacher could have seen Sanzō. Even if we allow that Sanzō saw the National Teacher it was merely a physical juxtaposition. Sanzō has yet to really see and meet the National Teacher.

Gensha said, "He was too close to see." True, he was too close, but it misses the point. What does "too close" mean? It seems that Gensha neither knew the meaning nor clarified it. He only knew that "too close" meant that there was no meeting of minds and vice versa. We should rather say that it is too far from the Buddhist Dharma. If the third question is too close the first two are too far. Let us ask Gensha, "What exactly is too close? Is it a fist? Is it enlightened vision? From now on you had better not say that something is too close to see."

Gyōzan said, "The first two answers were concerned with the objective world; Sanzō lacked *jijiyū samādhi* and couldn't see the National Teacher." Gyōzan, you lived in China but people in India think you are a little Shakyamuni. Nevertheless, your interpretation is very mistaken. There is no difference between the objective world and *jijiyū samādhi*. Therefore we should not say we cannot see one or the other because of some difference. There can be no adequate reason for distinguishing between the two. If we say that, when we are in *jijiyū samādhi* others cannot see us. Then we will be unable to experience *jijiyū samādhi* itself and not have practice and enlightenment. O Gyōzan, If it is true that you actually thought that Sanzō knew where the National Teacher was in the first two answers you cannot be said to be a true student of the Buddhist Way.

Daini Sanzō did not know where the National Teacher was not only in the third case but also in the first two answers—he neither knew nor saw him. If Gyōzan said that Sanzō did see him it means that Gyōzan did not know where the National Teacher was either. Let us question Gyōzan, "Where is the National Teacher now?" Before he opens his mouth to answer give him a loud "katsu!"

Gensha censured Sanzō by saying, "Did he know where the National Teacher was the first two times?" He had better think over his own words. They seem to be good, but actually it is like saying he saw something he did not. Gensha missed the point.

Myokaku Juken said about this, "Sanzō failed." This can only be properly said if Gensha's words were correct; If his words are mistaken then such a thing cannot be said.

Kai'ei Shitan said concerning this, "Why couldn't Sanzō see the National Teacher if he was on top of Sanzō's own nose? Because he didn't know that the National Teacher was already in his eye." This comment is also only concerned with the third question. The first two answers should also be criticized. How can the National Teacher know about being on top of Sanzō's nose or in his eye? If it is like that, we must conclude that Kai'e did not comprehend the National Teacher's words. Sanzō lacks both a nose [i.e., the essense of Buddhism] and eyes [i.e., enlightened vision]. Even if Sanzō attempts to keep his nose and eyes they will be shattered if the National Teacher penetrates them. If they are shattered then the National Teacher cannot remain there.

The five honorable priests mentioned above know nothing of the National Teacher. The National Teacher is an ancient Buddha for all generations and a Tathāgata for all the world. He illuminated and transmitted the Eye and Treasury of the True Law of Buddha and preserved the eye of enlightenment. He transmitted Buddha for himself and others. Although he lived in the era of Shakyamuni Buddha he has also practiced under all the Buddhas of past eras. Essentially he attained the Way before Kūō Buddha [the Buddha who existed before any worlds were created]. Although the National Teacher's home is originally in this world, this world is not always the ordinary world, nor is it covered by the ten directions of the entire universe. Shakyamini is master of this world but the National Teacher still heeps his home here and nothing obstructs him. For example, all of the Buddhas and Patriarchs who both preceded and came after Shakyamuni Buddha attained the Way together without obstructing one another.

There is proof that Sanzō did not know the National Teacher, and this also shows that śrāvakas, pratyekabuddhas and Hinayanists cannot even understand the outermost surface of Buddhas and Patriarchs. Remember this. We must clearly understand why the National Teacher scolded Sanzō. Why should the National Teacher only scold him the third time if he knew the answers the first two times? That is very strange.

If someone understands two-thirds of a question that is sufficient; then Sanzō should not be scolded. The scolding the National Teacher gave differs from that where nothing at all is known. If Sanzō thinks like that it is an insult to the National Teacher. If the National Teacher scolded him only because Sanzō could not answer the third question no one will have any confidence in the National Teacher. Rather, if Sanzō knew the answers to the first two questions the strength of those answers should cause us to scold the National Teacher.

The main point of the National Teacher's scolding of Sanzō lies in the fact that from the first question to the third, Sanzō did not know the whereabouts or body and mind of the National Teacher. He was scolded because he had never studied or learned the Buddhist Dharma properly. That is why the National Teacher repeated the same question three times.

Sanzō answered, "Why are you at Seisen watching the boat races?" The National Teacher did not say, "O Sanzō, you do know where I am," but rather only repeated his question. Without properly clarifing this principle many elders have formulated their own self-centered opinion of it for hundreds of years after the National Teacher.

Everything such elders have said runs counter to the intentions of the National Teacher and does not fit with the essense of the Buddhist Dharma. It is pitiful that such elders make such a mistake. If the ability to read others' minds exists in the Buddhist Dharma there also must be a corresponding ability to read others' bodies, fists, heads, and eyes.

If this is so there also must be the ability to read one's own mind and body. Like this, to freely control one's mind is to read one's own mind. If we can actualize such an understanding we can freely read others minds. Let us ask this question:

"Which is better: the ability to read others' minds or the ability to read our own? Answer quickly, quickly!" Yet it requires some time. "You possess my marrow," is the ability to read others' minds.

This was delivered to the monks at Daibutsuji, Echizen, on July 4, 1245.

ŌSAKUSENDABA

"The master's wish"

Speaking and silence, wisterias and trees, horses and donkeys, water and clouds; the relationship is the same. Therefore, we have the following story in the [*Mahaparinirvana Sūtra:*]

The World-honored One said, "When a king gives the order 'bring *sendaba*' to his attendants, that one word has four meanings: 1) salt; 2) a chalice; 3) water; 4) a horse. Like this, four things are contained in one word. A wise attendant knows this well. If the king wants to wash and says *sendaba*, the attendant brings water. If he wants to eat and says *sendaba*, the attendant brings salt. If after eating he wants to drink and says *sendaba*, a chalice is brought. If he wants to go out and says *sendaba*, his horse is prepared. Like this, a wise attendant understands the four inner meanings of the king's words."

This *ōsakusendaba* is the king's need and *shinbusendaba* is catering to the king's request. Such a custom has been practiced for a long time and it is similar to the transmission of the Buddhist kesa. Since Shakyamuni took up this subject, all of his descendants should study it. If we reflect upon this, we see that all who study under Shakyamuni practice *sendaba*. Those who do not study with Skakyamuni must continue their pilgrimage, and attain the first step of practice. *Sendaba* was first used between Buddhas and Patriarchs for a number of generations and then adopted by royal families.

The ancient Buddha Wanshi Shogaku of Mt. Tendō in Keigenfu of Sung Dynasty China said to an assemby, "Once a monk [Secchō] asked Jōshū, 'What is *ōsakusendaba?*' Jōshū folded his hands over his chest and bowed. Secchō said, 'Salt was requested but a horse was brought.'" Wanshi said, "Secchō was a great priest of a hundred years ago and Jōshū was a hundred and twenty year-old ancient Buddha. If Jōshū's answer is correct then Secchō is wrong and vice versa. Which answer is best?' Wanshi gave this interpretation: "If a mistake is made it will be huge. Using only words is like striking the grass to frighten a snake. Not using words is like melting coins to make the demons come out. Neither of them chose a wild field to roam in. They are like Gutei holding up one finger."

My late master, an ancient Buddha, once said about this story, "Wanshi is an ancient Buddha." However, the ancient Buddha Wanshi was only seen as an ancient Buddha by my late master. In Wanshi's time there was nother Zen master called Dai'e Shūkō of Kinzan. He was in the line of Nangaku. Most people of Sung Dynasty China thought that Wanshi and Dai'e were much the same. Occasionally, some people considered Dai'e superior to Wanshi. Such a mistake occurred because monks and laymen of the Sung Dynasty studied superficially, did not open their eyes to the Way, and lacked the ability to know others' inner states.

Wanshi's expression shows real determination. We must study the principle of the ancient Buddha Jōshū's folding his hands over his chest and bowing. At that time was Jōshū's action *ōsakusendaba* or *shinbusendaba?* We must also study the essence of Secchō's "salt was requested but a horse was brought." That statement is both *ōsakusendaba* and *shinbusendaba*. The answer to Shakyamuni's *sendaba* was Mahākāśyapa's smile. In answer to the first Patriarch's *sendaba* the four disciples brought a horse, salt, water and a chalice. When a horse, salt, water and a chalice became *sakusendaba* [i.e., were needed], they also became *hosendaba* [they were brought]. We must study this point.

One day, Toinchō came to see Nansen. At that time, Nansen pointed to a water pitcher and said, "There is a pitcher with water in it. Without moving the pitcher bring the water over here to this old priest." Toinchō brought the pitcher and poured the water over Nansen's head. Nansen said nothing.

We can see that Nansen asked for "water" [the water from an ocean that has completely dried up] and Toinchō brought a "chalice" [he poured out every drop in the pitcher]. Even if this occurs, however, we still must study "there is water in the pitcher" and "a pitcher in the water." Neither the water nor the picther has moved.

Once, a monk asked Great Master Kyōgen Shuto, "What is *ōsakusendaba?*" Kyōgen said, "Go over there!" The monk left. Kyōgen said, "That monk is making a fool of me."

Let's pose this question: Is Kyōgen's "Go over there!" *sakusendaba* or *hosendaba?* Please answer! Is "the monk left" *sakusendaba* or *hosendaba* or simply a statement in itself, independent of the initial question and answer? No matter if it is or not, we should not say "he is making a fool of me." Although this answer is based on the power of Kyōgen's entire life, it is like a general who has lost the war but is still proud in defeat. Often, [Buddhas and Patriarchs] say black when they mean yellow, and try to reveal enlightened vision. They explain *saku* [request] and *ho* [compliance] *sendaba* in very subtle and refined ways. Who can say that holding a staff or a fly whisk is not a type of *sendaba*? However, there are people who glue the bridge to the base of the koto or tighten the string too much [i.e., foolish people cannot understand *sendaba*].

One day, the World-honored One sat on the lecture platform without speaking. Then Mañjuśrī struck the gong announcing the end of the discourse, and said, "This is how to clarify the Law of the King of the Dharma." Then Shakyamuni left the platform.

Zen Master Myōgaku Juken of Mt. Secchō said about this, "Only the wisest sages among that assembly correctly perceived the Law of the King of the Dharma. However, if someone in that assembly knew about *sendaba* why was it necessary for Mañjuśrī to strike the gong?"

What Secchō meant was that if one strike of the gong is completely sufficient, then whether it is struck or not is still total detachment. If this is so, then one strike of the gong is *sendaba*. Then [Mañjuśrī] is the man who understands *sendaba* and all the sages in that assembly are his guests. They understand that "this is the Law of the King of the Dharma." The twelve hours of the day freely utilize and are utilized by *sakusendaba*. Requesting a fist brings a fist, requesting a fly whisk brings a fly whisk.

However, present day elders all over Sung Dynasty China cannot even dream of *sendaba*. This is very pitiful; the Way of Patriarchs has disappeared. Do not avoid difficult study; you must transmit the lifeblood of the Buddhas and Patriarchs. For example, if we say "What is Buddha?" there is the answer "Our mind is Buddha." What is the essence of this? It is *sendaba*, is it not? "Our mind is Buddha" must be studied in more detail. However, how many people truly know the meaning of *sendaba*?

This was delivered to an assembly of monks of October 22, 1245 at Daibutsuji, Echizen.

[58]

MENJU

"Direct, face to face transmission"

SHAKYAMUNI was once preaching to a large assembly gathered on Vulture Peak in India. He held up an udumbara flower without speaking and winked. Then Mahākāśyapa smiled. Shakyamuni said, "I possess the Eye and Treasury of the True Law and the Serene Mind of Nirvana. I now bestow it to Mahākāśyapa."

This is the principle of directly bestowing the Eye and Treasury of the True Law from Buddha to Buddha, Patriarch to Patriarch. It was handed down by each of the seven Buddhas and given to Mahākāśyapa; then it was transmitted through the twenty-eight Indian Patriarchs up to Bodhidharma. Bodhidharma came to China and passed it to Great Master Eka, Patriarch of the true teaching. It continued to Great Master Daikan Enō of Mt. Sōkei and then was transmitted by the seventeen Patriarchs that preceded my late master, the ancient Buddha Tendō of Daibyaku in Keigenfu of the Sung Dynasty.

On May 1, in the Hokke Gannen period of the Sung Dynasty [1225], I, Dōgen, made a prostration and offered incense before the ancient Buddha Tendō in his quarters. This was my first meeting with him. At that time my master faced me and said, "This is the actualization of the entrance into the Law of the Buddhas and Patriarchs. It may be compared to the holding up of the flower at Vulture Peak, [Eka's receiving Bodhidharma's] marrow on Mt. Sūzan, [Kōnin giving Enō] the kesa on Mt. Ōbai, and the bestowal of the Dharma to Tōzan. It is the direct, face to face transmission of the Eye and Treasury of the Buddhas and Patriarchs. Only I possess the True Law. For others it is just a dream."

The principle of this direct, face to face transmission of the Dharma is the same as Shakyamuni's possession and bestowal of the Law to Mahākāśyapa. It is the face of the Buddhas and Patriarchs.

If we do not receive the transmission of Buddha we cannot be a Buddha. Shakyamuni Buddha looked into Mahākāśyapa's heart and consequently bestowed the Law to him. Even the transmissions of Ānanda, Rāhula, and all the great Bodhisattvas cannot be compared to that of Mahākāśyapa. Shakyamuni and Mahākāśyapa shared the same seat and kesa; this is the most significant event in the proper transmission of the Buddhist teaching. Mahākāśyapa intimately received the transmission of Shakyamuni's face, heart, body, and eyes. Mahākāśyapa prostrated himself before Shakyamuni and devoted himself entirely and unsparingly to the transmission of the Law. His face is not his own but rather the face of Shakyamuni's direct, face to face transmission. Just as Shakyamuni looked into the heart of Mahākāśyapa, Mahākāśyapa looked into the heart of Ānanda. Ānanda prostrated himself before Mahākāśyapa's Buddha face. This is a real direct, face to face transmission. Ānanda preserved it and then passed it to Sāṇavāsa. Sāṇavāsa prostrated himself before Ānanda—this is truly direct, face to face transmission. Like this, Buddhas and Patriarchs in each generation, together with their disciples, see each other and directly transmit the True Law face to face. It even one Patriarch, master, or disciple does not receive the transmission directly, face to face, they cannot become Buddhas or Patriarchs.

For example, water flows from many different places to form a river; similarly, the many branches of Buddhism flow toward the Law. There is a continual inheritance that keeps the lamp of transmission eternally lit, but the transmitters differ only in form and not in essence. Knowing the proper time for transmission is like the mutual pecking of the shell by the mother hen and the baby chick at precisely the right time.

Therefore, we should prostrate ourselves before Shakyamuni Buddha and stay with him day and night. We will surely reflect the brilliance of Buddha's face and preserve his virtue all our lives.

The interdependence between the Buddha and ourselves cannot be measured. We should sit quietly and reflect on this. Through our devotion to Shakyamuni's face, we will reflect his eye in our own. When this occurs it becomes Buddha's vision and original face. This transmission has been handed down right up to the present time and has never been broken—this is the meaning of direct, face to face transmission. In each generation, every face has been the face of Buddha, and this original face is direct, face to face transmission. Therefore, we prostrate ourselves before this right transmission, the seven Buddhas, Mahākāśyapa, and the twenty-eight Indian Patriarchs. The original face and enlightened vision is like this. Seeing these Buddhas and Patriarchs is to see the seven Buddhas of Shakyamuni. At the proper time, Buddhas and Patriarchs have direct, face to face transmission. Direct, face to face transmission of Buddha transmits Buddha face to face. This transmission is like a tangled wisteria vine (*kattō*) that never ends. Open the eye, directly transmit through the eye, and receive the Law through the eye. Find the direct transmission of the face through the face. Direct transmission is the giving and receiving of the face. Open the mind, transmit and receive through the mind. Reveal the body, and transmit the body through the body. Regardless of the place or country, the transmission is always like this. From China towards the east, the inner essence of the right transmission of the Buddhas and Patriarchs is direct, face to face transmission and reception. It is bestowed when we prostrate ourselves before the true eye of the Tathāgata.

When we prostrate ourselves before the face of Shakyamuni Buddha, or the fifty-one Patriarchs, or the seven Buddhas, we should not compare them to each other. And we should not be concerned with the particulars of the transmission. Here is where we find direct, face to face transmission. If you have never seen a real master, you cannot be said to be a disciple and vice versa. By all means, masters and disciples must look into each other's hearts and directly transmit the Law, face to face. This is the "Mind" the Patriarchs use for the actualization of the right transmission. Therefore, the brilliant face of the Tathāgata is preserved in each generation.

Therefore, that is why we can see that throughout millions of years, direct transmission is the actualization and reception of Shakyamuni Buddha's face. The actualization of the Buddhas and Patriarchs, Shakyamuni, Mahākāśyapa, the fifty-one Patriarchs, and the seven Buddhas is the actualization of their own shadow, light, body, mind [and six sense organs]. Even if disciples cannot comprehend their master's "one word of teaching," the master is still able to certify their resolve to seek the Buddhist Way if the disciples are seeking the Way of Buddha with their entire body and mind. This also is right, direct, face to face transmission.

We must venerate this direct, face to face transmission. It is the imprint of Buddha's mind in the disciples' heart. Although it is not the highest and most precious form of life, it is accomplished directly, face to face, mind to mind; this face differs from the normal social face of the lay world. This face is the face of the Buddha's great enlightenment—it goes beyond inside or outside. Great enlightenment directly transmits great enlightenment face to face.

If we transmit the right eye of the Law and venerate the form of Shakyamuni Buddha, we become closer to him than he is to himself. Through that vision we can actualize countless Shakyamuni Buddhas in the past, present, and future. Therefore, if we truly venerate and seek out Shakyamuni Buddha, we must also profoundly honor the direct and right transmission [of the Buddhas and Patriarchs] which is extremely difficult to find. That is, make prostations before the Tathāgata and he will bestow the direct, fact to face transmission. When we look at the proper study and right transmission of the Tathāgata with a clear eye, we see that it is ourselves and others. We must value and protect it.

    The following are the words of the right transmission: "Prostrate yourself before the eight stūpas and you will throw off all sins and find the Way." The eight stūpas are those built where Shakyamuni Buddha actualized the Way: 1) at his birthplace [Kapilavastu]; 2) where he set in motion the Wheel of the Law [Migadāya]; 3) where he attained the Way [Buddha-gayā]; 4) where he entered nirvana [Kushinagara]; 5) at Kanyakubja; 6) Vesali [7] Jetavana; and 8) Rājagrha.][1]

    Shakyamuni's virtue is actualized throughout the earth and sky. In addition, his virtue appears in the "stūpas" of sound, smell, taste, sensation, mind, and form. We should prostrate ourselves before these stūpas and actualize the Way. In India everyone—monks, laymen, celestial and earthly beings—prostrate themselves before the eight stūpas as a general custom. The stūpas are the same as the entire canon of the Buddhist sūtras.

    Furthermore, the Buddhist Way is not only actualized in each life [in the prostrations before the eight stūpas], but also in the thirty-seven kinds of practice of the Dharma. Shakyamuni Buddha practiced enlightenment throughout the unlimited past and future, and his imprint is found all over and throughout history. That is why we are able to attain the Way. We should know that the stūpas are standing continually and constantly face many frosts and blossoms, wind and rain.

    Furthermore, Shakyamuni Buddha's virtue illumines the entire universe and actualizes the merit of the Buddhist Way. It is freely given to all without any loathing or begrudging. If we truly wish to practice, even if we are full of passions and defilements, the power of his virtue will give us strength to have practice and enlightenment.

    Shakyamuni Buddha's virtue is like this and the present direct, face to face transmission of his Way cannot be compared to prostrations before the eight stūpas, or the thirty-seven kinds of practice of the Dharma based on Buddha's face, mind, body, Way, light, or tongue. The virtue of the eight stūpas originates

---

[1] The ashes of Buddha were divided into eight portions and given to eight families who then constructed stūpas in the eight sacred places of Buddhism.

with Buddha's face, etc. In order to have the practice of free, unattached activity, students of the Buddhist Dharma must contemplate the virtue of direct transmission day and night in a quiet place. Then our Buddhist study will be full of bliss.

We may say that our country is superior to all others because our Buddhist Way is unsurpassed. Other countries have few people like us. The reason: our transmission is directly from the right Patriarch of Shōrinji [Bodhidharma] and the sixth Patriarch Enō. This transmission is even superior to the preaching of the Law on Vulture Peak delivered in the ten directions. This present time is the only opportunity we have to find the pure Buddhist Dharma. When else will we have such an opportunity? If we fail to cut off all passions now, when can we? If we lose this chance, when will we become Buddhas? If we do not sit like Buddha, how can we practice like Buddha? We must clarify this in detail.

When Shakyamuni Buddha gave his direct transmission to Mahākāśyapa he said, "I possess the Eye and Treasury of the True Law and the Serene Mind of Nirvana. I now bestow it to Mahākāśyapa." On Mt. Sūzan Bodhidharma said to the second Patriarch, "You possess my marrow." This was direct, face to face transmission. At the proper time, you can transcend your bones and marrow and have the direct, face to face transmission of the Buddhas and Patriarchs. Further, it is the direct transmission of great enlightenment which is the transmission of the mind-seal—this belongs to a very special world. Yet direct transmission cannot be expressed at all [in words]; even the principle of illusion cannot be found.

The Great Way of the Buddhas and Patriarchs is nothing but the direct, face to face transmission from master to disciple. Through direct, face to face transmission we will become full of joy and believe and venerate our own original face.

I, Dōgen, made a prostration before my late master, the ancient Buddha Tendō, for the first time on May 1, [1225]. The direct, face to face transmission was given to me, one who has mastered a small part of the vast Buddhist Teaching. I attained a certain degree of dropping off of body and mind and brought the transmission to Japan.

This was delivered to the monks on November 20, 1242, at Kippōji, Yoshida-gun, Echizen.

This principle of direct, face to face transmission of the Buddhist Way has never been seen nor heard until now. In the Keiyū period of the reign of the Sung Dynasty Emperor Jinshū [1034–1038] there was a Zen master known as

Jōko in Suipukuji monastery. Although he had many disciples, none had real practice. One day he ascended the lecture platform and said:

"The late Great Teacher Ummon Kinshin is still living. You monks have seen him recently, haven't you? If you have seen him you are just like me. After you have a certain measure of enlightenment you will be able to see him. If you do not see yourself you will never see him.

"Long ago, Zen Master Hyakujō, who was Ōbaku's teacher, was scolded by his teacher Baso with such a loud voice that it almost shattered his eardrums. Ōbaku heard this story from Haykujō and attained enlightenment. This is what we mean by saying the old masters are still living. Hyakujō then asked Ōbaku, 'Are you able to become the Dharma-heir of Baso?' Ōbaku replied, 'I've heard of Baso but have never seen him. If I become his Dharma-heir without seeing him then there will be no descendants of his Law.' At that time Baso had been dead for five years. We should know that Ōbaku's enlightenment lacks something since he had never seen Baso—only one eye is open. In my case, I have known and seen the Great Master Ummon and can be his Dharma-heir. The only difference between us is that about one hundred years have passed since his parinirvana.

"Now, all of you should understand why I teach this principle. I can see Ummon, and all of you who comprehend the Buddhist Law will certify this. Those who are simple-minded will have much doubt. If you have reached a certain stage of enlightenment you will not say anything; if you haven't attained enlightenment, is it possible to get there now or not? I hope this talk will help you find real peace."

Even if we allow that Jōko saw Ummon, I doubt that Ummon saw him. Ummon would not permit such a man to be his Dharma-heir. Jōko did not say Ummon saw him, so therefore, Ummon and Jōko did not have a direct transmission. Among the seven Buddhas and all the Buddhas of the past, present, and future there is not one who did not have direct transmission, is there? Do not say Ōbaku's enlightenment is incomplete. How can someone like Jōko tell what level Ōbaku has reached or what his words mean?

Ōbaku is an ancient Buddha and he sacrificed his life for the transmission of the Law. Jōko cannot even dream of beginning to study this principle of the Law. Ōbaku received the direct transmission after practicing under his master and meeting him face to face. In Jōko's case, he neither knows nor has ever seen a real master; therefore, he neither knows nor sees himself. He lacks Buddha's observation and has not fulfilled himself. Therefore, his transmission is incomplete.

Did Jōko know that Ummon is the descendant of Ōbaku? How was Jōko able to gauge Ōbaku's and Hyakujō's level of attainment? How can he gauge Ummon's? To be able to comprehend those masters' attainment one must have enough experience of the Way. If one has enlightenment one can know of others' attainment, but if one lacks sufficient study one can neither know nor measure.

Jōko said that less than five years had passed since Baso's death. Jōko was so stupid that he thought Ōbaku could not receive Baso's transmission. If you receive the transmission it must be received throughout all periods of time. If you do not do this you will be unable to keep it for half a day or even a minute. Jōko was a foolish and stupid man who did not know the meaning of sun-faced Buddha and moon-faced Buddha.

One hundred years had passed since Ummon's death and Jōko claimed to have received Ummon's teaching. He lacked the ability to transmit that master's teaching; his claim is nothing more than a dream of a three-year-old child. In order to inherit Ummon's Law it requires ten times as much ability as Jōko possessed.

Now I will try to explain the real meaning of Ummon's transmission to people like Jōko. What Hyakujō meant to ask Ōbaku was whether or not he intended to inherit Baso's teaching. Try to think about this with the same determination as that of a lion chasing small game, or changing your perspective like the cow and turtle who traded places to see what each other's habitat was like. Then there will be complete freedom and total detachment. In the Dharma-transmission such an ability is necessary. Ōbaku said, "Probably, I will lose my descendants." Since you do not understand at all, how can you know the meaning of "my" and "descendants"? You must study in detail. These words actualize the truth of direct transmission—nothing is hidden.

Unfortunately, the so-called Zen Master Bukkoku Ihaku, who lacked understanding of the transmission of the Buddhas and Patriarchs, designated Jōko as one of Ummon's Dharma-heirs. That was a mistake, but people in later days do not know about that. Do not think that Jōko studied under Ummon.

Recopied on June 7, 1244, in Kippōji by Ejō.

If we think like Jōko, i.e., it is possible to transmit the Way of Shakyamuni Buddha only by studying letters or reading sūtras, we are greatly mistaken. You must receive the transmission from a right master to be able to understand the sūtras. Jōko said that it was necessary to read Ummon's sayings, even though he did not read them himself. Not only did Jōko not see Ummon, he did not even see himself. He did not possess the eye of Ummon. He had much to clarify. What he really needed was to visit many temples, find the right master, and receive the transmission. He should never say that he received the transmission of Ummon. If he talks like that he is like a non-believer. Even if Hyakujō said the same things as Jōko, he still would be mistaken.

BAIGE

"Plum blossoms"

MY LATE master Tendō, an ancient Buddha, was the thirtieth Patriarch of Keitokuji of Mt. Daibyaku. One day he told the monks:

"This is my first address of the winter season. Yet even now an old plum tree with many tangled branches is beginning to bloom—one, two, three, four, five, countless blossoms appear. These blossoms are not proud of their purity or fragrance. The petals fall and it feels like spring as the wind blows through the flowers, trees and grasses. You monks are no doubt surprised to hear this. Suddenly, however, a great change occurs. A violent storm arises with driving rain and pounds the earth; it then turns into a blizzard and snow covers the earth. The old plum tree endures various conditions, even freezing cold that seems to cut off its very life."

The old plum tree mentioned here withstands all conditions—sometimes it blooms, sometimes it bears fruit, sometimes it faces spring, sometimes winter; sometimes it faces strong winds, sometimes storms; sometimes it surprises monks; sometimes it is the enlightened vision of the ancient Buddhas; sometimes it appears with grasses and trees; sometimes it is pure fragrance. It faces all these changes, all those that occur imperceptibly. Heaven and earth, the bright sun and pure moon—all aspects of the old plum tree— cannot be separated from one another.

When the old plum tree blooms the entire world blooms. When the world blooms spring comes. Then the five leaves bloom as one flower—three, four, five, one hundred, one thousand, countless flowers bloom. All these flowers grow on one, two, countless branches of an old plum tree. An udumbara flower and a blue lotus flower also bloom on the same branch. All these blooming flowers constitute the beneficence of an old plum tree. Such an old plum tree covers the worlds of human beings and celestials. These worlds appear within the old plum tree. Hundreds of thousands of flowers are the flowers of human beings and celestials. Millions of flowers are the flowers of the Buddhas and Patriarchs.

When this kind of plum tree blooms, all the Buddhas emerge in this world and Bodhidharma comes into existence.

Once, my late master said to the monks: "When Shakyamuni lost his ordinary sight and attained enlightened vision, one branch of a plum tree bloomed in the snow. But now small branches have appeared and the beautiful blossoms laugh at the spring wind blowing wildly."

"Now" is the time for the wheel of the Dharma of the ancient Buddhas to turn throughout the entire world and awaken all human beings and celestials—even clouds, rain, wind, water, all the grasses and trees, and insects will be influenced by the turning of the wheel of the Law. The turning of the wheel will enliven all the countries on earth and in heaven. Hearing this teaching for the first time causes such wonderful things. True attainment is to gain the understanding we lack. If there is no joy or virtue in our attainment it is not the wheel of the Dharma which we should study.

Presently in the Sung Dynasty there are one hundred and eighty provinces with a countless number of mountain and city temples. There are many *unsuis* and novices who know nothing of my late master, an ancient Buddha, and still more have never met him, much less learned his words directly or had a meeting of minds with him. Very few were accepted as disciples, permitted to make a prostration before him and allowed to receive his skin, flesh, bones and marrow or see his original face and clear vision.

My late master, an ancient Buddha, did not easily accept disciples in his monastery. If any of the monks were lax or lacked a Buddha-seeking mind he expelled them from the monastery. It is not necessary to help monks who are not real seekers, he said; they only disturb others and have no place here. I have seen many such people and often wondered what prevented them from staying in the monastery. It was very fortunate for me, a foreigner, to be not only accepted as his disciple but also allowed to visit him freely and observe his daily life. Since I am stupid and lack proper knowledge it was very good fortune to find such a master.

The influence of my late master was widespread throughout the Sung Dynasty and many gained the Way. Since his death the Sung Dynasty is darker than midnight; there is no ancient Buddha, past or present, who can be compared to him. Therefore, students of this latter age should know that such Dharma teaching cannot he heard or studied by others anywhere throughout the worlds of men or gods.

A plum tree blooming in the snow is the manifestation of the udumbara flower [which Shakyamuni held up before Mahākāśyapa]. We have the opportunity to see the Eye and Treasury of the True Law of the Tathāgata in our everyday life. Yet most of the time we lose the chance to smile and show our understanding. However, my late master has transmitted the principle of a plum tree blooming in the snow and that clearly reveals the enlightenment of Buddha. The wisdom of enlightenment is the supreme wisdom, and if we study the plum blossoms more deeply we will undoubtedly realize this. A plum blossom is the observation that "Above the heavens and throughout the earth I am the only honored one"—each thing is the most honored thing in the world.

Therefore, all flowers—in heaven, on earth, white lotuses, great white lotuses, red lotuses, great red lotuses—in the ten quarters of the universe are interrelated with a plum blooming in the snow; all flowers receive the beneficence of the plum blossom. All the million kinds of flowers are like subspecies of the plum blossom and can be called "little plum blossoms." Furthermore, flowers of sky, flowers of the earth, flowers of samādhi are large and small versions of a plum blossom. In one blossom countless countries emerge. In each of those countries different flowers bloom because of the beneficence of the plum blossoms. Only plum blossoms can give beneficence—not rain or dew drops. The continuous transmission of the Buddhist Way is based on this plum blossom. Do not only study the snow [in which Eka stood beseeching Bodhidharma] to teach him at Shōrinji on Mt. Sūzan. The snow itself is the enlightened eye of the Tathāgata—it illumines the sky over your head and the ground under your feet. Do not just learn about the Himalayan snow where Shakyamuni practiced—the snow itself is the Eye and Treasury of the True Law of Shakyamuni. The five eyes of enlightenment enable us to clarify all our studies, and the one thousand eyes of enlightenment allow us to complete them. The Divine Light of the body and mind of the venerable Shakyamuni must help us clarify all aspects of the phenomenal world (*shohō jissō*). Human beings and celestials have different viewpoints like that of ordinary people and saints. However, when the earth is covered with snow all differences disappear.

Snow must cover the earth and the earth must be full of snow. No snow, no earth. When snow covers the earth it is the enlightened eye of venerable Shakyamuni.

We should know that flowers and the earth transcend life and death. Since they transcend life and death the enlightened eye transcends life and death. This is called the supreme Buddhist enlightenment. The right time to comprehend this is when one branch of a plum tree blooms in the snow. Flowers and the earth are the life beyond life. "Covered with snow" means all over, back and front. The entire world is our mind, the mind of a flower. Consequently, the entire world is a plum blossom, i.e., the eye of Shakyamuni Buddha.

The eternal present is mountains, rivers, and earth—everywhere, at all times, these are the manifestation of [the flower of Bodhidharma]: "Originally I came here to save all sentient beings suffering in illusion; one flower blooms and five leaves begin to grow. This is true, natural time." The Buddhist Law came from the west to the east long ago but now is the time for the plum blossom to bloom.

When the tiny branches appear it is the time for the actualization [of enlightenment]. Among both large and small branches there are both old and new ones. We should study these branches; they cover everywhere in the eternal present. Among three, four, five or six flowers there are countless flowers. Each flower possesses its own deep and extensive virtue in its height and breadth. One plum blossom opens both the inside and the outside of the flower. While one plum blossom is on a single branch no other branches or seeds are necessary. Where the branch reveals itself it is the eternal present; this single branch is the one unbroken Buddhist Law transmitted from one to another.

Therefore, [Shakyamuni said,] "I possess the Eye and Treasury of the True Law and now bestow it to Mahākāśyapa" and [Bodhidharma said to Eka,] "You possess my marrow." If such a state is attained the entire world seems full of treasures. "One flower blooms and five leaves begin to grow." These five leaves are a plum blossom. Similarly, the seven Buddhas, the twenty-eight Patriarchs, the six Chinese Patriarchs and the following nineteen Patriarchs in China are the five leaves opening on a single branch. If you master one branch, you can master the five leaves and then you can learn the right transmission of the plum blossoms in the snow. Also we can study the world of the branch, achieve liberation, and find that the moon and clouds are the same, mountains and valleys are different.

Furthermore, a foolish person once said, "The five leaves are the five Chinese Patriarchs who came after Bodhidharma's flower bloomed." The "five leaves" refer to a point in time and are related to past and future. Such an understanding is not worth our time. That kind of understanding is not based on real effort; it is not studying the Buddhas and Patriarchs with the entire body. This is pitiful. Why should "one flower and five leaves" be limited to the five Patriarchs? Is it not necessary to count those who came after the sixth Patriarch? That is not even a good fairy tale. Do not cling to such an understanding.

My late master once said at the first address of the new year, "Congratulations on this new year. All things are made anew; prostrate yourselves and then the plum tree blooms and spring comes." If we quietly reflect upon this we can see that even though all Zen masters of the past and present may have transcended every attachment to this world, if they are not awakened to the inner meaning of "plum tree blooms and spring comes," they cannot be said to have clarified the Way. My late master alone is a true ancient Buddha among ancient Buddhas. The essence of his new year's greeting is that when the plum tree blooms the entire world is covered with spring. The virtue of just one or two plum blossoms brings spring everywhere. This is also the point of "all things are made anew." "All things" does not only refer to past, present, or future but also to time beyond time. Each and every moment, countless and limitless, is renewed. This "newness" goes beyond ordinary newness. That is why all the monks must examine the bottom of their hearts—this will reveal all things as they truly are.

My late master, the ancient Buddha Tendō, said to an assembly of monks: "If we are awakened to the one word of enlightenment, that state never changes. Buds sprout from the willow, and an old branch is full of plum blossoms."

It is said that in hundreds of kalpas of practicing the final goal is to be completely awakened, from beginning to end, to one word of Buddha. The goal is the same for a short time of practice. In spring the willow has new buds; they are "new" but they still are able to open the eye of enlightenment. That eye of enlightenment is nothing but ourselves. We should know that there is an eye of enlightenment in the new buds; their "newness" is the newness of all things. "An old branch is full of plum blossoms"; the plum blossoms penetrate the branches and the branches hold the plum blossoms just as they are, nothing else. The blossoms and branch grow and reach completion together. Blossoms and branches are one entity and form the entire tree. Shakyamuni's "I possess the Eye and Treasury of the True Law and bestow it to Mahākāśyapa" is the holding up of a flower; his smile is the full smile of the blossom.

My late master, an ancient Buddha, said to an assembly, "A willow is adorned with a beautiful belt and a plum tree wears an exquisite arm bracelet." Here "bracelet" is not made from jewels or jade but is the plum blossoms. The opening of the plum blossoms is the transmission of the Way—the marrow is passed from one to another.

Once, King Hashinoku of India invited the holy man Binzuru to partake of a meal with him. At that time the king asked him, "I have heard, O Honorable One, that you have seen Buddha. Is it true?" Binzuru raised his eyebrows and opened his eyes wide. My late master praised Binzuru with this gatha:

"Raising his eyebrows he answered the question;
That he once met and saw Buddha was not a lie.

His virtue is respected everywhere,
Spring is in the tip of a plum tree branch covered with freezing snow."

This story came about because of King Hashinoku's question. To meet Buddha is to act like Buddha; to act like Buddha is to stroke the eyebrows. Even an arhat, if he is not a real saint, cannot be said to have met Buddha. If he has not met Buddha he cannot act like Buddha. If he cannot act like Buddha he cannot show his understanding by stroking his eyebrows. We should know that a venerable man is one who receives the direct face-to-face transmission of Shakyamuni, has attained the four stages of practice and expects to become a future Buddha; he has met the Buddha, has he not? Meeting the Buddha does not just mean to see Buddha but also to arrive at his level. That is why the king realized that Binzuru was a good teacher. We must study the expression "to meet the Buddha" carefully. Spring does not only exist in human beings or Buddhalands, but also in the tip of a plum tree. How can we be sure of this? Because Binzuru showed us the condition of a frozen plum tree covered with snow by stroking his eyebrows.

My late master, an ancient Buddha, said, "Our original face possesses no life or death; spring is in the plum blossoms, as beautiful as a painted landscape." When we paint a spring landscape we must not only paint willows, or red and green plums and peaches; we must paint spring itself. If you only paint those objects it is not a real painting. It has to be nothing but spring itself. And there has been no one in either India or China who can paint spring like my late master. His skill was very precise. The "spring" we have been referring to is this "spring" of the painted landscape. Spring must occur effortlessly in the painting. Plum blossoms are necessary for this kind of painting. Spring must be put in the tree. Nyojō's skillful means are truly wonderful.

My late master, an ancient Buddha, clarified the Eye and Treasury of the True Law and transmitted it to the Buddhas and Patriarchs and all people in every direction throughout the past, present, and future. That is why he mastered completely enlightened vision and was totally awakened to the essence of the plum blossoms.

This was delivered to the monks on November 6, 1243 at Kippōji with three feet of snow covering the grounds.

If we are deluded and think that the plum blossom is not the enlightened eye of Shakyamuni we should ask ourselves if there is any other vision beside this. You should know that if you seek enlightenment outside of the plum blossoms you will not get it, even if it is right in your hands. Even if it is in front of your face you will not see it. Today is not our day, but the day of the Buddhist Way. Right now we must open the enlightened eye of the plum blossoms and stop chasing after other things. My late master, an ancient Buddha, said, "Clearly illumined, the plum blossoms no longer cast a shadow. Sometimes it rains, sometimes it is cloudy; but the plum blossom stands alone in the past and present. It lacks nothing!"

Rain and clouds are the forms and functions of the plum blossoms. They represent the plum blossoms' myriad changing forms. The plum blossoms form past and present.

Long ago, Zen Master Hōen said, "The icy north wind blows, and the bamboo grove in the valley trembles. The ground is completely frozen but there is no resentment. Only the wild plums in the mountains are full of life; they speak silently of the cold, lonely days of winter." We are familiar with the plum blossoms and therefore we can feel the cold, lonely days of December. The power of the plum blossoms cause the icy north wind to blow, the snow to fall, the months to pass, and the bamboo grove to exist in the valley.

The Elder Fu of Taigen said in praise of the Way of enlightenment, "Long ago I was not enlightened, and the sound of a flute made me very lonely. But now I have no time for such useless dreams even in my sleep. I let myself flutter in the wind with the plum blossoms." The Elder Fu was originally an itinerant preacher but finally attained great enlightenment under a kitchen monk who lived on Mt. Kassan. This is the spring wind blowing through the plum blossoms.

MUCHŪSETSUMU

"Explaining a dream within a dream"

THE manner in which all the Buddhas and Patriarchs appear is self-generated without origin; it has nothing to do with the opinions of old-fashioned and narrow-minded scholars. The virtue and continuous development of Buddhas exist in themselves, independent of time or space. They are not related to either eternity or instant flashes of time. It completely transcends the discrimination found in the world of ordinary people. Turning the wheel of the Law is also self-generating without origin. Therefore, it possesses unlimited merit and becomes an eternal beacon. This is "explaining a dream within a dream." Seeing enlightenment within enlightenment, therefore, is explaining a dream within a dream.

The place where the dream within a dream is explained is the land and brotherhood of the Buddhas and Patriarchs. In the Buddha land and Buddhist brotherhood and in the practice and teaching of the Patriarchs there is enlightenment beyond enlightenment, i.e., explaining a dream within a dream. While we listen to this teaching do not think that we are not already in the Buddhist brotherhood. This is the turning of the wheel of the Law of Buddha. This wheel of the Law turns in all directions; hence, the great oceans, Mt. Sumeru, land, and all the Buddhas emerge. This is explaining a dream within a dream before any dreams occur. Every manifestation of the relative world is a dream. This dream is the clear radiance of a hundred grasses [i.e., all forms of existence]. When we have doubt we have perplexity; then in dreaming of grass, grass explains grass. In order to study this we must learn that grass, roots, stems, branches, leaves, flowers, fruits, lights, and colors are one great dream. However, do not misunderstand this—it is nothing more than an ordinary dream.

Therefore, when those who have not learned the Buddhist Way hear about explaining a dream within a dream, they foolishly think that things exist where they actually do not. It is like illusion covering illusion. However, it is not like that. Although there is "illusion in the midst of illusion" and "illusion that covers illusion" we should first of all study and practice the path to enlightenment.

Explaining a dream within a dream is all the Buddhas. All the Buddhas are wind, rain, water, and fire. To keep those names is to preserve them. Explaining a dream within a dream is ancient Buddhas. Ride this precious vehicle and go directly to the dojo. Going directly to the dojo is contained within riding the precious vehicle. Right or wrong, there are only dreams. [Nyojō said that] tightly bound or completely free, the wind blows freely on and on. At that time, the wheel of the Law and the world of the Great Wheel is immeasurable and unlimited. It turns in the tiniest speck of dust and works incessantly. Although this principle turns the wheel of the Dharma in both immense and minute things, still "a smiling face, but a heart full of resentment" remains.

[Explaining a dream within a dream] affects all places; the wheel of the Law turns in large and small things, and blows freely like the wind. Therefore, the entire unlimited earth as it is incessantly proclaims the Law. This relative world of cause and effect is the supreme possession of the Buddhas. We should know that both the teaching and explanations of the Buddhas are being proclaimed incessantly, and establishing themselves everywhere. Do not look for its coming or going; when it comes it comes, when it goes it goes. Just as a tangled wisteria is bound together with other vines, supreme enlightenment is entwined with supreme enlightenment. As enlightenment is unlimited, so are sentient beings; they are also supreme. Attachment is unlimited and liberation is unlimited. "The actualization of enlightenment is to give you thirty blows." This is the proper explanation of a dream within a dream.

Hence, a rootless tree, a land without sun or shade, an echoless valley, etc. actualize the explaining of a dream within a dream. Such conditions are not in the world of men or gods, and are not known by ordinary people. Who can doubt the enlightenment of a dream, since it does not belong to the world of doubt? Who can certify it, since it does not belong to the world of ordinary consciousness? Since we have supreme enlightenment like this we use the expressions "dreams as dreams," "within dreams," "dreams explaining," "explaining dreams," and "dreams within dreams." If there is no dream within a dream, there is no explaining dreams; if there is no explaining dreams, there is no dream within a dream. If there is no explaining dreams, there are no Buddhas; if there is no dream within a dream, the Buddhas could not have appeared in the world or turned the marvelous wheel of the Law. This wheel of the Law is transmitted from Buddha to Buddha. It is the explanation of a dream within a dream. Within the explaining of a dream within a dream there are only supremely enlightened

Buddhas and Patriarchs. Furthermore, the continuous development of the Dharma-body is explaining a dream within a dream. Here, the most important aspect of Buddha transmitting Buddha is not to be attached to our head, eyes, marrow, brains, body, flesh, hands, or feet. When we are not attached to those things we can say, "Freely give and freely take"—this is called mystery of mysteries, wonder of wonders, enlightenment of enlightenment, a head above heads.

Such behavior is the essence of the Buddhas and Patriarchs. When studying this, ordinary people think of "head" as nothing unusual and not the "head" of various objects. If they cannot imagine it as the head of Vairocana Buddha, how can they imagine the head of the brilliant, radiant hundred grasses [i.e., all phenomena]? Moreover, they are unable to value their own heads.

From ancient times it is said that when foolish people hear the expression "head above heads," they think it means we should stop chasing worthless things. It is natural to think that certain things are not necessary and thus to doubt the expression "a head above heads." Actually this is a mistake. The actualization of explaining a dream within a dream is the same for ordinary people or saints. Therefore, ordinary people and saints live in explaining a dream within a dream, both yesterday and today. We should know that yesterday's explanation of a dream within a dream is interpreted in a manner that is beyond ordinary consciousness. Thus, the explanation of a dream within a dream is the value of seeing Buddha. It is a pity that fools cannot see that the brilliant, shining hundred grasses proclaimed by the Buddhas and Patriarchs are dreams which are clearer than hundreds of thousands of moons and suns.

The "head" in the "head above heads" is the head of a hundred grasses, a thousand kind of heads, ten thousand heads, and the head which is the entire body. That head is the entire world, and the ten quarters of the universe. It is [Sensu's] "one verse fits the head" and [Chōsa's] "The head of a hundred-foot bamboo pole." We must study and clarify the head above heads.

Therefore, that is why all the Buddhas with supreme and perfect enlightenment step out from the sūtras and become the head above heads and explain a dream within a dream. When these sūtras explain a dream within a dream, all Buddhas with supreme enlightenment emerge. All the Buddhas with supreme enlightenment proclaim this sūtra—it is decidedly "explaining a dream within a dream." If the origin of this dream is not clear, the fruits of enlightenment will not be clear. As the proverbs say, "One stone makes a thousand ripples" and "Ten thousand shots, but only one bullseye."

Like this, we should know that there are four kinds of explaining a dream within a dream: 1) things as they are; 2) people as they are; 3) not things as they are; and 4) not people as they are. These principles have been known for a long time. That is, the daily explaining a dream within a dream is the real explaining a dream within a dream.

An ancient Buddha said, "For your sake I, together with all the Buddhas of the three worlds and the six Patriarchs, explain a dream within a dream." We must clarify this saying. The holding up of a flower and [Mahākāśyapa's] smile is explaining a dream within a dream; [Eka's] prostration and his attaining the marrow is also explaining a dream within a dream.

Speaking of the Way with one verse, and comprehension that is beyond words and explanations are nothing more than explaining a dream within a dream. The thousand hands and eyes [of Avalokiteśvara] work spontaneously and he has the ability to see and hear through his ears and eyes. The explaining of a dream within a dream present in our body and contained within the proclaiming of the Law of the dream, is both totally bound and completely free.

"Direct pointing" is explaining the dream; hitting the bulls-eye is explaining the dream. We use totally bound and completely free to evaluate all things with equanimity. At such a level surely we have accurate judgment and then explaining a dream within a dream emerges. If there is no evaluation and no equality, then equanimity cannot be actualized. However, if we attain equanimity, we can see equanimity. We must know that to attain equanimity is to be independent of physical things, to abandon evaluation, and to have no base in potentiality; although this world is empty, if we do not have equanimity we cannot study the nature of equanimity. Just as subjectivity is present in emptiness, objectivity is also active and seeks its own liberation—this is explaining a dream within a dream. It is the actualization of the body of equanimity within emptiness; it is the Great Way of evaluating equanimity. Regardless of whether it is in the subjective or objective world, either with emptiness or form, each thing must be harmonized in explaining a dream within a dream. There is nothing other than the total liberation of explaining a dream within a dream. A dream is the entire great earth and the great earth is equanimity. Similarly, when we turn the head we turn the brain—there is no separation. This is enlightening the dream within a dream and believing, receiving, respecting, and following it.

Shakyamuni Buddha said, "The bodies of all the Buddhas are golden, covered with a hundred joys, and beautifully adorned. Listening to the Law and its proclamation to all people is their continual good dream. They also dream of the prince who abandoned his palace and relatives, renounced luxuries, and began austere practice. Then he sat under the Bodhi tree in the Lion's Seat for seven days seeking the Way. Finally he attained the wisdom of all the enlightened ones and entered the supreme Way. He then arose and began to turn the wheel of the Law. This proclamation continues to all sentient beings throughout the four directions for unlimited kalpas. He proclaimed the wonderful Law of the world of enlightenment and worked to save all sentient beings. Later on, he entered parinirvana; it was like smoke disappearing or fire blowing out. Now, anyone who proclaims the supreme Law in this sorry world will succor many and attain the virtue described above."

After we study this saying of Buddha, we must completely master the significance and depth of the community of Buddhas. This is not an allegory or metaphor. Since the wonderful Law of all the Buddhas is nothing but Buddha transmitting Buddha, all dharmas present in dreams and enlightenment form reality. Within enlightenment there is resolve, practice, awakening, and nirvana; also within dreams there is resolve, practice, awakening, and nirvana. Dreams and enlightenment form reality—there is no large or small, superior or inferior.

However, some people in the past or present read this story about the prince who abandoned his palace and focus on the power of proclaiming the supreme Law and conceive of a dream which is greatly mistaken. People form such misconceptions because they have failed to clarify the Buddha's proclaiming of the Law. Dreams and enlightenment are one and form reality. Even if the Buddhist Dharma is a metaphor, it still forms reality. If it is not a metaphor, still the dream mentioned in the above story is the truth of the Buddhist Dharma. Shakyamuni Buddha and all the Buddhas and Patriarchs have resolve, practice, and enlightenment within a dream. Hence, the Buddhist Way which instructs and leads this world was formed in a dream.

"Seven days" is the attaining of Buddhist wisdom. "Turning the wheel of the Law to save sentient beings" has been carried out throughout unlimited kalpas. We cannot accurately gauge the real condition within a dream. "The bodies of all the Buddhas are golden, covered with a hundred joys, and beautifully adorned. Listening to the Law and its proclamation to all people is their continual good dream." It is clear that this good dream is all the Buddhas. There is an eternal Way of the Tathāgata, not just a dream of a hundred years. Proclaiming the Law for all people occurs in the present body; hearing the sound of the Dharma is accomplished through our eyes and mind. It occurs in our ancient home before time.

"The bodies of all the Buddhas is golden, covered with a hundred joys, and beautifully adorned." The good dream which is the body of all the Buddhas cannot be doubted, even in the present age. There is a principle of unceasing instruction of Buddha within enlightenment, but the actualization of the Buddhas and Patriarchs is surely within a dream dreaming. We must study so that we do not slander the Buddhist Dharma. When we do this the eternal Way of the Tathāgata instantly manifests itself.

This was delivered to the monks at Kannondōri-Kōshōhōrinji on September 21, 1242. Transcribed on March 23, 1243, by Ejō, chief disciple.

RAIHAITOKUZUI

"Making a prostration and attaining the marrow"

WHEN we practice supreme and perfect enlightenment it is very difficult to receive instruction from a good master. It does not matter whether the master is a man or woman: The only requirement is attainment of the Way and accessibility. Nor does it matter if the master belongs to the past or present. [For example] a spirit of a wild fox was once changed into a priest of high virtue.[1] This is the true form of attaining the marrow of beneficial instruction. It is "karma never ceases" without thought of self or others.

After we have met a true master we must sever all old relationships, stop wasting time, and practice the Way earnestly with great effort. We must continue to practice regardless of how much or how little expectation we have. We should attend to this practice immediately with all our might. If we study like this those who slander the Law will not trouble us. The story about the Patriarch who cut off his arm and attained his master's marrow [Eka] is not about someone else. We are already the teacher who has cast off body and mind.

Attainment of the marrow of one's master and transmission of the Dharma is accomplished through sincerity and true faith. Sincerity and true faith do not come from either outside or inside. The Dharma is of far more value than our small body. Abandon the world and follow the Way. If we think we are of more value than the Dharma it will never be transmitted, received, or attained. Leaving aside all other teachings let us consider one or two examples of those who value the Dharma above all else.

We must value the Dharma above all else no matter what it is—a pillar, a stone lantern, Buddhas, wild foxes, demons, men or women. If such things possess the great Dharma and have attained their master's marrow we must receive and maintain their Dharma in our own body and mind throughout endless kalpas.

---

[1] See the chapter *Daishugyo* in Volume I.

We can easily gain a body and mind like the rice plants, hemp, bamboo or reeds that grow throughout the world. Yet it is very difficult to find the True Dharma.

Shakyamuni Buddha said, "When you meet a master who proclaims supreme enlightenment, do not be overly concerned with his social status or nationality, his appearance, his faults or his behavior. He should be highly respected because of his wisdom so provide him daily with good food. Honor him with heavenly food and celestial flowers. Every day pay him homage with three prostrations, and keep all evil thoughts from arising. If you do such things surely there will be a way to enlightenment. Ever since I first developed the resolve for enlightenment I have continually practiced like that and attained supreme and perfect enlightenment right up to the present day."

Therefore, you should ask trees and stones to proclaim the Dharma, seek out rice paddies and villages to hear their explanations, question round pillars, and study walls and tiles. Once Indra made a prostration to a fox and asked him about the Dharma. That fox was called a Great Bodhisattva. The fox's action was independent of noble or ignoble karma.

However, foolish people who have never heard the Buddhist Dharma consider themselves great bhikkus and refuse to make prostrations to young people who have attained the Dharma. They say, "We have practiced for many years and refuse to make prostrations to those who began to study late in life and then attained the Dharma. Since we have acquired the title of master we cannot make prostrations to those without that title. We are in charge of regulations and should not make prostrations to ordinary monks just because they have attained the Dharma; we are senior priests and cannot make prostrations to laymen or women who have attained the Dharma. We are like the three sages and ten saints so we should not be required to make prostrations to nuns who have attained the Dharma. We are decendants of the Imperial family and will not make prostrations to ministers or retainers even if they have attained the Dharma." Such foolish people, uselessly leave their fatherland and wander through other countries and never see or hear the Buddhist Way.

Long ago, Great Master Jōshū Shinsai of the T'ang Dynasty developed the resolve for enlightenment and began a pilgrimage. He said, "I will ask instruction from anyone with superior knowledge even if he is a child of seven, and will not talk with anyone who is inferior even if he is a hundred. Instead I will teach him."

Asking a child of seven about the Dharma and making a prostration before him even though we are much older is very praiseworthy and the right minded attitude of an ancient Buddha. Also, when a monk who is seeking the Way in the Buddhist brotherhood meets a nun who has attained both the Way and the Dharma and makes a prostration and asks her about the Law it is an excellent illustration of true Buddhist study. It is like quenching a severe thirst.

Zen Master Shikan of China was a senior priest of Rinzai. The first time Rinzai saw Shikan coming he asked him to stop by. Shikan said, "All right." Rinzai said, "I was about to give you a blow but decided not to." After this, Shikan become Rinzai's disciple. Later on, Shikan left Rinzai and went to Matsuzan [to see the nun Ryōnen]. Matsuzan asked him, "Where are you from?" Shikan said, "From the road's mouth [i.e., an undefiled place]." Matsuzan said, "Why don't you cover that mouth?" Shikan was unable to reply. Then he made a prostration and become her disciple.

Another time Shikan asked her, "What kind of mountain is Matsuzan?" She said, "Its peak cannot be seen." Shikan said, "What kind of people live on this mountain?" Matsuzan said, "They don't have the form of men or women." Shikan said, "Why don't you turn into a man?" She said, "I am not the spirit of a wild fox so how can I change?" Shikan prostrated himself before her, resolved to seek enlightenment from her, and studied under her for three years.

Later on, after Shikan returned to the world (as a full priest) he told his disciples, "I received a half-full ladle from that old follow Rinzai and another half-full one from the old woman Matsuzan, making one full ladle. Now I am completely satisfied and seek nothing further." Looking back on this old story we can see that Matsuzan, a top disciple of Kōan Daigu, transmitted her master's life blood and thereby become Shikan's "old woman." Rinzai was the Dharma heir of Zen Master Ōbaku Kiun and possessed strength derived from diligent practice. That is how he become Shikan's "old man." "Old man" means father, "old woman" means mother. Shikan's prostrations and seeking of the Dharma under Matsuzan is a high-minded illustration of Buddhist practice. It is an example of a monk's integrity and the breaking down of all barriers.

The nun Myōshin was a disciple of Gyōzan. Once Gyōzan was looking for a suitable candidate for the monastery's administrative chief. He asked the senior experienced monks to recommend a good person. Many opinions were offered and finally Gyōzan said, "The nun Myōshin from Waisu district is a woman, but she has a superior spirit and is the best qualified person for administrative chief." All agreed and Myōshin was appointed to the position. At that time there were many excellent disciples under Gyōzan but no one was dissatisfied with the decision. Although her position was not the most important one she did her best and loved others as herself.

Once she was working in the administrative quarters and seventeen monks from the Shoku district came to see her master. They wanted to climb the mountain right away but it was too late and they had to spend the night at the administrative quarters. At night they began to discuss the famous story of the sixth Patriarch and the wind and flag. All of the seventeen monks gave their respective opinions but all were off the mark. Myōshin overheard the discussion and said, "It's a pity that the seventeen donkeys have worn out so many pairs of straw sandals on pilgrimages and still cannot even dream about the Buddhist Dharma." A little later Myōshin's attendant told them what his master thought about their discussion, but none of them were dissatisfied, or resentful about it. On the contrary, they were ashamed at their lack of attainment of the Way. They straightened up their robes, offered incense, made prostrations and sought her instruction.

She said, "Please come closer." But before they could come closer she shouted, "The wind is not moving, the flag is not moving, the mind is not moving!" When they heard that all of them reflected on their own hearts, then bowed to her in gratitude and become her disciples. Soon after that they returned to Seishu without even visiting Gyōzan. Truly Myōshin's level is not surpassed by the three sages and ten saints and her actions are those of one who transmits the right stream of the Buddhas and Patriarchs.

Therefore, when present day chief priests and top disciples lack understanding they should ask nuns who have attained the Dharma to come and instruct them. What good are elders who have not attained the Dharma?

Masters who instruct many people must have enlightened vision. Nevertheless, there are many foolish masters who are attached to body and mind and are laughed at by even worldly people, much less given recognition as interpreter's of the Buddhist Dharma. Also among lay people there are some who question the practice of making prostrations to those monks who possess the right transmission. They do not know the Buddhist Dharma, they do not study, they resemble animals, and are far from the Buddhas and Patriarchs. Yet if anyone is willing to devote his entire body and mind to the Buddhist Dharma surely the Dharma will give him help. Even fools in heaven and earth can recognize true sincerity. Can it be possible for the True Law of all the Buddhas to fail to establish harmony among all things? Even soil, sand, and stones possess the ability to feel sincerity.

In present day temples in Sung Dynasty China there are nuns who have become famous for their practice and attainment of the Dharma. They are appointed masters of famous monasteries at the Emperor's request and give many lectures in the Dharma Hall. The chief priest and all the other monks assemble in the Dharma Hall and listen to their proclamation of the Law. The question and answer session will be conducted in the manner of bhikkhus. That is an established practice. After someone has attained the Dharma, i.e., become a true ancient Buddha, we should not or think about past meetings with that person [before he became an ancient Buddha]. When we meet that person [after his enlightenment] it is on special and new ground and we should only think about the new circumstances. That is why a nun who transmits the Eye and Treasury of the True Law and has been honored and instructed by arhats, the three sages and ten saints should receive our prostrations. What makes you noble just because you are man?

After all, universal emptiness is universal emptiness, the four elements are the four elements, and the five skandhas are the five skandhas; women are the same—attaining the Way can be accomplished by both men and women. Moreover, we must equally respect both attainments of the Dharma. Do not be concerned with the differences between men and women. This is a basic principle of the supreme and wonderful Buddhist Way. In China, there are also laymen who have not renounced the world yet still devote themselves to Buddhism. There are single people and couples living in huts practicing clean and pure lives in the midst of the dirt and pain of this world. Yet all of these people are trying to clarify the same things as masters who have become monks and gathered together to study, make prostrations and receive instruction. It makes no difference if they are men, women, or beasts. Those who have not seen the Buddhist Dharma even in their dreams—and this includes hundred-year-old bhikkhus—cannot surpass laymen or women who have attained the Dharma. Still they simply bow to them as a host bows to his guest.

Anyone who practices and attains the Buddhist Dharma, even a girl of seven, will be the leader and compassionate father of all monks, nuns, lay people and sentient beings. In [the *Lotus Sutra*] the daughter of a dragon king became Buddha. She should be venerated, honored, and respected like all the Buddhas and Tathāgatas. This is the ancient practice of the Buddhist Way. Those who do not know this and lack the right transmission are to be greatly pitied.

Written on one bright day in March, 1240, at Kannondōri-Kōshōhōrinji.

SANSUIKYO

"The mountain and river sūtras"

THE present mountains and rivers actualize the Way of the ancient Buddhas. Both mountains and rivers maintain their true form and actualize their real virtue. They transcend time and therefore are active in the eternal present. Since their original self is revealed, they are detached from their manifestation. Mountains possess the virtue of being high and wide yet the movement of the clouds and the blowing of the wind are free and not restrained by the mountain.

The priest Fuyo Dōkai of Mt. Taiyō[1] said to an assembly: "The green mountains are always moving and a stone woman gives birth at night."

The mountain possesses complete virtue with nothing lacking; therefore, it is always safely rooted, yet constantly moving. We must study the virtue of this "movement" in detail. Simply because the movement of a mountain is not like the movement of a human being, do not doubt that it exists. Dōkai's "moving" contains the essence of moving. We must clarify the meaning of "always moving." "Always moving" means eternal. The movement of "always" is faster than the wind, but those living on the mountain neither realize nor know it. Living on the mountain is analagous to "When a flower blooms, spring exists everywhere." However, those who are not on the mountain are also unaware of its movement. Anyone who does not see the mountain for himself cannot realize, see, or hear it due to this principle. If anyone doubts the movement of the mountain it is because he does not understand his own movement. People move and take steps but they are unable to understand it. When we understand our own movement we can understand the movement of the mountain.

Just as green mountains are not animate or inanimate, so are we. If we realize

---

[1] Fu-jung Tao-k'ai (d. 1118).

that, we will not doubt the movement of green mountains. The green mountains must be seen in relation to the entire world. We must closely examine the movement of the green mountains and our own movement—forward and backward. We must also examine the forward and backward movement that existed before heaven and earth were joined and time began.

If movement ceases, Buddhas and Patriarchs cannot appear. If movement came to a dead end, the Buddhist Dharma could not have been handed down to the present day. Both forward and backward movement have never stopped, and they are not opposed to each other. The virtue of the flowing mountains is this movement. Green mountains study their own movement, the east mountain studies its movement across the water. Therefore, this is the proper study of the mountain. It is not necessary to change the mountain's body and mind; the mountain learns about itself as a mountain.

Do not slander mountains by saying they do not move or walk across the water. There is doubt about this due to our shallow views. Since our understanding is inadequate we are amazed to hear the expression "flowing mountains." "Flowing mountains" is not completely understood by everyone, especially those caught in shallow observations and superficial understanding. Hence, when we say "mountain," we designate it so because of its increasing virtue and its maintenance of life. It moves and flows. When the mountain gives birth to a mountain, Buddhas and Patriarchs appear from this principle and emerge in such a manner.

Enlightened vision is actualized in the mountains, grasses, trees, earth, stones, fences, and walls. Do not have any doubt about it; yet it is not movement or total actualization. Even if the mountain is adorned with the seven precious jewels we still do not see its true form. Even if the Buddhas and Patriarchs practice there, do not become attached to it. Even if it possesses the highest form of all the Buddhas' unsurpassed virtue, it still has not revealed its true state. Like this, each observation depends on the respective viewpoint of the observer, and lacks something. It is not the work of the Buddhas and Patriarchs, but rather only one small part of total observation.

One-sided or narrow observations are not permitted by Shakyamuni. Discriminating between mind and nature was never done by the Buddhas and Patriarchs. Looking for one's mind and nature is the activity of non-believers. Attachment to words and letters is not the way of liberation. Like this, we can find the state that transcends such narrow views; i.e., "the green mountains are always moving" and "the east mountain walks across the water." Study this in detail.

"A stone woman gives birth at night." The barren woman gives birth at "night." In general, there are male, female, and neuter stones. These compensate for any lack in heaven and earth—there is also a stone of heaven and a stone of earth. Worldly people may pay lip service to this, but few people really know about it. We must be able to understand the principle of giving birth. When a child is born, is it a transformation of the parents? We study the idea that to become parents of the child is the actualization of birth, but we should also carefully study the practice and enlightenment of the birth when the child becomes the parent.

Great Master Ummon Kyōshin said, "The east mountain walks across the water." The essence of this actualization of the Way is that all mountains are the "east mountain" and all those east mountains walk across the water. Therefore, the nine great mountains and Mt. Sumeru [of India] actualize themselves and attain practice and enlightenment. This is the "east mountain."

However, can we be sure whether or not Ummon transcended the activity of practice and enlightenment in the skin, flesh, bones, and marrow of the east mountain? In the present day Sung Dynasty there are many groups of careless people whose number is increasing, and those who possess the truth cannot do anything to prevent it. Some people say that "the east mountain walks across the water" and the story of Nansen's sickle[2] are completely incomprehensible.

They point out that those words related to normal cognition are not the Zen words of the Buddhas and Patriarchs. Those words which are beyond comprehension are the sayings of the Buddhas and Patriarchs. Hence, Ōbaku's use of the staff and Rinzai's shouts are beyond comprehension. This is the great enlightenment that existed before time. All those skillful means used by our virtuous predecessors to cut off our entanglements are "incomprehensible."

That is not the teaching of a real master and not the eye of proper study. Such people are too foolish to mention. In the past two or three hundred years there have been many evil people and fake monks. It is very pitiful that the Great Way of the Buddhas and Patriarchs is perishing everywhere. The interpretations of those people are even inferior to those of Hinayanists and śrāvakas,

---

[2] One day when Nansen was working outside, a monk asked him, "Which way to Nansen's?" Nansen lifted up his sickle and said, "I bought this real cheap." The monk said, "I'm not interested in how much your sickle cost. Which way to Nansen's?" Nansen said, "I've gotten a lot of use out of it."

and their ideas are more foolish than those of non-believers. They are neither laymen nor monks, human beings nor gods. They are more stupid than dumb beasts who learn the Buddhist Way. What false monks term "incomprehensible" is only incomprehensible to them and not to the Buddhas and Patriarchs. Do not avoid the path of the Buddhas and Patriarchs just because you yourself lack comprehension. You might not be able to understand it now, but that does not mean that it is incomprehensible. There are many cases of such inadequate understanding in present day Sung Dynasty China. I saw many such cases with my own eyes. It is a very sorry thing that they are unaware of the inadequacy of their cognition; they do not realize that the words of the Buddhas and Patriarchs transcend ordinary cognition. When I was in China they kept quiet even if I laughed at them. What they consider incomprehensible is simply due to their evil minds. Who taught them such a thing? Since they lacked a master who possessed the truth they naturally became children of non-believers.

We should know that the east mountain walking across the water is the bones and marrow of the Buddhas and Patriarchs. All types of water are actualized at the foot of the east mountain. Therefore, all the mountains go beyond the clouds and walk over heaven. The peak of the water is various mountains. Climbing up and down is to cross the water. The toes of the various mountains walk over the water and the water splashes beneath their feet. This movement is natural and practice and enlightenment emerge. Water is not strong or weak, wet or dry, moving or still, cold or hot, existent or non-existent, illusion or enlightenment. When it is solid it is harder than the hardest diamond; when it melts it is softer than the softest milk.

Therefore, that is why we should not doubt the actualization of the water's virtue. Now we should study and observe for a time the water in the ten directions of the universe. It is not the study of the water seen by men and gods, but rather the study of water seen by water. Since there is a practice and enlightenment of water's water, there is a method to search for the water's water. We should actualize the Way of meeting ourselves through ourselves; others should study others following the path that moves freely and transcends itself.

Generally, when we look at mountains and water they are seen in a variety of ways depending upon the circumstances; the gods see it as their adornment, not simply as water. We see it as something else, we see it as water. For them it is an adornment and for us water. Some people see water as a wonderful flower yet do not use it as a flower. Demons see water as a huge fire or thick blood. Dragons and fish see water as a palace or beautiful halls. Water can be seen in many ways—as the seven precious jewels, forests, fences, the pure and undefiled liberation of Dharma nature, the true body of man, bodily form and essence of mind, or as the water seen by human beings. Different standpoint, different interpretation. Like this, the view depends on the eye of the beholder. Let us investigate this a little further. Does looking at one object give many different views or does it occur by mistakenly thinking one object possesses various forms? We must consider this carefully.

Therefore, that is why practice and enlightenment are not limited to just one or two kinds but encompass thousands of forms depending on the condition and nature of enlightenment. Further, if we consider this statement more closely we will find that even if there are various types of water, it is as if there were no true or original water, and no various types of water either. The various types of water, however, go beyond all this and are not mind, form, karma, themselves, or other things. Water is simply water, totally detached.

Hence, water is not comprised of earth, water, fire, wind, space, consciousness, etc. [matter]; it is not blue, yellow, red, white, black, etc. [color]; and it has no form, sound, smell, taste, sensation, perception, etc. [sensation]. Nevertheless, it is actualized in all those things. Consequently, it is very difficult to be able to clarify the nature of this present world and its palaces. Correct interpretation depends on the inner meaning of wind and space [emptiness]; it does not depend on ideas of oneself and others, and is far beyond superficial understanding. Do not limit your vision to some narrow range.

Shakyamuni Buddha said, "All dharmas are free and without attachment, abiding nowhere." We must know that all dharmas are free and without attachment; nevertheless, they maintain their true state. When human beings look at water they see only one kind of flowing. There are many kinds of flowing but human beings only see one kind. For example, land and sky are flowing, top to bottom, bends in a river flow, the deepest pools flow; above the clouds and at the bottom of the river all things are flowing.

In the *Monshi* it says, "Water ascends to heaven to make raindrops and descends to earth to flow in rivers." So-called descendants of the Buddhas and Patriarchs are not as wise as the non-believers who wrote that text, and it is shameful that they do not understand the principle of water. The point here is that water is not conscious of itself, but just manifests itself as it is.

"Water ascends to the heavens to make raindrops." We must know that water ascends, no matter how high it is, and makes raindrops. Raindrops change according to the circumstances; if someone says there is a place where water cannot go, it is just the teaching of Hinayanists or the false teaching of non-believers. Just as water penetrates flames it penetrates the mind of cognition and discrimination, and the enlightened wisdom of Buddha-nature.

"It descends to earth to flow in rivers." We should know that when water descends to earth it becomes rivers. If we can grasp the significance of "river" we can become sages. Foolish people out of the mainstream think that water is found only in rivers and oceans. This is not correct. Rivers and oceans are in the water. Consequently, water is not only in the rivers and oceans. When water descends to earth it takes the form of rivers and oceans. Again, since water forms rivers and oceans we should not study that there is no world or Buddha land in the water.

Even in one drop of water countless Buddha lands are actualized. Yet there is no water in the Buddha land, nor is there a Buddha land in the water. Where water exists it has no relation to past, present, or future nor to any particular world. Nevertheless, water is actualized as the absolute truth. Where Buddhas and Patriarchs go, water surely follows. Therefore, Buddhas and Patriarchs possess the body, mind, and thought of water. That is why "water never flows up" is not found anywhere in the Buddhist texts. Water flows everywhere—up and down, back and forth.

It also says in the Buddhist sūtras, "Heat rises, water flows downhill." What we must study is "up and down" i.e., the study of up and down of the Buddhist Way. Where water flows we think of it as down, but we should not say down before we see where it flows. Where heat rises is up. Although the world of existence does not actually correspond to the six directions, we use the four (five, or six elements) to tentatively divide the world in different directions. We cannot always say that heaven is "up" or hell is "down." Heaven and hell form the entire existence of the world.

However, when dragons and fish see water as a palace it is the same as human beings seeing a palace. No one sees a palace as flowing. If someone outside the palace tells the dragon or fish that it is flowing, they would be as surprised as human beings who hear the expression "mountains flow." Furthermore, the railing, stairs, and pillars of the palace are also flowing water. Quietly reflect on this principle. If we cannot separate ourselves from biased views, we cannot be separated from the body and mind of ordinary people, nor master the world of Buddhas and Patriarchs. We will not be able to master the world or palace of ordinary people. We may know what oceans and rivers are but dragons and fish do not. Do not foolishly think that simply because we know what water is, other beings also know. Those who study the Buddhist Way and learn about water should not limit their study to the observations of humans. Study all aspects of water in the Buddhist Way. How should we study the water observed by the Buddhas and Patriarchs? We should ascertain whether or not there is water in the enlightenment of the Buddhas and Patriarchs.

Mountains are the home of the great sages throughout the past and present. Saints and sages live together deep in the mountains; mountains are their body mind. Saints and sages actualize mountains. We may imagine that even though there are a great number of saints and sages gathered in the mountains, they meet no one else there. Only the vital function of the mountain appears without a trace of the saints' and sages' presence. Looking at the mountains from this world, and looking at them while standing on one of them are completely different. This type of speculation or actual knowledge of "not flowing" differs from the observation of dragons and fish. Men and gods live in their own respective worlds, and other things doubt or are unable to doubt their views.

Hence, you must study the verse "mountains flow" as the Buddhas and Patriarchs do, and do not base your interpretation on amazement or doubt. One opinion says "it flows," another says "it doesn't flow." Without proper study there can be no wheel of the True Law of the Tathāgata.

An ancient Buddha said, "If we wish to avoid evil karma we must not slander the wheel of the True Law of the Tathāgata." This saying pierces skin, flesh, bones, marrow, body and mind, emptiness and form, trees, stones, rice paddies and villages.

Although mountains seem to belong to the country they really belong to those who love them. When the lord of the mountain is loved, virtuous men and women will live there. When saints and sages live on the mountain, the mountain is their possession, trees and stones grow thick, and the birds and beasts flourish. The virtue of saints and sages influences all things on the mountain.

We should know that the nature of mountains is like that of saints and sages. There are many cases of emperors visiting a mountain to bow before sages and seek the counsel of saints. On those occasions they respect those sages as their masters and prostrate themselves before them. Here social customs or status are not binding. No matter how great the power and virtue of the emperor, sages are not moved by it. Those who live in the mountains are quite separate from society. On one occasion, the Emperor Kō of China visited the hermit Kōsei on Mt. Kōdō and approached him on his knees and bowed his head to the floor to show his humility.

Shakyamuni abandoned his father's palace and went to the mountains. The king bore no grudges, was not resentful of his son's actions, and did not question the sincerity of those who taught the prince in the mountains. Shakyamuni's twelve years of severe practice took place almost entirely in the mountains and his enlightenment took place in the mountains. Real kings never try to control or destroy mountains. We should know that mountains belong neither to the world of human beings or gods. Do not approach this using only your limited human ability. If you do, how will you be able to fathom "the mountain flows" or "does not flow"?

From ancient times saints and sages have also lived on the water. When they live on the water, some catch fish, some catch disciples, some catch the Way. This is the ancient tradition of water. Moreover, we must catch ourselves, catch "catching." By catching, "catching" is caught through the Way.

Long ago, the priest Tokujō suddenly left his master Yakusan and went to live on a boat on the Katei River. Soon a sage [Kassan] who lived there became his disciple. This is an example of catching fish, catching disciples, catching water, and catching yourself. Kassan saw Tokujō and found Tokujō in himself; Tokujō could see him because he met himself.

Not only is there water in the world, there is a world of water with a world in it. This is not true just for water, but for all material things—there are animate worlds in clouds, wind, fire, earth, Dharma worlds, one blade of grass, and a staff. Where there is an animate world there is a world of the Buddhas and Patriarchs. Study this principle well.

Therefore, water is the palace of the real dragon [enlightenment]. Water does not only flow: to think like that is to slander water. For example, if we choose a different perspective water does not flow. Water is its own true form. Water is the virtue of water and does not "flow." If we clarify this principle of the water's flowing or not flowing we can clarify all phenomena. There is a mountain hidden in precious jade and in streams, and in the sky and mountains. Study the mountain hidden in the depths of a mountain.

An ancient Buddha said, "Mountains are mountains, water is water!" These mountains are not the usual mountains. These mountains are the real mountains of the Buddhas and Patriarchs; therefore, study them. If we search for these mountains we can learn from them. Like this, mountains and water become saints and sages.

This was delivered to the monks at Kannondōri-Kōshōhōrinji on October 18, 1240. Transcribed on June 3, 1242, at Kippōji in the chief disciple's quarters by Ejō.

SHOAKUMAKUSA

"Refrain from all evil"

An ancient Buddha said, "Refrain from all evil, practice all that is good, purify your mind; this is the teaching of all the Buddhas." This precept has been kept by all the Buddhas and Patriarchs in the past and present, before and after the seven Buddhas. It has been handed down from Buddha to Buddha. This precept is not only the possession of the seven Buddhas; it is the teaching of all the Buddhas. We must clarify this principle. The Dharma Way of the seven Buddhas is the sum total of all their actions. There is an essential spirit in the continuous transmission and bestowal. That spirit is the teaching of all the Buddhas, and their practice and enlightenment.

"All evil" means the evil nature of good, bad, and neutral. That nature is unborn. The nature of good and neutral is also unborn, undefiled, and with true form. These three elements possess diverse forms. "All evil" means that the evil in this world and others, in the past and present, and among men and gods is not always the same. Between the Buddhist Way and worldly life there is a big difference in the ways of evil, good, and neutral. Good and evil are time, but time is not good and evil. Good and evil are the Dharma, but the Dharma is not good or evil. Good, evil, and the Dharma are equal.

Nevertheless, when we study supreme and perfect enlightenment we listen to the teaching, we practice, and we bear the fruits of enlightenment; this is profound, vast, and marvelous. We learn about supreme enlightenment from our venerable elders or from the sūtras. The first words we hear are "refrain from all evil." If we do not hear those words then it is not the Buddhist teaching, but the teaching of demons.

We should know that when we hear "refrain from all evil," it is the True Law of Buddha. Yet "refrain from all evil" is not what ordinary people attempt to do in the beginning. Only after hearing an explanation of enlightenment can we understand the meaning of the words which are based on the words of supreme enlightenment. Those words are enlightened words, and words enlightened. Supreme enlightenment is contained in those words, and by listening to them we can attempt to continually refrain from evil. Where no evil is produced, the true strength of practice is actualized. This actualization covers the entire earth, all the world, time, and all dharmas. The measure of its actualization depends on the amount of refraining from evil.

Those who have reached the state of refraining from evil can dwell in the midst of various evils without committing any evil themselves. Since refrain-from evil actualizes a certain amount of power, evil is restrained. Evil lacks the necessary requisites. It is the principle of sometimes holding, sometimes letting go. Those who arrive at this stage can clarify the principle that evil cannot break or taint them.

Simply by practicing with our entire body and mind we can accomplish eighty or ninety percent of our task without any conscious restraint. If we practice with our entire bodies and minds, the power derived from the four elements and five skandhas emerges; the four elements and five skandhas are untainted. Within the present four elements and five skandhas there can be continuous practice. The power of the four elements and five skandhas of our present practice can remake the previous conditions of those elements. This practice is carried out in the mountains, rivers, earth, sun, moon, and stars; indeed the mountains, rivers, earth, sun, moon, and stars make us practice.

Enlightened vision does not only occur in an instant, but is constantly active at all times. Since enlightened vision is active at all times, it enables the Buddhas and Patriarchs to practice, hear the teaching, and bear the fruits of enlightenment. The Buddhas and Patriarchs have never defiled teaching, practice, and enlightenment; consequently, those things present no obstacles. The Buddhas and Patriarchs have never avoided teaching, practice, and enlightenment in the past, present, or future. When sentient beings become Buddhas and Patriarchs [by refraining from evil] the actions of other Buddhas and Patriarchs are not obstacles. However, we must carefully consider the principle of becoming a Buddha or Patriarch through the daily actions of walking, staying, sitting, and lying. When sentient beings become Buddhas and Patriarchs they are not broken or lost—it is simply body and mind dropping off.

Practice is accomplished through the law of karma. That is, it is not moved by karma, nor does it create new karma. When karma exists it causes us to practice. When the original nature of karma is illuminated we see true refraining, impermanence, and the karma that ceases and never stops because there is only detachment. If we study like this we will see that we are able to refrain from all evil. When this understanding is actualized we can completely refrain from all evil and cut off all delusions through zazen.

Then from beginning to end, all our actions will be free of evil and evil karma will not arise from any condition. There is only non-creation of evil. It is not that evil is annihilated by conditions, but rather, there is simply non-creation of evil. If all evil is equal, then all dharmas are equal. Do not think that evil arises from certain conditions of cause and effect; if you do not realize that karma itself is non-created, you are to be pitied. The seed of enlightenment arises from the chain of causation, and vice versa.

There is no non-existence of evil, there is no existence of evil, there is no emptiness, and no form—there is only refraining from evil. Not refraining from evil becomes refraining from evil. For example, a spring pine, an autumn chrysanthemum, all the Buddhas, a pillar, a stone lantern, a fly whisk, a staff, and even we ourselves are not existent nor non-existent.

This kind of study enables us to actualize our koan, and vice versa. It must be studied both objectively and subjectively. Any regret or remorse we feel for creating evil, derives from the principle of refraining from all evil. This is the virtuous power of refraining from evil.

However, to think that we cannot refrain from evil is like heading north when we want to go south. "Refraining from all evil" is not just the donkey looking at the well, but also the well looking at the well, and the donkey looking at the donkey, human beings looking at human beings, mountains looking at mountains. Because such a principle exists, [i.e., the relationship between evil and its creation,] we must refrain from evil. Buddha's true Dharma-body is like space, or like shadows, or like the moon reflected in the water. Since all things are refraining from evil, all forms are refraining from evil. It is like space, existing no matter where you point. It is like the moon reflected in the water; the water does not disturb the moon. This kind of refraining from evil is surely actualized.

"Practice all that is good." "All that is good" is the good of the three natures [good, bad, and neutral]. Although good exists within the nature of good, it does not mean that good has some previous, independent existence and is waiting to be accomplished. When good is done, it contains all good. Although good is formless, when it is done it attracts more good faster than a magnet attracts iron. Its power is stronger than the strongest wind. All the accumulated karma throughout the earth, mountains, rivers, world, and lands cannot obstruct the power of good.

However, the interpretation of good depends on various circumstances; good is evaluated according to people's experience. Similarly, the essence of the

Dharma proclaimed by all the Buddhas of the three worlds is the same, yet the actual words used depend on the time and circumstance. Even though the life and quantity of Buddhahood varies according to the situation, the Dharma proclaimed is still that of non-discrimination.

Therefore, that is why the good contained in belief and the good of the Dharma are the same, even though they appear to be different. For example, "Keeping the precepts of the śrāvakas is the same as breaking the precepts of the Bodhisattvas."

Good is independent of the creation or cessation of karma. Although good is all dharmas, all dharmas are not good karma. Karma, arising, ceasing, and good have their own beginning and end. We should practice all that is good, but it should not be done consciously by ourselves or on the instructions of others. In the consciousness of self and others, there is knowledge and observation of self and others; therefore, each active enlightened vision causes the sun and moon to appear. This is to practice all that is good. When good is done at the proper time, enlightenment is actualized, but it is not the first or last actualization. This is called practice of all that is good.

Although practicing all that is good is necessary, we must not think of it analytically, and our enlightened vision must not be based on conjecture. In addition, it must not be used in order to evaluate the Dharma. Analysis with enlightened vision differs from general observations.

"Good" is not existence, non-existence, emptiness, form, etc.—it is just "practice." No matter where or when it is actualized, it is "practice." "Practice" surely actualizes all that is good. The actualization of practice is the koan that is beyond creation, destruction, or karma. Entering, staying, leaving, etc. are just like that. The practice of just one small good covers all dharmas, all bodies, the ground of truth, etc.—this is practicing all that is good.

Good karma is the actualization of enlightenment of practice. Although it is not possible to say that cause always precedes effect, both cause and effect are fulfiled and completed. Cause is usually thought of as preceding effect, but actually neither one comes before or after, due to the equality and identification of before and after.

"Purify your mind" is the self and purification of "refrain." There is a self of "your mind," and a refrain of "your mind." Also there is a mind, purification, and self of "practice." Therefore, we have "This is the teaching of all the Buddhas."

"All the Buddhas" are like the gods of total freedom. Even though they have some points in common, the gods of total freedom are not all the Buddhas.

Cakravartin[1] kings have great power and freedom but are not all the Buddhas. We must clarify this principle. Those who do not study the nature of all the Buddhas only create suffering for themselves and other sentient beings, and they do not practice the Way of Buddha. "Refraining from" and "practicing" mean "The donkey [evil] leaves, and the horse [good] arrives."

The poet Hakurakuten of the T'ang Dynasty was a lay disciple of Bukko Nyoman, who was the Dharma-heir of Kōsei Daijaku (Baso). When he was a high official in Kōshū he studied under Zen Master Dōrin of Choka.[2] Once Hakurakuten asked Dōrin, "What is the essence of the Buddhist Dharma?" Dōrin replied, "Refrain from all evil, practice all that is good." Hakurakuten said, "Even a child of three knows that." Dōrin said, "A child of three may know it, but even a man of eighty cannot do it." Hakurakuten bowed deeply.

Hakurakuten was a descendant of General Haku, and an outstanding poet. People say his work will endure forever, and he is sometimes considered to be another Mañjuśri or Maitreya. There is no one who has not heard of him; he has no equal in the literary world. Nevertheless, he was just a beginner in the Buddhist Way despite the fact that he was an old man. Furthermore, he could not even begin to dream of the inner meaning of "refrain from all evil, practice all that is good."

Hakurakuten thought that Dōrin was just like an ordinary layman after he heard Dōrin repeat such a common phrase; Hakurakuten failed to realize that the principle of refraining from all evil and practicing all that is good has been transmitted from ancient times to the present in the Buddhist Way. Since he had never practiced Buddhism he lacked its power and such a thing occurred. Although this discourse seems merely to be concerned with warning against evil and encouraging good, it is really the actualization of "refrain."

Generally, in the Buddhist Dharma both what we learn from virtuous people and from practice is the same. It is perfect from start to finish. It is called marvelous cause and marvelous effect, or Buddhist cause and Buddhist effect. Cause and effect in Buddhism differs from the ideas of *ijuku* [a cause making a different effect], *toryu* [a cause making an equal effect], etc. If there is no Buddhist cause there can be no Buddhist effect. Dōrin understood this principle and therefore possessed the Buddhist Dharma.

Even if evil blankets the entire world with many layers and absorbs all the elements, it is still the detachment of refraining from evil. Since good is good

---

[1] Chariot kings who control the four continents.

[2] Po-chu-i and Taolin (c. 740).

from beginning to end, the nature, form, shape, and strength of practice emerge as such. Hakurakuten lacked this understanding; consequently, he could say, "Even a child of three knows that." He said that because he lacked the power of attainment of the Way.

Miserable Hakurakuten, why did you say such a thing? Because you failed to learn the Buddhist teaching it is doubtful whether you know anything about the ability or natural talent of a three-year-old child. If someone can truly understand a three-year-old child he will know all the Buddhas of the three worlds. If you do not know those Buddhas you can never understand a three-year-old child. Do not think that we know a child just because we have met him and vice versa.

If we can understand a speck of dust we can know the entire world; one who truly knows one dharma can understand all dharmas. And if one fails to understand all dharmas, how can he understand one dharma? One who has total perception can see all dharmas, and he can see one dharma such as a speck of dust and learn about the entire world.

Anyone who thinks that a three-year-old child is unable to say anything about the Buddhist Dharma and that all his talk is simple is very foolish. To clarify the great matter of life and death is the central problem of Buddhism. An ancient worthy said, "When you were first born into this world you could roar like a lion. That lion's roar is the virtue of the Tathāgata's turning of the wheel of the Law and proclaiming the Dharma." Another worthy [Engo Kokugon] said, "The coming and going of life and death is the true body of man."

Therefore, clarifying the true body and possessing the virtue of a lion's roar is truly a great event and not at all easy or simple. Hence, clarification of a three-year-old child's actions and words is a great matter, since it is the same as (yet different from) the actions and words of all the Buddhas of the three worlds.

Hakurakuten foolishly misunderstood the meaning of a three-year-old child's attainment of the Way, was not puzzled by it, and therefore said such things. Dōrin's words peal louder than thunder but still Hakurakuten could not hear them. When he said, "Even a three-year-old child knows that," he meant "A three-year-old child has nothing to say about attaining the Way." He did not hear the child roaring like a lion, not the master's turning of the wheel of the Law.

The master could not help feeling pity for Hakurakuten and said, "A child of three may know it but even a man of eighty cannot do it." We must carefully study that point about the three-year-old child, and also the eighty-year-old man being unable to practice it. The child's attainment is entrusted to you, but his words are not typical. The old man's inability to practice also depends on you; but he also is not a typical person.

It is necessary to have this kind of principle—profound thinking, correct explanation, and basic understanding—in the Buddhist Law.

This was delivered to the monks of Kannondōri-Kōshōhōrinji, Uji, on the evening of August 21, 1239. Transcribed on March 27, 1243 at the chief disciple's quarters by Ejō.

[64]

SHISHO

"The seal of transmission"

Kannondōri-Kōshōhōrinji

ALL Buddhas surely transmit the Dharma to one another; all the Patriarchs have transmitted the Dharma to each other. This mutual pledge of enlightenment is the right transmission from master to disciple. Therefore, we have supreme enlightenment. If you are not a Buddha, you cannot receive the seal of enlightenment; if you do not possess the seal of enlightenment, you cannot be a Buddha. Who else besides Buddha can give the seal of enlightenment?

When the seal of enlightenment is received, there is the self-enlightenment with no master, and self-enlightenment of no self. That is why we say Buddhas transmit enlightenment and Patriarchs mutually pledge enlightenment. If you are not a Buddha you cannot clarify the essence of this principle. Even those people who are on the highest level or have the status of Buddha cannot easily grasp this, so how is it possible for scholars of the sūtras or abhidharma to conjecture about it? They may pretend to explain it but they have no real understanding.

Buddhas transmit to Buddhas, and only Buddhas can master the Buddhist Way. There is no place Buddhas are not. For example, stones transmit stones, jade transmits jade, chrysanthemums and pine trees transmit and hand down the seal of enlightenment. Each generation of chrysanthemums or pine trees passes its life to the next generation. If you cannot see this, you will never see the seal of enlightenment mutually possessed by all the Buddhas and Patriarchs. Even if they are confronted with the right transmission of the Way from Buddha to Buddha they do not question it. This is a great pity. They resemble Buddha but actually are not children or descendants of Buddha.

Once Sōkei [Enō] said to an assembly, "There are forty Patriarchs from the seven Buddhas to Enō, and from Enō to the seven Buddhas there are forty Patriarchs."

This principle is the essence of the right transmission of the Buddhas and Patriarchs. The seven Buddhas have emerged throughout countless kalpas of the past and present. Nevertheless, the Buddhist Way and Buddhist transmission exist in the direct transmission from master to disciple of the forty Patriarchs. Therefore, that is why from the sixth Patriarch to the seven Buddhas there is the Buddhist transmission of the forty Patriarchs, and from the seven Buddhas to the sixth Patriarch there certainly is a transmission of forty Buddhas. The Way of the Buddhas and Patriarchs is like this. If there is no mutual pledge of enlightenment between Buddhas and Patriarchs, there can be no Buddhist wisdom and no reciprocal understanding between them. If we lack Buddhist wisdom we cannot have faith or trust. If there is no reciprocal understanding between Patriarchs, we cannot have a pledge of mutual enlightenment.

We use the expression "forty Patriarchs" tentatively for those Patriarchs in this era. The transmission from Buddha to Buddha is ancient and profound, never retreating or turning, never stopping or cut off. This principle means that Shakyamuni Buddha attained the Way and transmitted it to Mahākāśyapa before the age of the seven Buddhas existed. Although it is said he attained the Way at the age of thirty, actually he existed before the time of the seven Buddhas; all the Buddhas simultaneously attained the Way at that time. That attainment of the Way occurred prior to, after, and at the same time as all the Buddhas.

Furthermore, that is the principle we must study in the transmission of the Dharma from Shakyamuni Buddha to Mahākāśyapa. If we do not know this principle we have not yet clarified the Buddhist Way. If we have not yet clarified the Buddhist Way we cannot know anything about the Buddhist transmission. "Buddhist transmission" means to be the heir of Buddha.

Once Ānanda asked Shakyamuni Buddha, "Whose disciples are all the Buddhas of the past?" Shakyamuni Buddha said, "All the Buddhas of the past are the disciples of me, Shakyamuni Buddha." This is true for all the Buddhas. To venerate, transmit, and accomplish the Buddha transmission is the Buddhist Way.

In the Buddhist Way whenever the Dharma is transmitted, surely there is *shisho*, the seal of transmission.[1] If there is no Dharma transmission, people will automatically become non-believers. If there had not been a definite, certifiable transmission of the Buddhist Way, how could it have been transmitted up to

---

[1] This is a certificate of enlightenment and Dharma transmission written by a master and given to his disciple.

the present day? Therefore, anyone in the line of Buddhist transmission must have received the seal of Buddha transmitting Buddha. Obtaining the seal of Buddha transmitting Buddha should be used to clarify the movement of the sun, moon, and stars and the attainment of skin, flesh, bones, and marrow. Sometimes a kesa, sometimes a staff, sometimes a pine branch, sometimes a fly whisk, sometimes an udumbara flower, sometimes a golden robe, sometimes a straw sandal, and sometimes a *shippei* is used to transmit the Dharma.

When a transmission occurs, the seal is made with blood from either a finger or tongue. It may be written with oil or milk. Either is acceptable. Both transmitter and receiver form the Buddhist transmission. Truly, the seal of transmission actualizes the Buddhas and Patriarchs and therefore the transmission of the Dharma is actualized. When such a transmission occurs Buddhas and Patriarchs bestow the Dharma freely without any motive or expectation. Where the Dharma transmission exists, Buddhas and Patriarchs exist.

The twenty-eighth Patriarch came from the west and the essence of the Dharma transmission of the Buddhist Way was heard for the first time in the east. Prior to that it was not known. Scholars of the abhidharma or teachers of doctrine never even thought about it. Even the ten saints or three sages cannot surpass that teaching. Students of the Tripitaka or reciters of secret chants cannot even begin to question it. It is shameful that although they are human beings and possess the ability to attain the Dharma as a birthright, they worry too much about obscure or minor teaching and know nothing about the Dharma or its occurrence. Hence, we must be very careful about the proper method of study and concentrate on developing a proper attitude for investigation.

When I was in Sung Dynasty China I had the opportunity to respectfully observe many seals of transmission. I saw several different types. One was the possession of the abbot Iichi who was invited to come to Mt. Tendō from his temple in Secchō Province. He was the former head (seidō) of Kōfukuji, and from the same hometown as my late master. My late master used to say, "If there is any question about enlightenment, ask the Seidō."

One day the Seidō said to me, "It is interesting to look at ancient calligraphy. Have you ever seen any?" I said, "Only a few examples." The Seidō said, "I have a scroll that happened to come into my possession. I'll show it to you now." Saying this, he brought out a seal of transmission. It was for the Hōgen line of transmission and was part of another old priest's possessions including his bowl and kesa. It was not actually Iichi Seidō's. On it was written, "The first Patriarch Mahākāśyapa was enlightened by Shakyamuni Buddha; Shakyamuni Buddha was enlightened by Kāśyapa Buddha."

When I saw that I became more determined and my belief in the right transmission of the Dharma from one to another was strengthened. I had not seen such a document before, but now I saw the necessity of protecting and preserving the Dharma-heirs of the Buddhas and Patriarchs. My deep emotion could not be expressed.

In the seal of transmission used in the Ummon line, I saw one after the elder Sōgetsu became the chief disciple on Mt. Tendō. On Sōgetsu's seal there was first the master's name and then a list of all the Buddhas and Patriarchs, ending with the new Patriarch. Therefore, there was a list of the forty-odd Patriarchs descended from the Tathāgata included along with the new Patriarch. It is as if the Patriarchs transmit their Law directly to the new Patriarch. Mahākāśyapa, Ānanda, and all the others flow together in one stream.

Then I asked Sōgetsu, "O Priest, there are five different Zen schools. What is the reason for this? If there is only one right transmission from India why do such differences arise?" Sōgetsu replied, "There seem to be differences, but we should simply study in the same manner as the Buddha on Mt. Ummon. Why did Shakyamuni Buddha respect others? Because he knew that all human beings possess the means for enlightenment. Why did Ummon respect others? For the same reason." After I heard this I was able to get some understanding of the seal of transmission.

There are some priests of large temples of the Kosetsu District who are said to transmit the lives of Rinzai, Ummon, and Tōzan. However, many self-proclaimed descendants of Rinzai are self-centered and dishonest. They study under a renowned master and then ask for his portrait or a sample of his calligraphy. This is what they use as their standard of transmission. Worse than that, there are some priests, no better than dogs, who visit many different masters and ask them for a portrait or a sample of calligraphy. Like this, they acquire a large stock of such things. As they get older they bribe officials in order to receive support for establishing a new temple and then become its abbot, even though they have not received a seal of transmission from a true master. In turn, they pretend to transmit the Dharma to well-known people, kings, ministers, and close friends without actually possessing it. They only covet fame. It is disgraceful that such malicious deeds occur in this evil age. Among those people not one can even dream of the Way of the Buddhas and Patriarchs.

Generally, samples of one's calligraphy or one's portrait are freely given to scholars, lay people, junior priests, merchants, etc. This can be seen in any of the annals of the various schools. Certain people who are unfit to receive the Law but are eager to gain profit from the Dharma transmission pester the master to give them a scroll. Those masters who have attained the Buddhist Way do not want to give them a scroll but sometimes resign themselves to the situation and write one. If they do so those masters are acting contrary to traditional practice; they are issuing only a simple certificate of one's being a disciple. Nowadays, it is the practice to give the Dharma transmission to anyone who has gained some power while studying under a master. Such a seal merely certifies that he has copied his master. The majority of monks have a tendency to stay with one master, listen to his lectures, live in the monastery, busy themselves with study, and try to clarify the Great Matter of life and death, hoping to receive the seal of transmission when actually they will not.

Once there was a monk named Den who was a descendant of Zen Master Butsugen Seion of the Ryūmon Branch. This Den was in charge of the sūtras and possessed a seal of transmission. In the beginning of the Kajō period [c. 1215] the elder Kōzen, a Japanese, took care of Den who had fallen ill. Kōzen looked after him very carefully and Den, wishing to thank him, took out his seal of transmission, placed it before Kāzen, and made a prostration. This kind of thing—looking at the seal and making a prostration—is done rarely.

Eight years later in the fall of 1223, I first came to Mt. Tendō and the elder Kōzen kindly requested that the sūtra-master Den show me his seal of transmission. On it was the following: The names of all the Patriarchs from the seven Buddhas to Rinzai were written; up to Rinzai there were forty-five Patriarchs. After Rinzai's name a large circle was drawn. Inside the circle the monk's name was written together with both their seals. After the name of the new Dharma-heir, the date was written. It seems that even such a distinguished master as Rinzai was not beyond producing such an inadequate seal.

My late master Tendō, the head abbot, was very strict concerning bragging about one's reception of the Dharma transmission. His community was a community of ancient Buddhas. He completely reformed the monastery. Nyojō himself never wore an elaborate kesa. Nyojō had received the Dharma robe of Dōkai of Mt. Fuyo but did not wear it even for his installation ceremony. He never wore any kind of expensive robe at any time in his life. Both those who understood the meaning of his actions and those who did not praised and respected him as a man of true knowledge and insight.

My late master, an ancient Buddha, always admonished the monks by saying, "In recent years many use the names of the Patriarchs, boastfully wear Dharma robes, keep their hair long, and chase after titles from the emperor in order to become well-known. That is a great pity. How can anyone possibly save those people? What a shame that elders everywhere lack a mind for the Way and have no real study. Even among thousands of monks there is not one who really comprehends the true meaning of the seal of transmission, or Dharma transmission. This is a perversion of the Way of the Patriarchs." He admonished all the monks in this manner, but none felt any resentment towards him.

Therefore, that is why if you practice the Way with a stainless mind, surely you will find the seal of transmission. When you find it, that will be real study of the Way.

In the Rinzai school's seal of transmission the family name is written first and then there is certification that the person in question had studied under the master, entered the community, received personal instruction, been given the Dharma transmission, or whatever the case may be. Then there is a list of the past Patriarchs. The essence being that it is not important who was the first or last to transmit the Dharma, but rather it is essential to certify that one has real insight and knowledge of the inner teaching. That is the style used in the Rinzai line. I have actually seen it and will reproduce it here.

"The Sūtra-master Ryōha of Ibu has become my disciple. [Setsuan] Tokko studied under Priest [Dai'e] Shūkō of Kinzan. Kinzan was Dharma-heir of [Goso Hō] en of the Yōgi Branch. [Hō] en was Dharma-heir of [Hokun Shu] zui of Kai'e. [Shu] zai was Dharma-heir of Yōgi [Hō] e. [Hō] e was Dharma-heir of Jimyo [So] en. [So] en was Dharma-heir of Fuyō [Zen] shō. [Zen] shō was the Dharma-heir of Fuketsu [En] shō. [En] shō was Dharma-heir of Nan'in [E] gū. [E] gū was Dharma-heir of Kōkei [Son] jō. [Son] jō was the outstanding Dharma-heir of the High Patriarch Rinzai."

This was written by Zen Master Bussho Tokko of Mt. Aiku and given to Musai Ryōha. When Ryōha was an abbot of Mt. Tendō, the novice Chikō secretly brought it to the monks' quarters and showed it to me. That occurred on January 21, 1224, and I cannot even begin to express how deeply impressed I was upon seeing a seal of transmission for the first time. It had the grandeur of the Buddhas and Patriarchs. I offered incense, made a prostration, and then reverently examined it.

I will now explain how all this came about. In July of the previous year, Shikō, the general secretary of the monastery, was speaking privately to me in one of the buildings. I asked him, "Is there anyone here now who has a seal of transmission?" He said, "Evidently, the abbot here possesses one. If you ask him politely, he might show it to you." After hearing that, I thought about it constantly, day and night. The next year I entreated the novice Chikō to show it to me and he finally acceded after seeing my great sincerity. This seal of transmission was wrapped in white silk, and placed on red brocade with a cylindrical piece of jade on one end. It was about nine *sun* in width and seven feet in length. Such a document is not shown to just anybody, so I was very grateful to Chikō. I immediately went to the abbot's room, offered incense, and made a prostration to show my gratitude to Priest Musai. Musai said, "It is very rare to have the opportunity to see a seal of transmission. Now you have arrived at real study of the Way." I was overjoyed when I heard that.

Later on, in the Hōkyō period [c. 1224] while visiting Mt. Tendai, Mt. Gato, etc. I arrived at Mannenji in Heiden. The abbot there was Gensu of Fukushū. After the elder Shūton retired Gensu was appointed and the monastery flourished. The first time I met him he talked about the traditions of the Buddhas and Patriarchs and he mentioned Dai'e and Gyōzan. He said, "Have you seen my seal of transmission?" I said, "No. How could I have seen it?" Then he stood up and held out his seal of transmission. He said, "I do not show this to even my closest friends or long-time disciples. This is a Dharma rule of the Buddhas and Patriarchs. However, once when I was in the city visiting the governor I had the following dream. The Zen Master Hōjō of Mt. Daibai was holding a branch of plum blossoms. He said, 'If someone comes a great distance by boat in order to locate the "real man" do not withhold these flowers.' He then gave me the branch. I remember saying in the dream, 'If he hasn't come by boat I'll give him thirty blows.' Incidentally, this occurred less than five days ago; I now see you here. Not only that, you have come a long way by boat and my seal of transmission is wrapped in silk decorated with plum blossoms. This is what Daibai was saying in the dream. Since the dream came true I brought out my seal of transmission. Furthermore, I will not hesitate to give you my transmission if you really want it."

Although my joy was inexpressible at being offered his seal of transmission, I did not take it but only offered incense, made a prostration, and paid my respects. The attendant monk who was carrying the incense tray said, "This is the first time I've seen the seal of transmission." Secretly I thought that all this came about due to the magnanimity of the Buddhas and Patriarchs. How else could a foolish foreigner like me be able to see someone's seal of transmission? Tears of gratitude wet my sleeves. When this occurred we were alone in the section of the abbot's quarters where an image of Vimalakirti is enshrined. This seal of transmission was made of cloth with a plum blossom design; it was about nine inches high and eight feet long. The rod was made of yellow jade and had a brocade border.

On the way back from Mt. Tendai to Mt. Tendō I stayed one night in the guest quarters of the novice training hall of Goshōji on Mt. Ōbai. I dreamed that the Patriarch Daibai Hōjō appeared and gave me a branch of plum blossoms. We must always be sincere when we talk about the seal of transmission. This branch was about a foot long. Are these plum blossoms different from an udumbara flower? Asleep or awake the reality must be the same. Both when I was in China and after I returned to Japan I told no one about this.

   The seal of transmission used in the Tōzan Dharma line differs from that of Rinzai or other schools. That which is kept in the inner lining of the robes of the Buddhas and Patriarchs is the seal of transmission, written with the blood from a fingertip of the High Patriarch Seigen, written by Sōkei [Enō] and bestowed to him. It was written with the blood of both Seigen and Sōkei. Seals of transmission written during the time of the first and second Patriarchs were done in a similar fashion. "My child transmits my law," etc. should not be written on the seal. All the Buddhas of the past used the above form for the seal of transmission.

   Therefore, we should know that the blood of Sōkei is mixed with the blood of Seigen and vice versa. Only the Patriarch Seigen received the seal of certification from Sōkei; no one else did. Those who understand this realize that the Buddhist Dharma has been rightly transmitted by Seigen only.

The seal of transmission:

   My late master, the ancient Buddha, Priest Tendō said, "All the Buddhas have surely received the Dharma transmission. That is, Shakyamuni Buddha received the transmission from Kāśyapa Buddha. Kāśyapa Buddha received it from Kanakamuni Buddha. Kanakamuni Buddha recieved it from Krakucchanda Buddha. Like this, Buddha transmits Buddha continually, up to the present time. This is what we must believe in and receive. That is the proper way to learn Buddha."

   Then I asked him, "Kāśyapa Buddha entered parinirvana before Shakyamuni Buddha was born in the world and attained the Way. How is it that the Buddhas of past aeons can transmit the Dharma to those in the present? What is the principle behind this?"

   My late master said, "Your standpoint is that of sūtra scholars or Hinayanists, but not that of the Way of the Buddhas and Patriarchs. Our Buddha transmission is not at all like that." We have learned that Shakyamuni Buddha received the transmission after Kāśyapa entered parinirvana, but we should also learn that Kāśyapa Buddha transmitted the Dharma to Shakyamuni Buddha before he entered parinirvana. To think that Shakyamuni Buddha did not receive the transmission from Kāśyapa Buddha is the belief of non-believers. How can anyone who thinks like that have confidence in Shakyamuni Buddha? The transmission from Buddha to Buddha has continued to the present time with each Buddha preserving the right transmission. It is not like many different things put in a line, or gathered together. The transmission passes from Buddha to Buddha without alteration; do not be concerned with the length of time involved or the number of years spent in practice—only Hinayanists do that. If we contend that Buddhism began with Shakyamuni Buddha, it is only about two thousand years old with only forty or fifty generations. That is not an ancient transmission, but rather new. Do not study like that about the Buddhist transmission. Rather, study that Shakyamuni Buddha received the transmission from Kāśyapa Buddha and that Kāśyapa Buddha transmitted it to Shakyamuni Buddha. If you learn that, you will know the real transmission of the Buddhas and Patriarchs."

Thus, I learned about the real transmission of the Buddhas and Patriarchs for the first time and also cut off all my old mistaken views.

This was written by Samana Dōgen, transmitter of the Dharma from Sung China, on March 27, 1241, at Kannondori-Kōshōhōrinji. Delivered to the monks on December 12 of the same year. Recopied at the chief disciple's quarters on February 25, 1242, by Ejō.

[65]

ANGO

"The training period"

My late master Tendō, the ancient Buddha, once said during the summer training period, "Now you monks are forming the structure of true practice and making a cave in universal emptiness. Complete those two things and you will have a lacquer bucket."

Therefore, if we experience the inner essence of the training period we can push on and all our actions—taking meals, stretching out our feet, and sleeping—will be forms of training throughout our lives. If we grasp this we will be diligent and not relax for even a moment. Such action is the ninety-day training period. This is the key point and original face of the Buddhas and Patriarchs; here we touch their skin, flesh, bones, and marrow. The days and months of a ninety-day summer training period carry the enlightened vision and essence of the Buddhas and Patriarchs. Even in just one term of summer training, people become known as Buddhas and Patriarchs. Both the beginning and end of the training period are the Buddhas and Patriarchs. Outside of this there is nothing, neither large nor small. The summer training period is not new, not ancient, and does not come or go anywhere. Its value is that of fist and its form is yanking the nose [i.e., universal and all-pervading].

When we begin a summer training period the entire universe is filled with that training period, nothing else. When the summer training period is finished the great earth has been turned topsy-turvy. Therefore, when the summer training period begins we have the actualization of enlightenment and after it ends all obstacles are broken—it is the same from start to finish. Nevertheless, there are some who are familiar with such practice and become attached to the beginning and end of the training period. Remember no weeds are found originally; do not limit yourself to a ninety-day training period.

Priest Shinshin Oryū said, "My pilgrimage of thirty years resembles a ninety-day training period—give or take a day." That is, the insight obtained after thirty years of practice can be condensed into a ninety-day summer training period. Even if we add or subtract a day, ninety days are sufficient and complete. Do not try to avoid those ninety days; simply concentrate on those ninety days as ninety days. The ninety days of a summer training period are the instrument of practice. It began before the Buddhas and Patriarchs and has been rightly transmitted by them up to the present day.

Therefore, to participate in a summer training period is to meet and see all the Buddhas and Patriarchs. The amount of time in one summer training period is immense, larger than one, ten, or even a hundred unlimited kalpas. Time functions within unlimited time. The ninety-day training period also functions within unlimited time and therefore someone who practices during a ninety-day training period and sees Buddha surely surpasses unlimited time.

That is why we must study that a ninety-day training period is absolute enlightened vision, nothing else. The body and mind of the trainee is exactly the same. We must both utilize and transcend the liveliness and freedom of the summer training period. It neither comes from, nor occurs at, some other place or time. If you seek the reason for it, or look for its basis, you will find ninety days, nothing else. Ordinary people and saints live within it; it is the root of their lives. Yet it goes far beyond the worldly conditions of either ordinary people or saints and it cannot be fathomed by ordinary thought, non-thought, or thoughtless thought.

The World-honored One was proclaiming the Dharma for all sentient beings in Magadha. At that time he wished to institute the summer training period and said to Ānanda, "I continually proclaim the Dharma for men, gods, my close disciples, and all sentient beings but they do not respect it properly. Therefore, I will now institute the practice of spending the ninety days of summer in one's room meditating. If someone has a question about the teaching, answer for me by saying, 'All things are without creation and without destruction.'" Saying this he returned to his room and began his meditation.

Two thousand one hundred ninety-four years have passed since then (up to the present year, Kangen sannen, [1245] in Japan). All those descendants who have not mastered the inner essence of this interpret the training period in one's room as "worldless proclaiming." Present day people also often misinterpret this, thinking that Buddha instituted a special training period in order to emphasize the inadequacy of words in explaining the Dharma; i.e., words are nothing more than "skillful means." They also say that the ultimate truth can never be explained with words; the truth only appears after the working of the mind has disappeared. Hence, "no words, no thought" is the way to ultimate truth. "Words and thought" lead us astray. The ninety-day summer training period is to be spent completely cut off from all other people. Such an interpretation completely misses Shakyamuni's real meaning.

Namely, if "words cannot describe the truth" and truth "appears only after the mind has stopped," then all social and economic activity cannot be explained in words and only appear after the mind has stopped its working. Actually, "beyond words" covers all words; "the mind stops working" covers all workings of the mind. Moreover, this story about Shakyamuni contains nothing about "wordless" proclamation. Shakyamuni entered the dirty water [i.e., this world] and with his entire body proclaimed the Law to everyone over and over. Turning the wheel of the Law was his sole intention. I would like to ask those "descendants" who say that the ninety-day summer training period is a wordless proclamation, "Please show me that ninety-day summer training period."

Shakyamuni said to Ānanda, "Answer for me by saying, 'All things are without creation and without destruction.'" Buddha's intention is not to be taken lightly. Why is the summer training period said to be a "wordless proclamation"? Let us put ourselves in Ānanda's place for awhile and ask what is the essence of, and how we should explain, "All things are without creation and without destruction." This is the way we should listen to Shakyamuni's words.

Buddha's concern here is with the ultimate and absolute truth of the turning of the wheel of the Dharma, rather than with "wordless proclamations." If we take his purpose as a wordless proclamation it becomes a pitiful, useless thing, something like Ryūsen's three-foot sword or an expensive antique sculpture.

Therefore, that is why the ninety-day summer training period is the eternal turning and proclaiming of the Law of the ancient Buddhas and Patriarchs. "At that time he wished to institute the summer training period." We cannot avoid those ninety days of summer training; anyone who does is a non-believer.

Shakyamuni spent his ninety-day training period in either the Heaven of the thirty-three gods [on the top of Mt. Sumeru] or in a quiet place on Vulture Peak with five hundred bhikkhus. Whenever he was in the five countries of India, he always had a ninety-day summer training period at the prescribed time. Present day Buddhas and Patriarchs also practice it as their most important work. This is the supreme Way of practice and enlightenment. The *Brahmajāla-sūtra* mentions a winter training period but that has not been established. Only a ninety-day summer training period has been handed down. This has been rightly transmitted up to the fifty-first Patriarch.

It is written in the *Shingi*, the rules for Zen monks, "Monks on pilgrimage who wish to participate in the summer training period must come to the monastery a half-month before the training period begins. It is important for monastery officials to note the applicant's behavior when he is served tea and permitted to stay overnight."

"A half-month before" means at the end of March. Therefore one must enter the monastery in the month of March. After the first of April the monks cannot go out and the gates are closed to all would-be entrants. By April 1, all monks should have chosen a monastery for training. Occasionally it happens that monks spend the duration of the training period at a layman's house. This has been done by both Buddhas and Patriarchs and it is permissible to follow their example. Diligent monks will be able to choose the proper monastery or other place for their training.

However, certain malicious people say, "The standpoint of the Mahayana is the essence of Buddhism, and the summer training period is only the practice and custom of śrāvakas; consequently, it is not necessary to participate in it." People who think like that have never seen nor heard the Buddhist Dharma at all. Supreme and perfect enlightenment is nothing other than the ninety-day summer training period. The ultimate goals in both the Mahayana and Hinayana are just the branches, leaves, flowers, and fruit of the ninety-day training period.

After the morning meal on April 3, the training session begins. The monk in charge of training must prepare a name board with the names and ranks of all the monks by April 1. After the morning meal is finished on April 3, the name board is hung in the monks' quarters on the left side of the window across from the entrance. All the windows must be latticed. After the morning meal the board is hung up and left until April 5 when it is taken down after the *hossu* bell (announcing the time allotted to interviews with the master is over) is struck. The board must be hung from the third of April until the fifth and taken down at the same time of day.

There is a special order used in writing this name board. One's rank does not depend on one's position as a *chiji* or *chosu*;[1] it only depends on one's years as a monk. If a monk has had some experience as one of the *chiji* or *chosu* his title

---

[1] There are six *chiji* (officers) in a Zen monastery: *tsūsu* (secretary-general) *kansu* (secretary), *fūsu* (accountant), *ino* (head of general affairs) *tenzo* (chief of kitchen), and *shissui* (chief of maintenance). The six *chosu* are in charge respectively of the trainees, documents, sūtras, guests, buildings, and the bath.

should be written after his name. If someone has been chief priest of some temple the title *seidō* should be written after his name. However, if the temple was very small, and the other monks would not recognize its name, it is not customary to write *seidō* after his name. Also, anyone who is training under his own master should have no title after his name even if he has been a *seidō* elsewhere. Occasionally the title *jōza* (elder) is placed after one's name. The attendant monks in charge of the clothing and incense should assist the master. This is an old established custom. Furthermore, all the other officers must follow the master's instructions at all times. If disciples of other masters or those with some previous administrative experience come to join the training session they should be appointed to some office. This is the proper procedure. It is not good for one to mention his serving as priest of a small temple; the other monks will laugh at him. A good monk will not mention such a thing.

The signboards I saw in China looked like this:

———— country, ———— province, ———— mountain, ———— temple
Preparations for this year's summer training period are now being made. The ranking of the monks is as follows:

     The Venerable Ajñātakauṇḍinya[2]
     ———— chief priest

Monks who received the precepts, summer ————:
———— jōza (elder)   ———— zōsu (director of sūtras)
———— jōza   ———— jōza

 Monks who received the precepts, winter ————:
———— seidō   ———— ino (director of general affairs)
———— shuso (director of trainees) ———— shika (guest master)
———— jōza   ———— yusu (bath master)

 Monks who received the precepts, summer ————:
———— shussui (director of maintenence) ———— jisha (assistant priest)
———— shuso (director)   ———— shuso
———— keishu (director of external affairs) ———— jōza
———— tenzo (kitchen director) ———— dōshu (director of monastery buildings)

---

[2] One of the five monks who became the first disciples of Shakyamuni after his enlightenment. Ajñātakauṇḍinya attained the Dharma before Shakyamuni finished his first sermon. He is held up as an ideal for for monks.

Monks who received the precepts, summer ———— :
———— shoki (director of documents)   ———— jōza
———— seidō   ———— shuso
———— jōza   ———— jōza

    The above was written with care and respect. If there are any errors please inform me. ———— year, April 3. Written by Bhikkhu ————.

This signboard should be written on white paper in block characters, not cursive or rough-style characters. The width of the string used to hang it should be about the thickness of two rice kernels. Attach the string to the board's edge and hang it vertically like a woven straw blind. After the bell is struck to announce the end of opening ceremonies on April 5, the board should be taken down and put away.

    A celebration is held on April 8, the anniversary of Buddha's birth. On April 13, after the midday meal all the monks return to their quarters and are served a light dessert. Then they chant some sūtras, acquiring merit thereby. The assistant monks must prepare the hot water and incense. Their rooms should be located in the central part of the monastery while the head instructor's quarters should be on the right side of the Mañjuśri image. Only the assistant monks should prepare the incense and the other officers should not attend this service. The officer in charge of general affairs should prepare the announcement board beforehand and place it on the upper half of the eastern wall in front of the monastery entrance in the space west of the entrance after the morning meal of the fifteenth.

    It says in the *Zenen Shingi:* "The officer in charge of general affairs must prepare the announcement board beforehand and adorn it with flowers and incense. After the midday meal of April 14, a board listing the names of the ten Buddhas should be hung in front of all the monastery buildings. That evening the monastery officials should offer incense and flowers before the board located in the Dōjidō.[3] All the monks should gather there to chant the names of the ten Buddhas. It should be done in the following manner. After the monks have gathered, the head priest offers some incense. Then the various officers and officials make their offerings in the same way as done for the ceremony of Buddha's birth. Then the officer in charge of general affairs rises from his seat, goes to the front, bows to the chief priest and finally, goes over to the Dōjidō.

---

[3] The hall where the god who looks over the monastery is enshrined.

He faces north and chants the following:

> "Imperceptibly, the autumn wind gently blows over the fields and the God of Fire [the sun] controls all directions. The Dharma King cannot leave. This is the day of Shakyamuni's birth. All the monks have gathered together and worship the spirits of the gods by chanting the names of the Buddhas that possess immeasurable merit. Pray that the virtue of the gods who protect this monastery and all its buildings will be transferred to us. We ask for protection throughout this training period and pray that it will come to a peaceful conclusion. Together let us chant the names of the Buddhas with respect and honor.
> The Pure and Undefiled Dharma Body, Vairocana Buddha.[4]
> The Perfect and Complete Bliss Body, Vairocana Buddha.
> The Unlimited Transformation Body, Shakyamuni Buddha.
> The One Who Will Come, Maitreya Buddha.
> All Buddhas of the Ten Directions and Three Worlds.
> The Great Saint Mañjuśri Bodhisattva.
> The Great Saint Samantabhadra Bodhisattva.
> The Compassionate Avālokiteśvara Bodhisattva.
> All the Honorable Bodhisattvas and Mahasattvas.
> The Mahāprajñāparamitā (the Great Perfection of Wisdom)."

The virtue obtained by chanting the names of the ten Buddhas protects the True Law and bestows on us the merit-transference of the earth-gods. We beseech them to share their spiritual power with us, that our deeds will be fruitful, our joy pure, and our bliss eternal and selfless. Let us chant again:

> "Praise to all the Buddhas of the ten directions and three worlds,
> All the Honorable Bodhisattvas and Mahasattvas,
> And to the Great Perfection of Wisdom."

Then the big drum is struck and all the monks take their seats in the monastery while hot water is being offered to the Buddha. The preparation and observance of this service is the resposibility of the secretary general. When the monks enter the monastery they should walk around it in single file before taking their seats. They should face front. One of the *chiji* will be conducting this part of the service and taking care of the incense.

---

[4] A small bell is struck after each name.

It says in the *Shingi*, "Usually the director of the monastery should officiate at the services but the secretary-general may take his place if necessary."

[There is another service held at this time.] A special announcement board is made for this service and taken to the chief disciple. When an officer or official meets with the chief disciple he must wear a kesa and take a *zagu* (prostration cloth) and make a set of *sokurei* and *ryoten*[5] prostrations before submitting the announcement board. The chief disciple then returns the said number of prostrations. After that the chief disciple takes the board and places it in a box with a cloth on the bottom. Then the chief disciple's assistant takes it away and the chief disciple dismisses the official.

The announcement board must be written in this style:

"This evening the secretary-general will hold a tea ceremony in the monastery. The chief disciple will answer any questions that monks may have, in order to prove his ability to succeed his master. I pray that the light of compassion will shine on us all. Written on April 14, ———— by the secretary-general, Bhikkhu ————."

The head official must initial it. After this announcement board is shown to the chief disciple it should be placed in front of the monastery, on the right hand side, by one of the assistants. On the southern side of the outside gate there is another board where announcements are made. This board should be painted. There is a lacquer box (*korosu*) for holding documents next to it. This box is hung on a bamboo nail. The characters on the announcement board must not exceed five *bun* (1.5 cm.). On the front of the lacquer box the following should be written:

"Invitation from the chief disciple to all the monks.
Sealed by the Bhikkhu ————."

After the tea ceremony is held the announcement should be taken down.

Before the morning meal of the fifteenth all officers, officials, senior monks, and the chief disciple should greet the chief priest. However, if the chief priest is too busy to compose a gatha and prepare a formal lecture, he may omit this observance. If he wishes to omit it he should place notices on each side of the

---

[5] A *sokurei* prostration is made by folding the *zagu* cloth into four sections, laying it on the floor, and touching the head to it. A *ryoten* prostration is made when the *zagu* is folded in half. A *daiten* prostration is made with the *zagu* laid out full length.

entrance to his quarters and in front of the monastery the previous evening.

After the Dharma talk on the fifteenth, the chief priest comes down from the lecture platform and stands in the center of the temple at the edge of the *haiseki* (the special straw mat used for prostrations by the chief priest). Then all the officers approach and give three *ryoten* prostrations. As they open their prostration cloths they chant, "Now we have entered the summer training period when it is forbidden to go out. We practice under you as our master because of the strength of your Law. We sincerely hope to complete our training without difficulty or trouble."

Again there is one more *ryoten* prostration; then the season's greeting is given, followed by three *sokurei* prostrations. After the *ryoten* prostration they fold up their cloths and say, "Summer has begun and it is growing warmer and warmer. You are looking fine, O Priest, and we are full of deep emotion when we consider the significance of this training period." Then they make the three prostrations and say, "It is good fortune that all of us can participate together in this training period. I pray that all the officers and officials will assist one another through the power of the Dharma and not experience any difficulties." Everyone participates in this ceremony.

After this the chief disciple, the officers, officials, senior monks, and all the other monks face north and make a prostration. The chief priest is the only one facing south. The chief priest's prostration cloth is spread out on the *haiseki* by an assistant. Next, the chief disciple and the rest of the monks make three *ryoten* prostrations to the chief priest. However, senior priests, top disciples, and novices stand aside (along the eastern wall of the Dharma Hall) and do not make a prostration. If laymen are already present and seated on that side, the senior monks, etc. should stand by the big drum or near the western wall.

After the monks finish their prostrations the officers return to their rooms but remain standing. Next, the chief disciple and the rest of the monks return to their quarters and make three *sokurei* prostrations. At the same time the senior monks, assistants, and top disciples make three *ryoten* prostrations to the chief priest. The disciples make three *ryoten* prostrations which are returned by the chief priest. The senior priests, assistants, etc. make nine prostrations, but the chief priest makes no prostrations in return. Novices should make either nine or twelve prostrations. The chief priest only makes a gassho to them.

The chief disciple now goes to the front of the monastery near the officers' seats (which are on the right hand side), faces south, directly facing the assembly. All the monks who are facing north make three *sokurei* prostrations to the chief disciple. Then the chief disciple leads the monks around the monastery to their respective seats (which are arranged according to seniority). After that, the officers enter the monastery and make three *daiten* prostrations before the image of Maitreya Buddha. Then they make three *sokurei* prostrations to the chief disciple. All the monks return the prostrations. The officers then walk once around the monastery and go to their seats where they stand in *shashu* (with the left fist held inside the right hand in front of the chest). The chief priest enters, offers incense before the image of Mañjuśri, makes three *daiten* prostrations, and then remains standing there. At that time the senior priests are standing behind the image. The rest of the monks follow behind. Then the chief priest makes three *sokurei* prostrations to the chief disciple and all the monks return his prostrations.

The chief priest walks once around the monastery and then goes out. The chief disciple goes to the southern gate to see the chief priest off. After the chief priest has left, the chief disciple and the rest of the monks make three prostrations to each other and say, "It is our good fortune to share the same training period; perhaps our three karmas [of body, words, and mind] are not good, but let us have compassion for each other."

During the above prostrations use the prostration cloth. After this, the chief disciple and the rest of the officers return to their respective quarters. The remaining officials and monks make three *sokurei* prostrations. The above chant is repeated.

After this, the chief priest begins to inspect the monks' quarters. All the monks follow behind until they arrive at the chief priest's room; then they return to their own. That is to say, the chief priest first visits the officers' quarters and gives a greeting. Then he continues his inspection with the officers following behind. They proceed to the eastern corridor but do not visit the infirmary. They move from east to west, passing through the main gate. The monks around the main gate then join in the procession. They move to the southern corridor and then towards the west. From there on, the various monks who live in the Anrō (elderly monks' quarters), the Gonkyū (former officers' and officials' quarters), the Idō (quarters for monks over one hundred years old), and the Tairyō (retired monks' quarters), and the other officials and attendants join the procession as it passess their residences. This is called "*Daishu Shōsō*," the Great Procession.

After all this, the chief priest climbs the western steps towards his quarters and takes a position directly in front of his room. He faces south with his hands folded across his chest. The officers face north in front of him with the rest of the monks lined up behind. All of them make a deep bow to the chief priest who returns their bow. Thereafter, everyone returns to his respective place.

My late master did not bring all the monks to his own room. He went to the Dharma Hall with the others, faced south with his hands folded across his chest, and then the monks made their prostrations. This is the old style. Then all the monks bow to one another.

Also, if it happens that monks from the same district meet in the monastery or in the corridor, they should not just bow to each other but also to the other monks present. They congratulate each other for attending the same training period. They may use the same greeting described above or they may use one of their own choosing. If a junior priest meets his master he must make nine prostrations; when the chief priest's senior disciples meet him they make three *daiten* or *ryoten* prostrations, and the other monks also make the same number. In addition, when fellow disciples (both senior and junior) meet, they must make the prescribed number of prostrations. Make prostrations whenever you meet neighboring monks and old or new friends. In the case of those who have separate quarters—e.g., the chief disciple, the various officials and officers, etc.—we must go to their rooms and make our prostrations. If there are too many people there when you make your visit you may leave a message written on white paper one *sun* (three cm.) wide and two *sun* in length. The form is:

   a) ———— quarters (*your name*)   congratulations (*haiga*)

Other acceptable forms:

   b) (*your name*) (*official's name*)   congratulations (*haiga*)
   c) (*your name*)   congratulations (*reiga*)
   d) (*your name*)   congratulations (*haiga*)
   e) (*your name*)   congratulations (*raihai*)

Actually there are many different styles of writing this greeting, but generally they follow the above forms. That is why there are so many name cards on each gate. They should not be placed on the left hand side but rather, on the right hand side of the gate. The name cards should be removed after the midday meal. On that day all the buildings, large and small, and each residence should have a rattan blind hung before the entrances.

Often, tea is served for the chief priest, or the secretary-general, or the chief disciple. However, if the monastery is in a remote or distant place, this service may be omitted. This service is used to show one's respect and is not absolutely necessary. If it is held, the retired elders and senior disciples should make the arrangements for serving the tea.

Like this, the training period may end but still they continue to practice the

Way. Although one may boast of the many forms of practice he has undergone, if he has not attended a summer training period he cannot be a descendant of the Buddhas and Patriarchs. Both Jetavanna Park and Vulture Peak were actualized by the summer training period. The dojo where the training period is held is the heart of the Buddhas and Patriarchs. It is the world where all the Buddhas and Patriarchs dwell.

The summer training period ends July thirteenth. On the evening of the fourteenth a tea ceremony should be held by that month's director of the monastery. On the following day a lecture should be given by the chief priest in the Dharma Hall. Then there is the same kind of greeting, inspection of the monastery, and tea ceremony as held at the beginning of the training period. The only difference is the wording of the announcements and the chants:

> "This evening I will hold a tea ceremony in the monastery to show my appreciation to the chief disciple and all the monks for their efforts during this past training session. I sincerely hope that all the monks will show their compassion and attend this service."

The following verse should be chanted in the Dojidō:

> "The autumn wind blows across the fields and the god of the autumn equinox controls all directions. The king of enlightenment emerges and on this day the Dharma has been fulfilled everywhere. Nothing disturbed us for ninety days and all monks were at peace. We chant the names of the Buddhas and bow to the god who guards our monastery. Let us say ... (the same verses used on the first day are now chanted.)"

After the chief priest finishes his talk, a word of thanks is offered by the officers to the chief priest: "Joyfully the Dharma has been fulfilled everywhere and nothing has disturbed us. The power and virtue of your teaching protected us and we are deeply grateful, unable to show our appreciation." Then the head priest replies, "The Dharma has been fulfilled, and I deeply appreciate the efforts of all the officers and officials. I thank everyone from the bottom of my heart."

Then the chief disciple and the director of monks address the chief priest, saying, "All of us have come together for this ninety-day training period. Our karma is not good and we have caused trouble for you, but we now ask for compassion and your forgiveness."

After this the officers and officials say to the monks, "All of us are brothers on the same pilgrimage. Today our training period is over. After our tea ceremony is finished please feel free to go wherever you wish." (However, they may stay if they are incapacitated for some reason.)

This ceremony has been the highest form of Buddhism handed down from the immemorial past. It is the most significant event of the Buddhas and Patriarchs. Non-believers or demons cannot obstruct it. All true descendants of the Buddhas and Patriarchs in the three countries [India, China, Japan] have participated in this ceremony. Non-believers have never learned about such a ceremony. Because that ceremony is the main work of the Buddhas and Patriarchs, the summer training period itself contains everything from the attainment of the Way in the morning to the entering of nirvana in the evening. Monks of the five schools in India may disagree, but all who have undergone a ninety-day training period share the same practice and enlightenment. There are nine sects in China but none failed to observe the summer training period. If you do not experience a ninety-day summer training period sometime in your life, you cannot be called a bhikkhu or a disciple of Buddha. Training is not undertaken in order to become enlightened; training itself is practice and enlightenment beyond enlightenment. Shakyamuni Buddha, the World-honored One of great enlightenment, had practice and enlightenment in every summer training period throughout his life, without missing one. Here, we must know that the practice and enlightenment of Shakyamuni is Buddha's enlightenment beyond enlightenment.

However, those who do not understand the practice and enlightenment of the ninety-day training summer period and still call themselves descendants of the Buddhas are laughable, or worse. We should not listen to the words of such fools, nor talk, sit, or walk with them. In the Buddhist Dharma we should convert such evil people with silence.

Keep in mind that the ninety-day summer training period is nothing but Buddhas and Patriarchs. The right transmission has been handed down continuously from the seven Buddhas to Mahākāśyapa, then passed to the twenty-eighth Indian Patriarch. The twenty-eighth Patriarch came to China and transmitted the Law to the second Chinese Patriarch, the Great Teacher Taiso Shōshū Fukaku. The transmission continued intact and without alteration from the second Patriarch up to the present time. I went to China and brought the right transmission of the Buddhas and Patriarchs to Japan. If you spend the ninety-day summer training period as the right transmission, it becomes the right transmission. Whenever the summer training period is spent with experienced monks it is a real training period. Truly, the same training period that existed in the time of Shakyamuni has been rightly transmitted directly, face to face, from the Buddhas and Patriarchs. Since the body and mind of the Buddhas and Patriarchs is bestowed interiorly, to see a training period is to see Buddha. To enlighten the essence of the training period is to enlighten Buddha. To practice in the training period is to practice Buddha. To hear the training period is to hear Buddha. To learn the training period is to learn Buddha.

The ninety-day training period is the one thing that all the Buddhas and Patriarchs must be very careful about. Therefore, that is why kings, Indra, Brahma, etc. become bhikkhus and monks and attend at least one summer training period. In other words, they see Buddha. Anyone—men, gods, dragons—who becomes a bhikkhu or bhikkhuni and has just one summer training session can see Buddha. Those who join the Buddhas and Patriarchs and spend ninety days in training also see Buddha. It will be our great fortune to have had at least one summer training period because it means that the skin, flesh, bones, and marrow of the Buddhas and Patriarchs becomes our own skin, flesh, bones, and marrow. The Buddhas and Patriarchs come to us and make us practice the summer training period. Our individual practice of the summer training period and the summer training make us practice. Hence, the summer training period can be said to be the origin of countless Buddhas and Patriarchs. The summer training period is the skin, flesh, bones, and marrow of the Buddhas and Patriarchs and comprises their mind and body, their head and enlightened vision, their fist and nostrils, and their complete and perfect Buddha-nature. The summer training period is a fly whisk, a staff, a *shippei*, and a zazen cushion. The summer training period is not made of new things nor does it use only ancient things.

The World-honored One said to Perfect Enlightenment Bodhisattva, a great assembly of monks, and to all sentient beings, "Anyone who experiences a three-month summer training period will attain the state of a pure and undefiled Bodhisattva right from the beginning. That state of mind is different from that of a śrāvaka. Without relying on the power of others, when the day for the summer training period arrives, one may confidently stand before Buddha and say, 'We bhikkhus and bhikkhunis, lay men and lay women, are all living as Bodhisattvas and are practicing the way of liberation. We have entered the state of purity and undefilement, and dwell there. Great and perfect enlightenment is our home, and this body and mind is where we carry out the training period. We are in a state of equanimity; our wisdom and nirvana has no attachment. We respect virtue and without depending on the teaching of śrāvakas join all the Tathāgatas and Bodhisattvas of the ten directions in this ninety-day training period. In order to practice supreme and perfect enlightenment and have great karma, we should not follow foolish people. Virtuous people! This is how to actualize the summer training period of the Bodhisattvas."

Therefore, that is why bhikkhus, bhikkhunis, lay men and women who practice in a ninety-day training period surely practice supreme and perfect enlightenment and great karma with all the Tathāgatas and Bodhisattvas of the ten directions. Here, notice that it specifically mentions that lay men and women should participate in the training period.

Where the training period takes place, great and perfect enlightenment exists. That is why in both Jetananna Park and on Vulture Peak there is the same great and perfect enlightenment of the Tathāgata. All the Tathāgatas and Bodhisattvas of the ten directions practice together in the summer training period in accordance with the instructions of Shakyamuni Buddha.

Once, the World-honored One held a ninety-day summer training period and on the final day, when forgiveness is asked by all, the Bodhisattva Mañjuśri came to join the training session. At that time Mahākāśyapa asked him, "Where did you spend the training period this summer?" Mañjuśri replied, "This summer I practiced in three places: [one month in a palace, one month in a nursery school, and one month in a brothel]." Mahākāśyapa was about to strike the *byakusui* to cell the monks together and have Mañjusri expelled, when suddenly innumerable stupas and temples appeared out of nowhere. In each of the buildings both Mañjuśri and Mahākāśyapa could be seen, with Mahākāśyapa poised to strike the *byukusui*. Then Shakyamuni said to Mahākāśyapa, "Which Mañjuśri are you going to expel?" Mahākāśyapa was unable to answer.

Zen Master Engo interpreted this story like this: "If the bell is not struck there is no sound. If the drum is not hit we can hear nothing. Mahākāśyapa got the point—that Mañjuśri actualized unlimited zazen. Both of them revealed their Buddhist insight but one thing is lacking. That is, when the old sage Shakyamuni asked, 'Which one are you going to expel?" he should have struck the *byakusui* himself and said, 'Look! Is there anyone here who can kill both Mahākāśyapa and Mañjuśri?' "

Engo also composed this verse:

"A great elephant cannot walk on a rabbit's path.
How can swallows or sparrows know anything of a great swan?
Both monks observe the rules, like a stonecutter at work,
Or an archer taking aim and shattering his target.
This world of relativity is Mañjuśri,

It is Mahākāśyapa.
Both face Buddha, there is no gap between them.
Why should Mañjuśri be expelled when the *byakusui* is struck?
The Golden Buddha [Mahākāśyapa] drops off all hinderances."

Therefore, that is why Shakyamuni's training period in one place is the same as Mañjuśri's practice in three places. If there is no training period there are no Buddhas or Bodhisattvas. All descendants of the Buddhas and Patriarchs must practice in a summer training period.

If we participate in a summer training period we are the descendants of the Buddhas and Patriarchs. To practice in a summer training period is to possess the body and mind of the Buddhas and Patriarchs. It is their enlightened vision and the root of their life. If we do not practice in a summer training period we are not the Dharma-heirs of the Buddhas and Patriarchs, and cannot become Buddhas and Patriarchs. All the Buddhas and Bodhisattvas made with clay, wood, gold, or the seven precious jewels are present in the three-month training period. During that training period we live within the Three Treasures of the Buddha, Dharma, and Sangha; it is our justification and method of teaching.

All who wish to be true disciples of the Buddhas and Patriarchs surely practice the three-month training period.

This was delivered to the monks of Daibutsuji, Echizen, on June 13, 1245, during the summer training period. Transcribed at Shinzenkōji, Nakahama, Echizen, on May 20, 1279, during the summer training period by Giun.

INDEX

Ajñātakauṇḍinya, 70, 191
Ānanda, 38, 40, 138, 179, 187, 189
Anavatapta, 118
Aśoka, 118
Aśvajit, 70
Avālokiteśvara, 155, 193
Avataṁska Sūtra, 87, 91, 109, 124

Banzan Hōshaku, 4
Baso, 6, 64, 74, 84, 175
Bhadrika, 70
Binzuru, 117-8, 149-50
Bodhidharma, 18, 24, 37-41, 52-4, 68, 82, 94-7, 101, 104, 113, 120, 135, 146, 180, 199
Bodhisattva vehicle, 26, 104
Bokkuku Ihaku, 143
Brahma, 83-4
Brahmajāla Sūtra, 189,
Bukko Nyoman, 175
Butsugen Seion, 182

Chikō, 183-4
Chōrei, 35
Chōsa, 154
Chimon Kōso, 5, 35

Dachi, 96
Daibikku Sanzen Iigi Sūtra, 87
Daibutsuji, 16, 133, 136, 202
Dai'e, 11, 41, 53, 55, 87, 184
Daishō, 120
Daśabalakāśyapa, 70
Den, 182
Devadatta, 75, 80, 82
Diamond Sūtra, 14-5, 82, 107, 135
Dōchō, 107-9

Dōfu, 38-9
Dōgo, 5, 97
Dōiku, 38-9
Dōkai, 3, 33, 163, 182
Dōrin, 175-6
Dōshin, 97

Echū, 126-132
Ego, 36
Eightfold Path, 79
Eiheiji, 7
Ejō, 7, 16, 20, 32, 42, 46, 51, 57, 71, 86, 98, 101, 119, 125, 143, 157, 159, 170, 177, 186
Eka, 18, 37-40, 54, 68, 71, 94-7, 104, 113, 135, 155, 158, 199
Engo, 31, 32-6, 108-9, 176, 201
Enō (the sixth Patriarch), 5, 9, 39, 52-3, 74, 81, 87, 94-5, 123, 161, 170, 185

Five faculties leading to proper conduct, 76
Five powers of the five faculties, 77
Five vehicles, 104
Four right efforts, 74
Four steps to supernatural power, 76
Four types of meditation which eliminate false views, 72
Fu, 151
Fumyō Zenshō, 85

Ganto, 3
Gensha, 49, 94-7, 126, 130
Gensu, 184
Giun, 202
Golden Light Sūtra, 14

Gozu Hōyū, 6
Gutei, 96
Gyōzan, 127, 130, 160-1, 184

Haku, 175
Hakurakuten, 175-7
Haryō, 23-4
Hashinoku, 117, 149-50
Hōbō, 107
Hōen, 36, 109, 124, 151
Hōgen, 2, 111-2, 180
Hōjō, 3, 33, 184
Honei Jinyū, 118
Hōon, 80
Hosshin, 11
Hōtatsu, 9
Hotei, 35
Hotori, 98
Hyakujō, 32, 142

Iichi, 180
Indra, 83, 159, 200

Jinshū, 141
Jizō-in Shinō, 49-50
Join Kobaku, 3-4, 33
Jōko, 142-4
Jōshū, 10, 18, 40-1, 43-6, 91, 119, 126, 130, 134, 159

Kai'e Shitan, 127, 131
Kanakamuni Buddha, 185
Kannondōri-Kōshōhōrinji, 7, 15, 20, 28, 32, 42, 46, 93, 157, 162, 170, 177-8, 186
Kassan Butto, 36
Kāśyapa Buddha, 180, 185
Kippōji (Yoshiminedera), 42, 57, 66, 84, 102, 110, 125, 170
Kō, 15
Kō, Emperor, 169
Kōan Daigu, 160
Kōsei, 169
Kōzen, 182
Krakucchanda Buddha, 185

Kūō Buddha, 32, 67, 75, 120 131,
Kyōgen, 135-6

Lotus Sūtra, 9, 14-5, 112, 114-6, 162

Mahākāśyapa, 10, 22-3, 37, 39-40, 49, 52, 58-62, 86, 104-5, 118, 135, 137, 147-8, 155, 179, 201-2
Mahanamam, 70
Mahaparinirvana Sūtra, 134
Maitreya, 83, 175, 193
Mañjuśri, 13-4, 83, 136, 175, 196, 201-2
Musai, 183-4
Myōkyō Shori, 107
Myōshin, 160-1

Nangaku, 94-5, 113, 119, 130, 135
Nansen, 27, 43, 97, 112, 135
Nine teachings, 27
Ninnō Sūtra, 15
Nyojō (Tendō), 11-2, 37, 71, 97, 99, 135, 137, 145-9. 153, 182, 185, 187, 197

Ōbaku, 6, 109, 142, 160, 165

Prabhūtaratna Buddha, 115-6
Prajñātāra, 10, 37
Pratyekabuddha vehicle, 25, 104

Rāhula, 92, 138
Rifuba, 81
Rinzai, 3, 41, 56, 97, 116-7, 124, 160, 165, 181-3
Roya Ekaku, 100
Ryōnen (Matsusan), 160

Samantabhadra Bodhisattva, 114, 193
Sāṇavāsa, 73, 138
Sanzō, 126-32
Śariputtra, 83, 89
Secchō, 35, 41, 61-2, 107, 127, 131, 135-6
Seidō, 78
Seigen, 25, 27, 58, 110, 130, 185

Sekitō, 5, 25, 27
Sensu, 154
Seppō, 3, 19–20, 41, 94–5
Seven ways to enlightenment, 78
Shakyamuni, 9, 15, 22–3, 26–8, 30, 37, 43, 47–9, 58–61, 69–70, 73–7, 79–80, 82–5, 92–3, 96, 101, 104, 111, 113–4, 117–8, 120, 122–3, 134, 137–140, 146, 155–6, 159, 167, 169, 179, 181, 183, 187, 189, 193, 199–200
Shikan, 160
Shikō, 183
Shinsan, 52
Shinshin Oryū, 185
Shinzenkoji, 202
Shiva, 84
Shōshō, 58–9
Shūko, 107–9
Shūshō, 94
Shūton, 184
Sōgetsu, 181
Sōji, 38–9
Sōun, 41
Sōzan, 4, 27
Śrāvaka vehicle, 25, 104
Súbhavyuha, 116
Sūbhuti, 83
Suramgama-samādhi-nirdesa Sūtra, 109
Suvarnaprabhāvāsottama-raja Sūtra, 15

Tandō, 36, 107
Three vehicles, 22, 24–6, 104
Toinchō, 135
Tokujō, 170
Tokusan, 3, 41
Tōzan, 1–4, 11–2, 33–4, 52, 55, 57, 79, 100, 110, 123–4, 133
Twelve teachings, 12, 24–6, 104

Ummon, 2, 35, 41, 107, 116–7, 142, 165, 181
Ungan, 1, 4, 97, 100
Ungo Dōyō, 4, 12, 58–9
Unrai-onshuku-okechi Buddha, 116

Vairocana Buddha, 193
Vimalikirti, 80, 83–5, 184
Vimalikirti Sūtra, 12–3

Wanshi, 34, 135

Yabu Dōsen, 12
Yakuō Bodhisattva, 113
Yakusan, 5, 8, 12, 15, 80, 97, 170
Yōka Shinkaku, 74
Yūbunko, 81

Zenen Shingi, 90–2, 189, 192
Zenjihō, 51

SHŌBŌGENZŌ

英訳　正　法　眼　蔵　巻二

昭和 五十二 年 九 月 十五日　初版発行

昭和 五十二 年 九 月 一 日　初版印刷

訳者代表　　西　山　広　宣

ジョン・スティーブンス

印 刷 者　　カワタ・プレス

発 売 元　　仏教書林　中山書房
〒113 東京都文京区湯島 2-14-4
ＴＥＬ (03) 833-7676
振替口座　東京 180328